Packaging Baseball

Packaging Baseball

*How Marketing Embellishes
the Cultural Experience*

MATHEW J. BARTKOWIAK and
YUYA KIUCHI

McFarland & Company, Inc., Publishers
Jefferson, North Carolina, and London

ALSO OF INTEREST

The MC5 and Social Change: A Study in Rock and Revolution, by Mathew J. Bartkowiak (McFarland, 2009)

Sounds of the Future: Essays on Music in Science Fiction Film, edited by Mathew J. Bartkowiak (McFarland, 2010)

LIBRARY OF CONGRESS CATALOGUING-IN-PUBLICATION DATA

Bartkowiak, Mathew J.
    Packaging baseball : how marketing embellishes the cultural experience / Mathew J. Bartkowiak and Yuya Kiuchi.
      p.   cm.
    Includes bibliographical references and index.

    ISBN 978-0-7864-6132-5
    softcover : acid free paper ∞

    1. Baseball — Economic aspects. 2. Baseball — Management.
3. Baseball — Social aspects. 4. Major League Baseball (Organization) I. Kiuchi, Yuya. II. Title.
GV880.B35 2012
338.4'3796357640973 — dc23   2012020869

BRITISH LIBRARY CATALOGUING DATA ARE AVAILABLE

© 2012 Mathew J. Bartkowiak and Yuya Kiuchi. All rights reserved

No part of this book may be reproduced or transmitted in any form or by any means, electronic or mechanical, including photocopying or recording, or by any information storage and retrieval system, without permission in writing from the publisher.

Front cover image: Baseball signing for MLB fans in Citi Field, New York © 2012 Shutterstock

Manufactured in the United States of America

McFarland & Company, Inc., Publishers
  Box 611, Jefferson, North Carolina 28640
  www.mcfarlandpub.com

To Sara, Ella, and Porter
— Mat

To Nichole Kramer-Kiuchi and Noriko Kiuchi
— Yuya

Acknowledgments

We wish to express our sincere gratitude to Nichole Kramer-Kiuchi, Sara, Ella, and Porter Bartkowiak, Hugh Mechesney, Hiroko Kato, James Vlasich, Anna Komanecki, Gary Hoppenstand, Shawn Novak, Brad Horn, Jim Small, Steve Dall, Kitty Geissler, Jane Oitzinger, Barbara Ehrenreich, Mark and Sandy Krueger, Adam Nelson, Baaron Schulte, Holly Hassel, Ron Briley, Stacey Oelrich, the University of Wisconsin–Colleges, the UW–Marshfield Wood County Foundation, the UW–Colleges' English Department, MSU's WRAC and English departments, and the UW and MSU librarians. We would also like to thank our moms on both sides of the Pacific, and our fathers, whose influence and encouragement continues to be with us. Finally, we would like to thank Praeger and McFarland, who published earlier versions of what would become two of the chapters in this book.

Table of Contents

Acknowledgments vii

Introduction 1

1. More Than the Crack of the Bat: "Walk-on Music" and Popular Music in Major League Baseball 9

2. Bobbleheads and the Bottom Line: Giveaways in Major League Baseball 26

3. Everything but the Players: The Game-Used Memorabilia Market 42

4. Making the Mark: The Life of MLB Logos 59

5. From Pastime to Obsession: Major League Baseball and Its Media Strategy 77

6. Telling the Story: Creating the History of Baseball 94

7. Commodore Selig: The Importance of Japanese Baseball Players in Major League Baseball 114

8. It's All About the Capital: Major League Baseball and Its Capital-Driven International Strategies in the World Baseball Classic and the Olympics 132

9. MLB in Japan and Around the Globe: An Interview with Jim Small of MLB 151

10. The Globalization of MLB and Its Consequences	166
Conclusion	186
Afterword	188
Works Cited	191
Index	203

Introduction

While we both were completing our graduate work at Michigan State University, Yuya and I were sitting in a computer lab in Linton Hall one day when Yuya's phone rang. Both of us were students in the American Studies Ph.D. programs and TAs in the same class. Our research interests, despite our commonalities, didn't really match up. I was completing work on my dissertation, looking into music as a potential tool of social change and development, while Yuya was working on the effects of cable access television on a specific metropolitan center.

As Yuya spoke on his phone, I did my best to focus on my work. Still, I was intrigued as I heard terms like: "baseball," "translator," "salary," etc. As a graduate student at that time, the last term was especially interesting ... perhaps Yuya could be the guy to always buy the first round now. After he hung up, I couldn't help but ask, "What was that about?" He replied that it was a Major League Baseball team looking to hire a translator for a newly signed player from Japan. In addition to his academic work, Yuya also does an extensive amount of professional Japanese/English translating work.

Yuya couldn't take the gig, and after I cursed him a bit for not dropping everything else in his life to do it, we started talking, a bit in disbelief, about what had just happened. We both were reading Walter LaFeber's *Michael Jordan and the New Global Capitalism* at the time and talked about how sports function in the modern world. We found it infinitely fascinating that such considerations as translators are a facet of making an entity like Major League Baseball work. For me, an avid baseball follower, it was as if the glowing halo surrounding the baseball diamond had been momentarily lifted, revealing the inner workings of the machine ... like a behind-the-scenes tour at Disney World or opening up the back of a pocket watch.

Yuya's involvement with several professional soccer leagues internationally as a referee bounced off of my thoughts on baseball and the call he received. Two years later when we were still talking about it, we decided to commit to writing this book. As we searched further and found out more about the small and not-so-small practices of marketing Major League Baseball that make it what it is today, we discovered that these practices were far from top-down impositions pushing MLB on the world.

Instead, momentary practices like employing "walk-on" music to more over-arching events like mediation reflected a complex interweaving of use values. Fans, players, teams, owners, and corporate sponsors all seemed to have a vested interest/investment/literacy in how Major League Baseball continues to live its life in our global, capital-driven, mediated world. Far from static events/texts to deal with academically from the top down, these events constitute living/breathing, as De Certeau would say, "dark rock[s] that resists all assimilation." The sport is "cultural" in nature; the marketing practices/realities of Major League Baseball, to the chagrin of many and to the delight of others, become part of the sport itself and part of the participants as well. They help us to decode baseball today, and not just the sport itself, but the experience that constitutes Major League Baseball today.

The events that we deal with are not carefully guarded marketing secrets. They are widely known by businesses, fans, players, and a good portion of the general populace. It is no secret that players use walk-on music, that MLB depends on broadcasting/media, and that fan-giveaways exist. It is our aim to understand better the processes that are at play in these occurrences. The study is not intended to be comprehensive in terms of the entirety of Major League Baseball marketing. The following pages are case studies that have pulled us in because they involve distinctive marketing elements and cultural use values. What happens in these events that propels and/or challenges MLB financially, and as an inherently important cultural event in the United States and abroad? By pinning down several parts to the whole, we aim to explore the role of Major League Baseball in its current state for numerous disciplines and for the merely curious, and in the hope of contributing to the literacy of this important economic and cultural force. MLB was consulted frequently itself, and whenever they were offered, we included their perspectives. In a world of decreasing public spaces, the MLB ballpark offers a spot of collective celebration, identity, and escape ... as long as you have your ticket, or your channel tuned to the right station.

To begin, we start with what some may consider small or fleeting instances in constructing today's Major League Baseball experience. These events are ones you may not think twice about when attending a game, but prove to be important facets of the MLB experience. Beyond any romantic notions of the game, one can be greatly overwhelmed walking into any major or minor league baseball stadium in the United States. Stadiums, new and old, have become powder-kegs of merchandising and popular culture forms. By the time one gets to his seat, he will have been ambushed by t-shirt giveaways tied to credit card enrollment or newspaper subscriptions, audio of the game or of highlights being piped throughout the stadium, and television kiosks featuring the newest official merchandise. The onslaught continues as fans get themselves settled in for the game. Clips from popular film and television products show up on the JumboTron, along with a veritable jukebox of songs echoing throughout these massive entertainment complexes.

The first chapter, "More Than the Crack of the Bat: 'Walk-on Music' and Popular Music in Major League Baseball," deals with constructing the MLB ballpark as a themed, mediated, potential utopian experience and escape. Amongst many other concerns, an auditory soundtrack is created for the MLB experience. Five to twenty second clips of all kinds of music create an auditory/mediated experience at the ballpark. Beyond few moments of silence, the ballpark is meticulously managed as a mediated event when it comes to the use of music. The first chapter explores the central importance of music as a mediated device for those in attendance. As much as we might like to construct our own narratives of the game as fans, a process of framing and narrative surrounds us all.

The chapter considers many elements at play. The few short seconds provided as a player steps into the box are an example of a much larger structure of musical packaging that is created in all parks great and small. This small, reoccurring event is a testament to larger processes of mediating the stadium experience. Though momentary, the event creates a remarkably functional space for audiences, players, team owners, music industry interests, and music publishers to fulfill multiple wants and uses. From players carving out a space for motivation, to teams creating a continuous soundtrack to keep avid and not-so-avid fans immersed in the festivities, walk-on music is, in many ways, a focus of great investment for numerous populations associated with the game.

The second chapter, "Bobbleheads and the Bottom Line: Giveaways in Major League Baseball," continues the theme of the supposedly small event reflecting much more complex economic and cultural realities than one might shake a springy head at. Giveaways have even showed up as an aspect of managing one's season in the video game world. Why? Attendance, marketing tie-ins, branding of players and the team — all are connected to this world of bobbleheads, garden gnomes, and free apparel. Beyond the economic payoffs of giveaways, fan use of these giveaways represents a spectrum of values or lack thereof. Whereas some fans may curse the fact that they have to lug around a bobblehead likeness of the San Diego Chicken for three-plus hours, others will plan their yearly attendance based upon the giveaway schedule listed in each MLB team's printed and online schedules. Nor is it an uncommon experience to see people waiting outside the gates when attendees come out at the end of the game, offering cash for the latest giveaway. Fan sites, the memorabilia industry, and a whole host of eBay auctions speak to the cultural cache of a good themed giveaway. In turn, so do the turnstile numbers.

Chapter 3, "Everything but the Players: The Game-Used Memorabilia Market," builds on the tactile realities of Chapter 2. The distance between the first row of seats at the ballpark and the field seems to create a severe psychological distance between player and fan. For devoted followers of the Church of Baseball, there is a premium to pay for bringing a piece of the promised land into your home or office. At stadiums, memorabilia shops/sites, and in packs of baseball cards, fans can literally own a piece of the game. Bases, bats, helmets, jerseys, from your favorite player, and even scoops of dirt from your favorite infield can all be obtained for the right price. Above and beyond autographs, Major League Baseball clubs realize fans will do a lot to add a physical presence to the para-social relationships they have with their favorite players.

Chapter 4, "Making the Mark: The Life of MLB Logos," looks to the epicenter of MLB team branding: the team logo. At the front of every marketing assault rests the brand identity of the team. From Braves to Padres, team logos not only entail a need to concisely encapsulate a product, but also can become almost sacred images to the fans devoting themselves to their respective teams. Based upon one's nostalgic feelings of youth, to aesthetic wants, these logos become important representations of teams' narratives, along with their fan's own personal narratives as well. Realizing this, MLB teams encourage such events as "Throw-Back Jersey" nights, and the MLB is happy to sell consumers their favorite iconic representation of their team from throughout the ages. Sometimes the introduction of a new logo can be remarkably polarizing for fans, as it can challenge or seek to rebrand a text that may feel above such capital-hunting marketing attempts. It can also be a refreshing breath of fresh air to a stagnant organization looking to increase interest in the club. Like the chapters preceeding it, teams, players, investors, and fans all have a voice in the discussion to consider.

Chapter 5, "From Pastime to Obsession: Major League Baseball and Its Media Strategy," is a historical overview of MLB's relationship with media, with a special emphasis on how media have allowed baseball to take place outside of ballparks. Radio, broadcasting television, cable television, the Internet, and other forms of media have brought the game to living rooms, offices, and even to the fingertips of fans. Because of this omnipresence of the MLB in the American consciousness, it has changed its status from America's favorite pastime to America's favorite obsession. This new obsession is a large capital-generating enterprise with a few key players. This chapter reveals how MLB's media industry is a closed and expensive business that keeps the ball rolling.

Chapter 6, "Telling the Story: Creating the History of Baseball," examines the role of the National Baseball Hall of Fame in Cooperstown, New York, through an interview with its senior director of communications and education, Brad Horn. Although MLB captures so much media and fan attention as a global for-profit entity most of the time, the Hall continues to be the place where baseball of various forms is remembered, catalogued, and commemorated. Its scope is inclusive. A female Little League player has a chance to have her jersey displayed at the Hall, just as the winning pitcher of this year's World Series. Similarly, baseball players outside of the U.S. have a chance to be featured in this sacred place of the sport. Horn explains that this is not an easy task. As an independent and non-profit entity, it is responsible for recording true baseball history, even if it might include an embarrassing moment for MLB. He states, however, that MLB and the Hall maintain a very positive relationship with mutual respect.

The Hall helps teams celebrate former players, hosts events, and offers fun experiences to their fans. In return, both teams and players consider it an honor to be asked to donate an artifact to the Hall. On a project basis, teams may offer financial assistance. What the interview reveals is that behind the popular stories about MLB, a reality remains that MLB is just a form of baseball that is only part of this American experience. Even for MLB players, to get to Cooperstown is a journey. Located in the countryside of upstate New York, the Hall reflects baseball's symbolic value as American pastoral idealism to its over 300,000 annual visitors.

The seventh chapter, "Commodore Selig: The Importance of Japanese Baseball Players in Major League Baseball," opens up the discussion of the economic and cultural realities and ramifications of marketing Major League Baseball as a global game. Much like the "smaller" events dealt with in the book up to this point, the influx of Japanese talent in MLB has introduced new economic and cultural challenges/benefits to the game. The chapter looks into the economic and cultural milieu surrounding the arrival and success of Japanese players in MLB history, with a focus on contemporary figures like Ichiro, Daisuke Matsuzaka, and Hideki Matsui. Identity politics, global politics, and nationalism speak volumes about the practice of baseball diplomacy today.

Chapter 8, "It's All About the Capital: Major League Baseball and Its Capital-Driven International Strategies in the World Baseball Classic and the Olympics," argues that MLB's main focus in its international strategies has been the expansion of its business market, rather than in the pursuit of increasing a sport market. In both case studies on the WBC and the Olympics, it is evident that MLB plays a leadership role in the quality of baseball but even more in its marketing. Success is frequently defined by generation of capital, rather than pure expansion of the baseball fan base. Even when the U.S. national team failed to perform well in two WBC tournaments, MLB considered the event to be a successful one because they generated a great deal of revenue for the League. The same focus on capital explains the relative indifference by MLB in the exclusion of baseball from the Olympics. This chapter reveals the shifting role of MLB in contemporary baseball.

Chapter 9, "MLB in Japan and Around the Globe: An Interview with Jim Small of MLB," explores the significant growth of MLB Japan in the last decade. MLB Japan is but one arm of a global influence for the league, and is one that coincides with the book's contemporary examination of MLB as a popular culture product and as a business entity. Much like other global powers, MLB has received both welcome arms and criticism. The interview with Jim Small, the head of MLB Japan, provides a voice in this debate and our focus on the extent of the actions outside of the white lines of baseball.

The last chapter, "The Globalization of MLB and Its Consequences," examines various facets of MLB's international operation. As Toby Miller, et al., stated:

> Discussions about globalization need to address the following: transnational capital; opportunities for nation-states to control capital and information flows; pressures on nation-states to adopt neoliberal policies; the growth of extra-state bodies to monitor and regulate production and exchange; differentiated impacts at the local level of exported culture; the role of the triad; the interconnectedness of locations around the world, reducing the importance of space and time; increased flows of people across national boundaries; consumer consciousness of the international culture industries; and counterknowledges based on national interest [29].

This final chapter of this book attempts to add complexity and more layers to the existing scholarship on MLB and its internationalization. It examines the flow of players, talents, and personnel. It also examines global media, merchandising, licensing, and other business opportunities as well as studies resistance by the local leagues, communities, fans, and other interested parties. Just as has been the case with any example of globalization, MLB's global business plans as mentioned have been both welcomed and resisted. Resistance can come when fans potentially feel they are losing promising players from their domestic professional league. Many Latin Americans feel that their market is exploited both by MLB teams that try to recruit young players at low contract fees and by baseball businesses that takes advantage of inexpensive labor.

While admittedly we don't believe we have unlocked any Da Vinci Code in Major League Baseball, we have examined important elements concerning the process of marketing the sport that shape how we see, feel, hear, and understand the modern state of the game. Whether one aesthetically considers the practices dealt with in the book as significant or not, the topics tenaciously prove to be concerns of the encoders and decoders of this professional and official take on American's pastime. In terms of reading Major League Baseball as an economic and cultural product, one has to step back and look outside of the neatly chalked baselines of a typical game of baseball to the complex interweaving of economic and cultural realities that create, frame, and order the life of Major League Baseball today.

1

More Than the Crack of the Bat*

"Walk-on Music" and Popular Music in Major League Baseball

Going through the turnstiles of any Major League Baseball stadium, you are met with a multi-mediated assault on the senses. The din of thousands walking the concourses is interspersed with a symphony of announcements and flat-screen televisions showcasing current promotions and merchandise. Beer makers and credit card companies, respectively, hawk commemorative glasses and free shirts with an application for the "your insert team name here" Visa or MasterCard. Eventually you can gaze at the pure majesty of the diamond. Perhaps you did not realize you were sitting in the "Toyota Tundra Zone" or "Big Mac Land," but alas the choreographed world that surrounds you is replaced by the relatively untouched sacred space of the playing field.

But it is here where another precise choreography begins: the creation of space and experience for you and your 40,000 neighbors. It is a contested dance, one that has been with the game for years. Today, in the shadow of the massive scoreboard, alive with advertisements, public service announcements, and snippets from popular culture films and television shows, stretches out an additional soundtrack. Sometimes a familiar organ plays some jaunty tunes; other times popular music stadium faire like Gary Glitter's "Rock n Roll Part 2" or the Ramones'

---

*Chapter 1 is a revised and expanded version of "More Than the Crack of the Bat: 'Walk-On Music' and Popular Music in Major League Baseball" by Mathew Barkowiak and Yuya Kiuchi in *Rockin RBIs: Popular Music in Baseball* (Praeger). © 2012 by Danielle S. Coombs and Bob Batchelor. Reproduced with permission of ABC-CLIO, LLC.

"Hey Ho, Let's Go" reminds us of the way we have been trained to "hear" baseball over the last several decades.

The next three-plus hours will reflect a rich, interwoven, and precisely choreographed dance of media, consumption, and yes, baseball. The following pages will deal with a small part to the whole of this precise, meticulous experience. As players make their way from the dugout or on-deck circle to the batter's box, or from the bullpen to the mound, they are joined with the sounds of their selected "walk-on" (also referred to as "walk-up" or "walk-out") music. As Elvis did with "Also Sprach Zarathustra" during his later shows, these players are walking on stage with a focused soundtrack. This chapter will examine the practice, history, debate over, and the multiple uses of "walk-on" music in Major League Baseball. This practice, which has filtered down to all levels of play, from professional to beer-league, is a pragmatic case study in the mediation of sport in society. Though only a part to the whole, walk-on music represents a space in which multiple use values and interpretations make short clips of music a living, breathing entity to the mass of people gathered around you and those few on the field. It is a poignant lesson in not only uncovering the multiple use values of fans, players, etc. of a game, but it is also a remarkable reflection of media and mediation in everyday life, as well as a the creation and maintenance of identity in public commemoration and celebration. Note for note, the practice of "walk-on" music, though supposedly ephemeral, has much more to say than its momentary nature might otherwise supposedly allow.

The Practice of Walk-On Music

"Hearing" a game of baseball as an attendee at any Major League Baseball stadium is a proving ground for our collective, remarkable media literacy. Between the announcer's voice introducing players or directing our attention to the flag for the national anthem is a complex symphony of sound. Audio from clips and advertisements for upcoming park promotions on the JumboTron percolate between plays, pitching changes, and innings. Any space left in the air during play is filled with a veritable jukebox of organ interpretations of popular standards, birthday wishes (including The Beatles' "Birthday"), "charge" chants, and a well-spring of popular music played whenever time allows ... sometimes for literally only a few seconds. It seems as if the only moments of silence come into play during moments of focus or in the icy silence that comes when the opposing team's players step into the box. Here, the noise of the crowd easily could make a visiting team member feel small and remarkably insignificant. Teams may actually make use of other songs to mock an opposing player coming to the plate as well, as is the case for John Mayberry when opposing teams may play the theme from the *Andy Griffith Show*: "The Fishin' Hole." Of course, there is also the sobering, chilling silence that envelopes the stadium when a visiting player triumphantly rounds the bases after a home run.

Walk-on music is a part of the popular music cacophony in modern baseball. It is similar to the ever-present soundtrack we subject ourselves to while watching a film, a television show, or in our cars on the morning commute. Major League Baseball is continuously propelled forward with music. Filling in the gaps, an attendee never has to worry about any lulls or "dead-air," just like the television viewers watching the game at home. This includes the microscopic amount of time batters take as they make their way into the box. Walk-on music is absolutely a part of larger sound politics at the ballpark.

This momentary event actually reflects the larger meticulous employment of media in the stadium. Far from the announcer and organist set near the press boxes, the norm for the Major Leagues is for individual teams to have "media departments" and "directors of entertainment." In a piece done for NPR called "Take Me Out to the Rock Concert: Baseball Now Part of a Multimedia Experience," Oriole Park "producer" Jason Siemer, along with his crew of twelve, "essentially creates a soundtrack for the game as the action unfolds" (Katz). The crew is entrusted with creating a soundtrack from before the game, throughout the game itself, and as fans exit the stadium. Siemer states that the musical presence in the stadium is far from a cursory practice: "We'll play more low-key type stuff and as the later innings approach, and we're trying to get the team more pumped up and the crowd's into it. Say it's a Friday night, we're going to build it, slowly build it" (Katz).

Much like a DJ on college radio or at a wedding, Siemer and crew are actively searching out and planning the soundtrack of the day, as part of the media onslaught called a MLB game. The practice seems to be replicated in numerous forms around MLB. In Milwaukee's Miller Park for instance, Aleta Mercer, Senior Director of Broadcasting and Entertainment, is "in charge of everything that goes on around Miller Park on game day from the pre-game band concerts in the parking lot to the Klement's Racing Sausages race" (Kass). According to a 2005 *Los Angeles Times* article, a thirty-person entertainment and pyrotechnics crew runs the "electrified as the Las Vegas Strip" Angel Stadium, "with flashing billboards, fireworks, geysers, videos and a deafening soundtrack" (Rivenburg). Such insights reveal a well-planned and coordinated science in creating the "experience" of the ballpark. As Angels announcer David Courtney states, while following a thirty-page game-day entertainment script, "The only thing we can't script is the final score, unfortunately" (Rivenburg).

Walk-on music is part of this musical script, existing alongside music used during rallies, walks, steals, and errors. Walk-on music, opposed to more scripted uses of popular music in baseball, can be a continuously shifting entity. Players, depending on the stadium/franchise, are allowed to request specific songs as their "personal soundtracks" in the brief lull that exists as they make their way to the batter's box. Regular attendees may notice that the music can change quite frequently, sometimes to the chagrin of those responsible for the music. Bruce McGuire of the Angels discusses his lack of patience with some songs selected by players: "They're the biggest thorn in my side." McGuire then goes on to describe, in regards to then-infielder Dallas McPherson's request for music from *The Dukes of Hazard*, that "If it works for him, great. But for me, hearing it three or four times a night, just shoot me now" (Rivenburg). Such requests for music are brought to the entertainment/media department by or on behalf of players. Depending on licensing concerns (which will be discussed shortly), the music could change from game to game or even from at-bat to at-bat. As Rob Walker explains in *Slate Magazine*, "Players can pick several songs as personal themes for their plate appearances, sometimes a rotation of four different tracks a game." An example of this fluidity of game-to-game use is an impromptu tribute to a fallen popular culture star by the then–Brewer Prince Fielder. When Isaac Hayes of "Shaft" fame passed away in 2008, Fielder was able to successfully request that the "Theme from Shaft" be played for his walk-on music following news of Hayes' death (Cryns). The turnover can be a quick one, pending licensing concerns, and a quality assurance check to make sure the content is "family friendly" enough for the ballpark.

As will be discussed in the "Use Values" section, teams are able to do this through agreements with performing rights organizations like BMI and ASCAP. Though many details are confidential, agreements with

Major League teams and MLB itself allow the team and/or league to play selections from the publisher's catalog. In the case of BMI, as reported by the organization, this represents 6.5 million works.

The technology that allows for such updating of walk-on music and for the general sound of baseball today is an industry within itself as well. Companies such as Click Effects provide teams/organizations with "the best in technology oriented solutions for live event presentation in the world of sports"; services include prerecorded music, multimedia storage/use devices that can handle video (including replay), audio, and graphics ("Product"). Entertainment departments are able to instantaneously react to plays or change walk-on music during batting order changes from booths that include, as Rivenburg lays out in his look at the Angels, "banks of TV monitors, assorted clapping sound effects, video editing bays, push-button song selectors and canned organ music, including 'Take Me Out to the Ballgame' in 12 keys."

The music seems to be a place where, for good or for ill, players can "personalize" the game. Still, this is a practice that is far from an organization simply playing music to keep their players happy. Instead, it represents a vast intersection of player usage, fan usage, and business interests. Though the practice of walk-on music seems simple enough, and abrupt enough, this specific practice within the larger usage of popular music in baseball is like all forms of popular culture, a contested site for all taking part. Here label interest, gate interest, publisher interest, player interest, and fan interest can repeatedly intertwine with the announcement of each home player on his way to the batter's box or the pitcher's mound.

History: Baseball as a Quiet Game

Despite today's omnipresence of music in popular American sports from baseball to basketball and to ice hockey, and from the local high school to professional league levels, sporting events remained "fairly music-free" until the mid-twentieth century. While marching teams and drill teams played the national anthem and some music before, during, and after sporting events, it was not as prevalent and coordinated as it is today. African-American sport leagues were the exception to this social trend with their use of jazz and blues music, as well as dancing among the audience. Apart from those segregated games in the 1950s and earlier, music had a very limited place in American athletics. It was only in the

1970s that popular music began to enter sporting venues en masse. After the rise of the rock 'n' roll in the 1960s and the increasing attention to cultural production by youth audiences, the professional sport leagues saw the convergence of music and athleticism (Ehrenreich 240–241).

Even after the popularization of music as collective entertainment, music at sports venues was not, however, always welcomed. Even baseball games that saw brass bands playing music while moving through spectators as early as the 1890s were not an exception. Although listening to and singing the national anthem, hearing passionate fans cheer, and hearing music during an extended interval were not uncommon by then, frequent exposure to music at a ballpark did not gain popularity immediately. Players who were used to standing at bat, surrounded only by fans' cheers, felt that they could no longer focus enough on the game because of the music (Ehrenreich 240; Rivenburg).

The main culprit in music's infancy as an increasing presence in the game were organists at ballparks who played music to add more entertainment to America's pastime. It was at Wrigley Field in Chicago in 1941 that American baseball fans first heard organ music (Rivenburg). The arrival of organ music at a baseball game signaled a shift in the meaning of baseball. On the one hand there was a new layer of entertainment value in the sport. On the other there was an unprecedented debate over what baseball meant as a social space.

It was evident that singing songs and listening to music in the forming ritual of baseball increased the level of participation by spectators. While the term "pastime" commonly suggests baseball fans' relatively passive way of enjoying the game, they played a more active role in establishing a new social context in which the ballgame happened. Singing "Take Me Out to the Ballgame" at any baseball game or singing "Sweet Caroline" during the eighth inning at Fenway Park allows fans to create a special space in which they experience baseball. The "epitome of Boston" is not simply what Emile Durkheim calls "collective effervescence," or a special sense of energy felt at a sporting event. It is, rather, a means of participation. Charles Steinberg, the vice president of public affairs for the Red Sox, summarizes this role of music well explaining, "[Fans] thought [singing] 'Sweet Caroline' might inspire a win ... I thought this song was powerful enough that it might change the atmosphere regardless of how far down we were" (Beggy and Shanahan).

The historical debate around the increasing use of music during a baseball game has been two-fold. On one level, it has raised pragmatic concerns about how it affected the concentration of players. Letting music interfere with, and possibly compromise the quality of, the game was not permissible to many passionate traditional fans. They saw music as a distraction and a sign of baseball "abandoning its roots" (Rivenburg). Many players agreed with these traditionalists. Studying the role of music as "collective joy," Barbara Ehrenreich explains that players frequently frowned upon the noise where decibel levels can be as high as a rock concert in today's game (242). Many players and fans originally considered, and some still believe, that popular music did not have a place during a baseball game because it could distract the players and the "main task" at hand.

The second kind of debate was based on an argument that baseball was a sacred sport that had no place for loud music. Its slow-paced, family-friendly, and inclusive nature, at least in theory, reflects the agrarian idealism of the United States that has long been associated as one of its sacred values. Concurrently, baseball parks as a place to gather with family members and close friends were often considered to be part of an American way of life which frequently included traditional and pastoral lifestyles. Unlike soccer, ice hockey, football, or basketball where violence is supposedly more likely, if not expected, and linguistic profanity is more common, baseball showcased American's sacred "good old days." To borrow Durkheim's theory of dichotomy between the sacred and the profane, baseball without a doubt was regarded as a sport that offered a sacred collective arena. Although Stefan Szymanski and Andrew Zimbalist's historical analysis on the reality of baseball as not so religious and not so orderly is an accurate one, American society has had a gentrified image about the sport (20–25). It is not only in the movie *Fever Pitch* that an American boy is essentially brought up in a ballpark while interacting with family and friends. What Major League Baseball games look like today with their commercialism, loud music, and a JumboTron, could be seen as not mixing well with baseball idealism.

Music disrupted this quiet space. Even organ music was considered sacrilegious and profane. The debate surrounding music that started with the first organist's "concert" at Wrigley Field in the early 1940s continues to exist. *The Los Angeles Times* quotes letters sent to the *Sporting News* describing fans' disapproval of organ music in baseball. Calling it a distraction and one individual said organs had to be "removed and put back in church where they belong" (Rivenburg). One can see in their frustrations that in some ways ballparks are more sacred than churches.

Although the earliest examples of music in baseball, such as bands, date back easily to more than a century ago, Major League Baseball's more formalized use is only a bit more than a half a century old. The use of a more popularized and regularized form of entertainment music, including walk-on music, during an MLB game is only a few decades old. This short history, as this section has demonstrated, has been a history of contestation. Even today the relationship of music and MLB is problematic. Rick Schlesinger, the Milwaukee Brewers vice president of business operations, in the *Business Journal of Milwaukee*, says there was a fine balance between entertaining spectators and not "[annoying] intense fans" (Kass).

Constant negotiations between appreciating the game and adding more entertainment and excitement, between allowing players to focus and engaging less passionate baseball fans, and many other issues have never resulted in an absolute consensus. As capitalism continues its intimate relationship with the game and the conversion of various media outlets and sports takes place at a rapid speed, music has become a major part of the baseball experience. Fans expect to hear music every time a new batter walks to the box. Players know they cannot let music get in the way of performing well. Team interests and officials know that through music they can generate a larger profit. The decades-old debate on music usage is, therefore, a history of locating baseball's identity.

Debate on Usage: Making a New Baseball Environment and Losing the Baseball Sound

In contemporary baseball, music can become a topic of intense focus/debate, just as much as RBIs, ERAs, hitting streaks, and on-base percentages are thoroughly discussed. Players, fans, and team employees definitely concern themselves with what music brings to the game and what it disrupts both pragmatically and ideologically. Many of the debates are relevant to the original concerns about organ music's intrusion to the game. Fans and employees concurrently see benefits associated with music. They discuss quite extensively which player has the best or the worst walk-up music, what those songs mean, and so on. All music is not created equal though. Fans can debate at length which player has the best walk-on music and whose tune is less than optimal.

In other instances, the idea of baseball as a sacred space continues to prevent music from being a holistically welcomed part of the ballgame even today. Music in contemporary baseball parks continues to be a double-edged sword. On the one hand, it is "a medicine" to borrow Aristotle's idea on music and leisure. Walk-on music provides entertainment and "amusement" in the midst of work, or a professional baseball game. It is a "movement of the soul" that brings "a relaxation, and because we enjoy it, rest" (Aristotle 456). On the other hand, the new baseball environment interferes with the traditional idealism about baseball.

The general debate concerning music during a baseball game, as discussed, including walk-on music, has a strong connection to the organ debate in early baseball. It is a question about authenticity. What is an authentic baseball experience? What kind of memories should fans take home after a game? Is it about the game as a sport? Is it about the game as pastime whose value is enhanced by music? Does baseball lose its authenticity when there is what Jeffrey Katz calls "a high-tech cheerleader" leading the collective experience? While the use value of music is apparent, as the following section will show, there is yet to be a consensus amongst fans, players, and team officials.

The baseball walk-up music practice debate is multi-faceted. On one level, the presence of music itself is contested. Although there is perceived benefit in walk-up music, not everyone agrees what the benefits truly entail. Some argue that it increases revenue. Music coordinators at ballparks have significant influence on spectators' game experiences. Schlesinger, of the Milwaukee Brewers, stated in 2007 that Aleta Mercer, senior director of broadcasting and entertainment for the Brewers, "impacts every single person who comes to Miller Park." Considering the impact of in-game entertainment, Mark Kass, of the *Business Journal of Milwaukee*, states that the amusement factor of a baseball game, including music, is a way to generate more profit through its business operations. Don Walker of the *Milwaukee Journal Sentinel*, on the other hand, holds a different view. Rather than attracting new fans and increasing profit, he believes that the music is a way to not alienate existing fans ("Brewers Hope"). As Walker once explained, music as a predictable service plays its role as an assurance that "serve[s] to make the sport experience, from stadium to stadium to stadium, as consistent as a McDonald's Happy Meal."

Team officials and players are not the only ones that have a stake in walk-on music. Obviously, team officials would like to make the most of this custom to generate as much profit as possible. They are concerned about balancing the appeal to not-so-avid baseball fans that enjoy the atmosphere and making sure that enthusiastic fans do not feel distracted by the music. Players choose music they like and they can feel energetic about. Even if music is nothing but a distraction for those players, it has come to the point that it is a necessary evil that is here to stay in the capitalism-driven baseball business ("Los Angeles"; "Oakland"; "Pittsburgh"). Major contributors to this enterprise, fans, also discuss and debate walk-up music too.

Many fans engage themselves in casual online conversation about what music they would choose as their walk-on song if they were a Major League Baseball player. Walk-on music is very frequently a means for them to feel a part of the game, even outside of the turnstiles. Graham Womack, a baseball fan who runs a fan blog site, showcases such fans. He wrote in one of his entries, "I'll listen to a song and find myself wondering if it would make good walk-up music." On *Yahoo! Answers*, there are numerous topic threads asking very similar questions: "What would be your walk-up music?" At the same time, many fans are looking for a list of player walk-up songs. "What is some good walk-up music?" "Do you know why [player name] chose this song as his at-bat song?" and other discussions are very frequent. Both ESPN and MLB have featured numerous articles on their websites on "good" walk-on music and "bad" walk-on music. They have interviewed players to explain to baseball fans the reasoning behind their choice. For instance ESPN.com's "Name that tune in MLB" explains:

> We know you've wondered. Heck, we wonder all the time ourselves.
>
> You're out at a big-league ballpark, and you hear a few seconds of some song as the batter steps into the box. Immediately, you find yourself wondering, "What the heck was that song?" or "Who sings that tune again?"
>
> And in many cases, you're wondering, "Why in the heck did he pick THAT song as his entrance music?"
>
> Well, wonder no longer because Page 3 is here with the answers. We've talked to the music folks for all 30 major-league teams, and we've got a list of the at-bat music for every team in the big leagues. For some players, we've even got the "story behind the story" about how the song was chosen. We even got some pitchers to tell use [sic] what their entrance tune is when they come in from the 'pen.

In this regard, Schlesinger's view on the positive impact that music has over the general baseball experience seems accurate. A forty-four-year-old Angels fan is quoted saying, "Loud? [Baseball music] could never be too loud" (Rivenburg). As long as the delicate balance is kept, music has much to offer to the game to many fans.

The debate on walk-on/walk-out/walk-up music is also a part of the larger debate on the sacred nature of the game. JumboTrons, fireworks, and other forms of entertainment have been subject to scrutiny in the history of baseball. Is music necessary? Does it compromise the sacred nature of the game? Even organ music was considered to disrupt the serenity of baseball decades ago. Now that electronic technology has begun to replace organists, there is an added layer to the debate. Not many fans are aware that the organ music that they hear during the game is often actually pre-recorded. Technology has shifted the baseball park into an outdoor concert hall where fans collectively listen to a veritable top forty music radio station. Even music DJs are now aware that the sacred root of baseball has been affected by music. White Sox organist Nancy Faust reflects on this on-going debate of usage when she laments, "We're losing a sound associated with the game.... Now, we're hearing the same music you hear at the shopping malls. There's nothing baseball about it" (Rivenburg).

Use Values

As stated earlier, walk-on music is a meaningful case study in the use and practice of momentary events in popular culture. Whether it be a commercial, a line in a film, or the momentary employment of popular music as MLB players make their way to the plate, these brief events play host to a myriad of uses for various audiences. Indeed, it can be an event that does the following: provides a euphoric collectivism amongst 40,000-plus fans, can be easily ignored as one focuses on adding condiments to their hot dog, annoys media departments, excites the player making their way to home plate, and can be a great revenue/marketing tool. These brief moments in the game continue to bring feverish debate over the secular sacred space of the ballpark. This section will examine some of these segments, but like many products of popular culture, this discussion only reflects some of the *many* uses of this specific practice.

To begin, let's look at the person most obviously connected to this practice, the MLB ballplayer. The uses here can vary as well. Depending on the player's connection to the music being played, the music could act as a customized soundtrack readying the player to enter into this intensely focused-on part of the action. Players can use this customized event as a psychological tool to prepare for the pressures at hand. In 2001, NPR chronicled one such use: "As Orioles third baseman Jeff

Conine comes to bat, Devil's Dance by Metallica blasts from the stadium speakers. But rather than distracting him from the task at hand, the heavy metal melody drives Conine to excel. 'I hear my song and it gets me focused even more." (Katz). Of course, in addition to getting focused, facing an opposing pitcher with thousands of eyes on you along with numerous cameras could solicit a want for any level of comfort or focus that could be provided. Perhaps too, like hearing a favorite song on the radio on the way home from work, these songs/melodies could provide some relaxation or comfort. Joe Lemire of SI.com writes that, regardless of the need, walk-on music is a concern for many players such as Torii Hunter: "Before the start of the 2009 season, Torii Hunter was consumed with an arduous chore: finding the perfect song to introduce him for his at bats at Angel Stadium. 'It's like research,' he later explained. 'Google all day. iTunes all day. Man, it took all of spring training [that year] to find a song. Then I was just listening to it in the car one day and was like, 'Wow, rewind that.'"

As mentioned before with Prince Fielder's choice of the "Theme from Shaft," the practice of walk-on music could represent small places within a massive spectacle for players to personalize the game. Songs can be homages to friends, family, heroes: a mass dedication and/or request line for players and their personal needs from game to game. These possibilities reflect a micro usage by players of the popular culture product at hand. However, the practice extends far beyond the uses of the individual themselves.

These brief songs also become a part of larger structures of usage at the meso and macro levels. For instance, a player, much like a team, is interested in "packaging" or branding their individual identities for fan usage. From Rollie Fingers' mustache to "Wild Thing" being played in the fictional baseball world of Ricky Vaughn in *Major League*, players/marketers/owners know the power of packaging players into sellable identities. As Lemire explains: "the walk-up song is also an essential part of a player brand and, along with his batting stance, a chance for personal expression. Thus, the music played when a home players [*sic*]walks to the plate can be an explanation of self, audition for support, anticipation of the moment, exhibition of beats, proclamation of faith or fodder for pranks." Walk-on music can be seen as effectively creating a soundtrack for each player. One's roots may be reflected in song: an Outkast track for an Atlanta-raised player, or a "country" song by Trace Adkins for a player from the rural South. Players's identities as being focused/intense, team-jokesters, young/old, etc. can all be expressed in song. Between seasoned veterans, and young up-and-comers, the soundtrack is a diverse and meaningful in carving small slices of space within the game to create/maintain/market an identity.

These spaces are opportune for creating individual, commodifiable characters in the everyday narrative of Major League Baseball. Then-Toronto Blue Jays pitcher Dan Plesac commented that when his kids go to a game: "They hear a song, they know who's coming up to bat. They know Carlos Delgado's song when he bats and they know a pitcher when he's coming into the game because of the song that he picked, so you know it's becoming part of baseball" (Katz).

Media and marketing departments realize this potential as well, and are able to easily build upon and help create the personalities on the field. It helps the teams, in turn, to create a multi-mediated, entertainment-rich environment that can assist in keeping the turnstiles moving. As Alexomanolaki, Loveday, and Kennett found in their study. "Music and Memory in Advertising: Music as a Device of Implicit Learning and Recall": "Results indicate that music is effective in facilitating both implicit learning and recall of the advertised product, showing that, under non-attentive conditions, there appears to be a certain mechanism of unconscious elaboration of the musical signal" (51). In terms of creating an atmosphere of multi-mediated entertainment and selling their entertainment product, music at MLB games can create definitive associations with a player as a specific product or with the entirety of the "entertainment experience" that is encountered by the fans.

The continued mediated carnivalization of the MLB ballparks has been a continuous project in baseball's recent history. As Aleta Mercer of the Brewers states: "Baseball is at the center of what we do, but at the same time we know that not everyone who comes to Miller Park is a hard-core baseball fan. We have to appeal to families, young adults and others who just want to come for the experience" (Kass). She cites owner Mark Attanasio's efforts to put "an added emphasis on in-game entertainment as part of his push to increase revenue earned from stadium operations, such as concessions, retail and ticket sales" (Kass). Walk-on music is part of this media/entertainment onslaught across MLB as seen in Katz's previously mentioned observation that the media teams are essentially creating a soundtrack during the games. This soundtrack is meant to maintain interest and create momentum as a mediated entity surrounding the attendees.

Silence is not golden; in fact, it is the enemy of a multi-mediated mechanism meant to keep consumption and entertainment constantly enveloping the crowd. Beyond marketing or packaging players, walk-on music makes good entertainment sense to include for those non-hard-core fans that Mercer speaks of above. It helps to set a norm for seeing a normally mediated event (television) in person. It essentially mediates the immediate and direct experience for a modern audience's comfort and their expectations of "entertainment." Much like TV viewers at home, the modern baseball park is a concisely mediated event that does count silence as dead air.

Music industry interests are increasingly seeing wasted auditory space at the ballpark as wasted business as well. An intricate network of music industry interests are invested in popular music in baseball, including the practice of walk-on music. In 2002, for instance, *Billboard* featured an article on "Pro Sports Music Marketing," a company that is "attempting to transform sporting events into a platform for helping break new hits by servicing music to professional sports franchises in the same way other promotion firms service radio stations" (Olson). The Baha Men's "Who Let the Dogs Out" is cited by a client at Atlantic Records as "a record that was totally broken at sporting events, and there will be another song like that. It's just a matter of time" (Olson). The *Billboard* article states that in terms of working with labels, "Pro Sports has quickly cemented a reputation for digging down deep, often to the individual players, to get a song or an act noticed" (Olson).

The aforementioned Click Effects program, along with numerous other industries, all the way down to manufacturers of stadium prerecorded tracks and even prerecorded organ music, have made the sound of baseball an industry to reckon with. There are many companies vying for a role in the "soundtrack of baseball." The formality of a seemingly informal event like a player picking a song to walk onto the field, is further reflected in the legal realities of the practice as well.

For instance, performing rights organizations such as BMI, ASCAP, and SESAC are employed to ensure that fair compensation occurs for even such brief musical events as walk-on music. According to the Better Business Bureau, "Anyone whose business in one way or another performs music for its customers or members should be aware that they may be called upon by one or more of the major performing rights organizations to license the performance of copyrighted works in their respective repertories" ("Music in the Marketplace"). Businesses and operators can be held liable for copyright infringement in places like concert halls, bars, and Major League Baseball stadiums. Infringement can result in civil suits and damages "of up to $30,000 for each copyrighted song performed without a license" ("Music in the Marketplace").

Though some details of contracts with MLB and the teams are not public record, one can see the economic realities of incorporating popular music into the game, including the practice of walk-on music in BMI's "Professional Team Report Form." This is a form that can be obtained from their website for any professional team looking to utilize BMI's massive library and finding a ballpark (pun intended) figure. The standard equation is: "Total Attendance (rounded to the last full thousand) / 1,000 × $7.00 Per Thousand = Total" (BMI RF-2009/Nov-36S).

Considering this is one of three major performing rights organizations, the costs add up for teams quite quickly, though MLB and teams do normally have blanket contracts that could differ easily from the equation above. Of course, many details are unknown about the agreements between the teams and these organizations, but this basic model indicates that teams are willing to make a significant financial investment in the usage of popular music, including for the ability to play walk-on music.

So why the investment? First, there is the need for the teams and MLB to protect themselves from potential infringement lawsuits. In the case of BMI, "violators face fines of anywhere from $750 to $150,000 per song" (Bowe). More so though, this is a profitable marketing move for the ball clubs. As Ben Anderson observes in his research on music and utopia, "Perhaps the most vivid example of the link [between music and utopia] is the consistent use of music as a strategy of explicit political resistance or in the construction of self-consciously utopian happenings and events" (212). MLB teams are creating a transcendent experience that pulls in fans, whether they are interested in the game or not. It is an immersive experience that creates and focuses in on the merits of their product: entertainment. It is also an experience that gives players, at times, a sense of autonomy, a hand in the creation of their individual being as a "product" of consumption and/or a shot of confidence as they approach the plate. To stop at these two levels though, would ignore the most prevalent usage of this music within a MLB park, the usability of the music by fans. In addition to the audience uses chronicled earlier on such sites as Womack's, other uses abound.

For fans the music can be embraced, ignored, or used to retain information, along with numerous other usages. In the case of a Brewers game attended as part of our research, there definitely was a utopian moment that reoccurred throughout the game. Each time the Brewers' Frank Catalanotto stepped up to bat, the song "Your Love" by the Outfield played. This seemingly struck a chord (no pun intended) with fans, as each time the music was played during his walk-ons, portions of the crowd took control of the song and sang along for the few brief moments it was played, and then *continued* to sing the song after the official use had finished. Fans in our nearby section closed their eyes to the game, sung at the top of their collective lungs, and swung their beers in unison as they made the moment theirs. It was an inspired moment, and one in which the participants had momentarily completely lost focus of the game. From background noise for the purist to definite narrative of an experience, walk-on music fulfills numerous wants and needs.

As Stan Savran explains in the *Pittsburgh Post-Gazette*, "Songs at stadiums and arenas are part of our sporting culture. And I don't mean 'Take Me Out to the Ball Game.' I'm talkin' rock-and-roll." Beyond the utopian experience of those Brewers fans, popular music is simply an expectation of a MLB game for many fans (along with many other levels of play). Popular music has become an expectation of a remarkably mediated audience. In essence, walk-on music, like other forms of popular music employed during the game, has become (for good or for ill/to some s chagrin, to other delight) the soundtrack of watching baseball at a MLB park. Fans may take part in the music, as team, label, and artist interests may want. They may take the raw popular culture material presented in walk-on music for their own. Whatever the case, though, the practice of walk on music has become and remains a profitable, usable, and increasingly canonized form of the baseball experience for those in attendance.

Where Does America's Sacred Pastime Go from Here?

Over half a century after the first organist played music at the Wrigley Field in the early 1940s, walk-on music and other forms of baseball music have become a staple of the game just like peanuts and hot dogs. Fans expect to hear loud at-bat music, and many would argue it is a natural part of the game. Players have learned to turn the potential distraction into a means of self-motivation. Team owners and operation personnel see it as a means to generate revenue. Music has become an invaluable aspect of America's traditional pastime.

While walk-on music undoubtedly adds values to the game, it raises questions about what it means to have an authentic baseball experience. The nostalgia about baseball from the "good old days" lingers. Baseball purists would argue that introducing organ music and distracting fans from the game alone was lamentable. To have recorded organ music, let alone rap, country, and rock music blaring, could be viewed as almost sacrilegious. The only way to make sense of this development in the baseball culture is to consider at-bat music as a creature beyond such purist's control.

The momentum that music possesses at baseball stadiums appears unstoppable. Our ears have been normalized to the contemporary soundtrack of the game. Although there have been and continue to be, discussions of sacrament and ritual from parishioners from the Holy Church of Baseball, the music of the game, like any product of popular culture, stands too amorphous, too shifting, and too remarkably useable/un-useable to pin down into one absolutely discernable form. Walk-on music in baseball is at once a practice for all, for one, for none: all at the same time. It, like other events in popular culture, is a reminder that a vast audience, in the stands, in the booths, in corporate America, and in the business offices of Major League teams, exists beyond the experience of our singular experience and our numbered seat.

2

Bobbleheads and the Bottom Line

Giveaways in Major League Baseball

Major League Baseball understands and capitalizes on the spectrum of fans and fan experiences that are part of each game. In order to effectively generate income and fan connection to the product at hand, baseball relies on a whole host of practices to keep not only the turnstiles turning, but also to maintain a high level of emotional and financial investment once fans have entered the park. In the case of walk-on music chronicled in the previous chapter, investments are made into game/fan experience to meet the needs of as many fans as possible, from the very casual to the firmly invested, with small practices or events becoming remarkably significant parts to the MLB whole.

Another case that exemplifies the culture of modern Major League Baseball for fans and clubs alike comes in the formalized free-for-all called the giveaway. Over the last several decades this undertaking has delighted some and bewildered others in its increasing formality and development not only in MLB, but also in the NBA, NFL, and other leagues. "Free" is obviously not a new development. One can see that on the predominance of Major League team pocket schedules and team websites that giveaway days are seemingly a significant concern for a diversity of potential clients of all ages, economic backgrounds, and levels of dedication.

On the way into a recent game I was handed a surprisingly large box. Inside was a bobblehead of one of the team's starting pitchers. By this point of the season, the pitcher could comfortably be considered by most fans as "struggling." As we made our way through the concourse snide jokes were coupled with some attendees marveling at the free gift they had procured on their way through the turnstiles. Opinions within our own party differed greatly. Some were genuinely impressed, some wondered who exactly this person depicted as a bobblehead was, and some actually damned the fact that they had to lug a box with a bobblehead of a player inside that they may have not been too fond of that year.

Throughout the game, the bobbleheads (some out of their boxes) were used/abused/coveted in many ways. Some fans held tightly to their giveaway as a treasured keepsake or checked on them frequently beneath their seat to assure no spills or peanut dander was affecting the box's integrity. Adults and kids alike played with them. Others easily stuck them out of sight in favor of a cold beer or a foam finger.

On the way out, the boxes/figures remained a common sight. Clear bags full of other merchandise became handy carriers for some fans' bobbleheads. Fans also doggedly struggled with the boxes while handling kids or just while looking for their keys. We all carried a memento of the day, of that season, and of that specific player (who would later be traded the next season). My interest was keen throughout by the whole day, but it was not until getting outside of the park that I understood the full extent of a Major League team's giveaway day. On the way back to the car, we were approached by a woman holding out a fan-shaped collection of dollar bills. She was pleading to buy a bobblehead from one of the exiting attendees from that day's game. Amazed, yet still tightly clutching my keepsake, we made our way out to begin the long ride home.

Major League Baseball and its franchises partake in an intricate dance season to season. The ability to get fans to invest, live, and attend the 162 games that make up the season demands a vast network of people, labor, and marketing. The practices of MLB and its teams color and affect the experience and culture of modern baseball. Such is the case with the events of that day. Though my experience at the park indicated that some may find it arbitrary, silly, and/or confusing (why are they giving me something free?!?), the game-day giveaway is an expectation and a cornerstone reality of each season for fans and teams. How and why has it entrenched itself so completely in the marketing of MLB and as a cultural event? What makes it such a success and why do some fans even structure their attendance plans around these giveaways? Why is it that even video games like *MLB: The Show* have incorporated giveaway days as something gamers can manage/plan in their virtual MLB baseball seasons? How much of a part of the baseball experience does this represent?

This chapter examines the Major League giveaway. Though its very name may conjure up connotations of cheap and fleeting, we'll see that giveaways actually represent, like other subjects dealt with in this book, an interconnected web of use values on all sides of those invested in Major League Baseball, and an important part of understanding this American pastime as a popular culture event today. Beyond RBIs and ERAs, widely accepted practices in MLB like the giveaway constitute the current life of MLB and the realities of placing and packaging the game in American and global culture as both a marketable product and a cultural rite.

A Brief History of Giveaways

"Free." Perhaps this is a word that excites some as taking advantage of the system or something of the sort. Perhaps it is a word that conjures up suspicion and doubt as an antithetical term in the capitalist world order. Whatever the case may be, the practice of free that is exemplified in the Major League giveaway has been a familiar concept in the last century of marketing practices. Chris Anderson in his book *Free: The Future of a Radical Price* traces the mass incorporation of free as a marketing strategy to the beginning of the twentieth century, when first Jell-O and then Gillette razors sparked "one of the most powerful marketing tools of the twentieth century: giving away one thing to create demand for another" (Anderson 9–10). By giving away cookbooks and creating demand for disposable blades by giving away the razor, these two brands entrenched themselves as household names (9–10). Such industries as the banking industry and the restaurant industry over the years have become synonymous with the practice of "free." The effects of this initial practice are, of course, all around us still today. Though it may create a sense of doubt in some consumers, "free" has been and continues to be a powerful /term that pulls in consumer interest. Whether it is online with offers of "free" shipping or premiums given away at major sporting events, the allure lingers on.

Of course, not every industry found the practice as useful or effective as Jell-O or Gillette did. In fact, Major League Baseball was known for its lack of, or at least modest use of, marketing and promotions, such as giveaways throughout the first half of the twentieth century. As Chacar and Hesterly argue, MLB isolated itself from the larger structures of marketing and promotions during this time period:

> The owners did little to increase the appeal of the game and their revenues, despite a constant increase in promotional expenses in other American businesses from the 1860s. As Heylar notes, promotions were practically non-existent: "Typical was the Cincinnati Reds' idea of promotion: a three-foot square sign on the front of Crosley Field that said: Game Today.... Baseball people believed, essentially, that real men didn't market" [422–423].

Chacar and Hesterly, along with numerous other authors, point to Bill Veeck as the party crasher that brought down the veil of purity in Major League Baseball in the mid–twentieth century, and made way for common marketing practices in MLB today, including the giveaway (423).

Veeck was the owner of three major league teams throughout his career as a baseball impresario. He also "introduced ballpark crowd-pleasers like fan-appreciation night, player names on uniforms, fireworks displays, electronic scoreboards, and culinary alternatives to peanuts and Cracker Jacks" (Brewster). Veeck was seen by the baseball establishment as cheap and pandering even though he pioneered more "official" acts like being the first owner to sign an African-American player in the American League (Chacar and Hesterly 423; Novak). Veeck was a flashpoint of promotions and marketing practices that would become standardized in both minor league and MLB stadiums. The onus was taken off the purity/absoluteness of the game with his practices, as funds were directed towards creating an entertainment experience for a spectrum of attendees, including families. The game, of course, maintains the epicenter of action, but becomes one of the many entertainment possibilities in a modern MLB park, along with kids' areas, restaurants, and shopping opportunities.

Giveaways were part of Veeck's motus operandi. From barnyard animals to more accepted items like bats, Veeck worked with the theory "You can't win every game but you can make every game entertaining" (Novak). Pete Williams of the *Sports Business Journal* places the responsibility for the giveaway significantly on Veeck's shoulders: "More than a half century has passed since Bill Veeck helped create the promotional giveaway in sports, handing out 6,000 baseball bats to children accompanied by adults at a St. Louis Browns game." Williams adds that since that time the practice of the giveaway has become an entrenched part of the MLB stadium experience: "Since then, fans have received countless T-shirts, hats, keychains, beach towels, retail coupons, calendars, Beanie Babies, bobbleheads, magnet schedules and other knickknacks, with sponsors usually covering the cost, if not plastering their logo upon the product." Williams' comments aptly point out the financial realities of the giveaway, realities that are closely tied to corporate sponsorship. The following pages review the financial life of the giveaway and beyond. Teams, other business interests, and fans have created an immense network of relationships and understandings that are part of the successful packaging and cultural use of baseball as a popular culture product, national pastime, and utopian entertainment event.

The Business of the Giveaway

In this era of the life of MLB, in addition to thinking about broadcast rights, merchandising, and other numerous facets of the game, teams also still hold the core responsibility of keeping the turnstiles moving. Much like the prior discussion on walk-on music highlights, MLB teams are responsible for reaching a vast spectrum of fans and immersing them in a themed entertainment experience pushing consumption. From baseball purists to community center children's groups, the cavernous parks fuel a myriad of fan expectations for those in attendance. So how could a bobblehead or a grilling apron ensure financial success and meet customer demand for entertainment experiences? The simple answer, of course, is to pull fans in. But does this *really* work? Are people that anxious to get "free" merchandise even if it means paying seventy bucks for a lower-level seat?

The simple answer is "yes." According to a study in the *Journal of Sport Management*, promotions, in general, "increased attendance by about 3,893 fans per game, all else equal. In other words, the average increase in attendance is about 14 percent from having a promotion" (McDonald and Rascher 17). Teams appear to have such numbers in mind when they prominently feature giveaway and promotional nights like "Fireworks Night" on their printed pocket schedules. Promotions prominently are featured even as a "search" function on MLB team websites for many clubs. Fans are able to track down promotional nights as their base from which they can choose specific games to meet their giveaway and promotional needs. The same can be said of ticket packages like the San Francisco Giants 2010 Tim Lincecum and Pablo Sandoval Bobblehead mini-pack plans. Each plan featured six games including the specific date those respective bobbleheads were featured. According to a customer service agent from the team, all such packages were sold out early in the season.

According to some MLB sources, the correlation can be seen immediately and used strategically throughout the season. Patrick Klinger, vice president of marketing for the Twins, discussed the strategy in a 2004 interview: "We sit down at the beginning of the season and review our opponents and our game times; weaker opponents get stronger promotion support" (Taylor). Klinger reaffirms the strategy in an interview in 2006, stating that promotions (in this case, figurines) "move tickets on days that need some help" (qtd. in Williams). Other teams in 2006, such as the Cubs, "who pack Wrigley Field each game," looked at the practice as less of a seat-filler and more so as a "value add" (Williams). In the case of the Red Sox, no giveaways were listed on their team MLB.com schedule, a rare exception in MLB. The Twins have found a great deal of success in utilizing this strategy to fill up seats and increase revenue not only through ticket sales, but also further populating chances for these seat occupants to take part in concessions, entertainment, and retail opportunities.

Other approaches/strategies involving the giveaway look beyond the low-drawing single game strategy. Richard Tedesco in *Promo Magazine* discusses that although giveaways have been part of MLB marketing for some time, "The frequency of ballpark promotions took off in the mid-'90s, as baseball teams sought to rekindle the interest of disaffected fans after the 1994 strikes." Giveaways were thought of as value-added items that could be included in the Major League Baseball entertainment experience that would bring fans back. The bad PR felt from the elongated strikes was met with a concentrated focus on welcoming fans and creating a sense of goodwill in those fans that may have had their visions of the purity and sacredness of the game tainted by the perceived greed. *Time* diagnosed the feeling of some fans when the magazine wrote, "Never before has the naked power struggle between players and owners seemed so heedless and self-destructive" (Shapiro et al.). Plummeting attendance due to this perception of greed and the wants of individuals at the expense of the game was partially countered by the strategic use and draw of bobbleheads and other giveaways.

According to Tedesco, giveaways were, and are still, part of the promotional methods meant to help MLB compete for revenues against the National Basketball Association and the National Football League, especially in the past two decades. Baseball has had its work cut out for it due to the 1994 strike and more recently from negotiating the choppy waters of the fallout from the steroid era in baseball. The rise of NASCAR, the rise of ticket prices, and other factors come into play as well when trying to figure out the centrality of the giveaway as a marketing tactic meant to help keep MLB above water in the 1990s and 2000s. MLB has generally successfully overcome these said challenges, but has retained practices, like the giveaway, that were meant to reestablish a symbiotic relationship between the fans and the product.

The reestablishment of this relationship reflects Major League Baseball's ability (like many professional leagues) to look beyond the purity and nostalgia of their product and to view baseball as an entertainment industry (Chacar and Hesterly 432). Much like Disney World, the MLB and its teams aim to create cohesively themed environments where establishing and creating consumer ties to the brand can be facilitated. The ability of fans to feel connected and welcome in the ballpark translates into financial dividends for teams. Robert Alvarado, the Angels vice president of marketing, frames it as such: "Your loyalties as a baseball fan actually lie in whatever emotional connection you make in the ballpark" (qtd. in Tedesco). That emotional connection, as Mark McDonald and Daniel Rascher explain, has to overcome numerous variables, including the potential quality of the game itself: "To be successful, a team must offer a variety of peripheral products in case the game itself isn't of high quality. This helps smooth out the value of the overall experience from game to game" (15). Such is the case in other forms of ballpark culture today, such as children's play areas, restaurants, and shopping outlets. Giveaways can be a formidable first wave of attack for fans making their way into the festivities, by creating a sense of investment that is developed and encouraged throughout their time at the stadium. If teams and MLB can catch multiple market segments with the diversity of any of these hooks, that means that there is always something to come back for and some level of investment (in a multiplicity of forms) in the massive project/brand/experience at hand.

Developing the brand of MLB and its teams as living, caring entities is a central concern of the baseball world today. Rein, Kotler, and Shields in *The Elusive Fan*, describe this targeting of fans as a need to reflect macro and micro concerns, since the "MLB macro brand embodies the core attributes of family and youth, history and nostalgia, and summer and leisure. Its micro brands include its 30 different teams, players, managers, executives, and the sport itself. While the Oakland Athletics are an MLB micro brand centered on youth, irreverence, and innovative management, ideally they still must represent and reinforce the macro brand of MLB" (136). Enticing fans with special events, ballpark amenities like kids' areas, and giveaways are all meant to be resources to create these emotional connections between the fan and the team along with their connection to MLB as a brand itself (not to mention the packaging and marketing of individual players). For some families and individuals, some of the sting of paying for a MLB ticket can be partially alleviated by this "value-added" process. These items and a carnival atmosphere from which to escape the realities of the world outside of the turnstiles are meant to immerse attendees and hopefully create dedication to the brand. Of course, if a team runs out of giveaways or only offers a certain number, PR departments may find themselves attending to disappointed fans as the value-add can become a point of contention for those missing out on the "value-add" process.

In a 2009 *USA Today* article, MLB showcased a new level of selling the experience to families struggling with the economic downturn. In lieu of more lavish trips, MLB sought to "entice fans to make the ballpark their vacation destination this year" (Ortiz "Sales"). The ballpark is no longer a mere spot to watch a game of baseball, but has become a vacation destination entertainment center. Look out, Disney World, the party has moved to Tropicana Field, Safeco Park, and Target Field. Certainly, for some, these amenities and the idea of MLB parks as urban or suburban entertainment complexes reflect the rise of needless distractions taking away from the majesty of the game. Still, events like giveaway nights, as part of this carnivalization of baseball, reflect the need to create a welcoming and personal brand at the micro and macro levels that can pull in a spectrum of fans.

More than creating a brand and pulling in people to fill the seats, the giveaway reflects numerous other possibilities for concerned parties. Corporate sponsors, teams looking to fill out sponsorship packages, premium makers of the products themselves, and the fans all can benefit and actively take part in the spoils of this culture of "free." Much like the previous chapter exemplified with walk-on music, giveaways are a deceptively simple part of the culture of baseball, that in actuality are ornately orchestrated flashpoints of use values for all of those taking part, whether it be from the top or from the turnstiles.

Corporate sponsors, for instance, are an important part of figuring out the puzzle. A good number of the premiums given away at ballparks carry with them a prominently featured corporate sponsor's logo. This is the case for products themselves, along with any packaging that is used as well. These sponsored promotions, according to a source in a 2006 *Marketing* article, are ripe places for giveaways to act as "tangible touch points for integrated campaigns" (qtd. in Bashford). Even if a logo is not featured, "value to sponsors now comes from associating with the big-event night itself" (Williams). Companies are able to sponsor giveaways as part of ongoing campaigns that associate their brand with MLB and its teams. Although Chevrolet may have little to do with the "Carlos Pena Toothbrush Holder" product that they are sponsoring, the company benefits from its association with the team, MLB, goodwill from fans recognizing the promotion positively, and from the fact that a prominent Chevy logo will now be featured on the bookshelves, and in this case, in the bathrooms of thousands of young fans, since the promotion was aimed at children 14 and under ("Rays Schedule").

Any danger that may come in not getting fans to create a concrete link between a company and a product that may have nothing to do with their specific brand, such as the case above, is countered by the company's name being linked to the entertainment experience of MLB ballparks. The companies that sponsor giveaway nights will often be companies whose name is seen in other parts of the park and potentially on televised games as well. Though a constant concern exists that there may be a "watering down effect" when too many promotions crowd teams' schedules (McDonald and Rascher 17), and that the practice may fall out of favor, the numbers tend to prove that the system is still working fine for sponsors. Ken Belson highlights this in a piece for the *New York Times* that discusses Gold's Mustard and bobblehead giveaways. According to Belson, "[Marc] Gold said the bobbleheads had helped increase mustard sales about 10 percent a year since the company started sponsoring them. Sales have grown regardless of the team's performance or the commemorated player." In addition to sales, a more ongoing branding campaigning is associated with the giveaways for Gold: "People are going to put it on their fridge or desk and connect it to Gold's" (Belson).

Teams and sponsors also find mutual benefit in offering the giveaway as part of company sponsorship packages. These packages help to guarantee revenue for teams from sponsors, while it provides sponsors with a variety of choices in presenting their brand to consumers. Sponsors like Delta Airlines apply funds to giveaways along with "tickets, suite costs, print signage, arena signage, etc" (Williams). MLB.com, individual team's MLB sites, and schedules (print, magnet, etc.) feature giveaway dates and their sponsors then prominently throughout the season. Tedesco cites the fact that this has equaled out to a big business, explaining, "Teams typically create events and giveaways and then get corporate sponsors to match." This includes, in 2007, $505 million in sponsorships (Tedesco). This amount of money reflects a process that is mutually beneficial for sponsors, teams, and MLB. Revenue streams come into the ballpark, while exposure to individual brands leaves with the fans on bobbleheads, caps, and toothbrush holders. Even in the most recent economic downturn, when fans and sponsors alike were struggling the practice of the giveaway did not subside and was focused on by many teams as key additional value to add to the price of tickets ("Can Baseball"). Even in economic mire, companies kept the bobbleheads bouncing, since their connection between their brand and the giveaway remained intact.

According to Belson, premiums like bobbleheads are relatively cheap individual items to produce and deliver (about three dollars each). Promotional businesses that create these premiums can see a significant amount of money changing hands, especially if they are able to employ Chinese labor in the production process. A 2001 piece in The *Wall Street Journal* on bobbleheads in numerous sports leagues described that "Alexander Global Promotions Inc. of Bellevue, Wash., makes most of the dolls— 280,000 a month, in China. The company is developing prototypes for the Women's National Basketball Association and the PGA golf tour, and PepsiCo has contracted it to make dolls of about 40 college mascots, including Stanford University's tree" (Fatsis). Today, the company continues to provide bobbleheads along with snow globes, tote bags, drink ware, apparel and many other products to teams in various leagues that continue to be targets for professional league use thanks to their relative affordability.

Bensussen Deutsch & Associates is cited by an ESPN piece as producing "most of the bobbleheads given away at major league ballparks. The company says it is scheduled to deliver more than 1 million dolls combined for at least 44 promotional dates this season" (Caple). To reinforce the continued demand for promotional items like the bobblehead, the ESPN piece describes that demand for the company's production includes six Mariners games in 2010, with 30,000 bobblehead dolls given away at each date (Caple). Though the concern remains that promotional items may produce a watering down effect in some of the research on giveaways, MLB believes the giveaway is a viable marketing option for most teams. If any concern was there, the majority of teams promotional schedules did not reflect any lessening of the practice of the giveaway in 2011.

Fan Demand for Giveaways

Amidst this elaborate dance of relationships, profit margins, and marketing, some attention needs to be paid to those creating the demand for giveaways: the fan. The opening narrative of our ballpark experience attests to the fact that there is no way to reduce the baseball fan into one discernable identity or group. Giveaways can prove to be an add-on in value for some fans as well as be considered a needless exercise in team and corporate pandering. As DJ Gallo put it in a piece for *ESPN.com*, "As American sports fans we hold these truths to be self-evident, that all teams are created equal on Opening Day, and that we are endowed by our Creator with certain unalienable Rights, that among these are Life, Liberty and the pursuit of Free Crap."

Gallo's piece was part of an impressive number of media and fan discussions about the upcoming season's giveaways across the nation. A significant amount of effort is put forth by media outlets as well as in fan outlets as each new season beckons on the horizon. Commentary ranging from praise to disdain is directed towards teams and their choices for the year's free merchandise. ESPN and SI.com both have featured pieces on giveaway promotions. Local news outlets, blogs and fan discussion forums as well offer a whole host of fodder for fan discussion, whether it be on the totality of the coming year's program of giveaways, discussions of a specific date, trading/selling discussions, or the lasting effects of a giveaway.

ESPN.com offered a preview of the best and worst giveaways for the upcoming year in an April 2010 piece. The author, DJ Gallo, admonished the Cubs' "W" Banner giveaway, stating, "It's the Cubs. *The W here can't mean Win, can it?* I think they accidently left off the T and F." Gallo then praises the White Sox' "Mothers Day White Baseball Hat," by stating, "A promotional item for females at a baseball game and it is NOT the color pink? This might just be the best promotional item of all time!" Though Gallo offers a top-down assessment of the giveaway season, other major news outlets allow for a good deal of fan influence and reflection when discussing this and many other subjects.

In the case of *SI.com*, users are able to see a comprehensive list of rankings. One of the rankings available is done to rank teams via quality of promotions. In 2008, for instance, the rankings depended on the quantitative responses rating "the quality of the promotions/giveaways offered by the home team." Each team's quantitative information was set off by a small section allowing for qualitative data from fans as well. In response to the questions "What is the best promotion/giveaway your team has offered? What is the worst? What is a promotion you'd like to see?" fans decidedly did not hold back their thoughts on the subject. Fans both praised and lamented their team's giveaway practices. The Angels, ranked sixth on the list, solicited the following comment on a favorite giveaway: "Thundersticks during the playoffs were great, because they created a pumped-up atmosphere the team lacked before 2002." The twenty-second ranked Yankees had a fan complain, "The worst was one of the bobblehead nights when they only gave them out to kids. I hate paying 10-year-olds $10 to get a bobblehead." A Minnesota fan described both sides in one post: "Worst: Minnesota Road Map Night. The road maps turned into giant airplanes sailing down from the upper deck. Best: Dairy Queen Spatula Night. The clink, clink of the 10,000 spatulas was incredible." To showcase the potential disdain or apathy for giveaways, one can look to a Tigers fan's post that "I don't really care about promotions since they usually only apply to the first 10,000 people.... I'm not going to sit around for four or five hours before the first pitch just to get a bobblehead." ("MLB Ballpark"). The *SI.com* rankings showcase a mixture of industry and fan interaction, which is not a rarity by any means in a sports media industry that looks to encourage fan participation through sports talk radio, comments on websites, etc. Still, we can see that major media outlets are dedicating space and effort to measure and analyze the giveaway culture of MLB. They are providing opportunities to keep the conversation and the investment in this marketing practice going for consumers/fans of Major League Baseball and their respective teams.

Local media outlets as well cater to the demand from fans to cover and provide a forum for discussion when it comes to giveaways. Like the examples above, these events have become news events and an expected part of the consumption of baseball season to season. Fans were alerted to the team's bobblehead giveaway schedule in the *Milwaukee Journal Sentinel's* Brewers' Blog in February 2008 (Walker "Brewers Announce"). The *Palm Beach Post* helped fans deal with the fallout of a scandalous giveaway of the vuvuzela, (otherwise known as the World Cup Mosquito Noise-Makers of 2010). The Marlins gave away 15,000 noise-makers, with everyone seeming to have an opinion about the subject. While the president celebrated the giveaway, second baseman Dan Uggla stated, "That was the worst handout or giveaway I've ever been a part of in baseball," and fans either blew away happily, wore earplugs, and/or complained (D'Angelo). Tom D'Angelo's article "Opinions Mixed on Florida Marlins' Vuvuzela Giveaway," in this case probed not only into the effect of the giveaway on fans, but also into the possible implications for the players and the sacred ground in the middle of the vuvuzela madness. Though decreed a success by some, the culture of the giveaway is also highly interrogated as one practice stepping beyond its supposed boundaries in the cultural practice of baseball.

Fans frequently look outside of national and local media sources as well to partake in the discussion and investment in the giveaway. Perhaps some of the greatest indicators of the developing fan cultures and communities concerned and invested in giveaways can come from fan forums discussing all facets of the subject, or in immense networks of giveaway memorabilia sales. Networks of traders, buyers, commentators, and discussants abound, showcasing the formality of this seemingly fleeting detail of the MLB season.

A discussion forum that is especially active are the bobblehead message boards. A steady stream of forum users post bobblehead trades, sales and alerts, and archive bobblehead information. "The Only Accurate Bobblehead Collectors Board," "The Bobble Board," and "Bobble Bums" are some of the few spots in which the giveaway community can get together to discuss their wants and conquests. The search can be expanded beyond bobbleheads by using the acronym "SGA" to search out stadium giveaways of all varieties. These message boards will often deal with multiple sports and the giveaways associated with various leagues and teams.

Seemingly the most traffic for giveaways comes on secondary-market sites like eBay where giveaway items past and present are available for sale. Stadium giveaways like schedules, apparel, and bobbleheads are available to fans for purchase. Collectors wanting a certain giveaway from a game they were not able to make it to that day can often find giveaways posted within hours of the completion of the game. The *St. Petersburg Times* chronicled such an event when demand for Tampa Bay Rays Championship Ring replicas (given out in the stadium two days before the publication of the article) pushed prices up to $125 on eBay for the replica ring made of zinc alloy (Nipps). The *Wall Street Journal* chronicled in 2001 the popularity of bobbleheads on eBay, stating, "Bobbleheads are fresh meat for collectors and dealers. Limited runs—teams generally don't give away more than 10,000 dolls based on the likenesses of the most popular players—create the instant scarcity that collectors covet. Some new dolls have sold for hundreds of dollars in Internet auctions" (Fatsis).

With potential money to be made, and a wealth of willing collectors to obtain giveaways in person and through other secondary methods, demand (especially for bobbleheads) can be sometimes intense for MLB clubs. In the case of the 2006 Tigers, the want for rally towels by Comerica Park attendees necessitated some quick, fancy footwork, "After Major League Baseball originally planned a different giveaway for the first two games of the World Series this weekend at Comerica Park, MLB and the Tigers announced on Friday that they'll be giving away the towels after a surprising demand from the fans" (Beck). MLB was cited as normally taking over giveaway responsibilities in the World Series. Up to that point the Tigers provided fans with giveaways during the Division Series and ALCS. Thankfully, MLB and the Tigers were able to provide the coveted towels to attendees.

Demand for Minnesota Twins bobbleheads in the late '90s and early '00s brought a feverish response from Twins fans and others trying to get their hands on a doll. According to a VP of marketing for the Twins: "We had lines of people at the ballpark farther than the eye could see. We gave away 5,000 bobbleheads in five minutes, but we had huge security issues, with line crashers and bobblehead snatchers who ran through the concourse literally stealing the dolls out of our customers' hands" (qtd. in Taylor). The team also came up in The *Wall Street Journal* piece mentioned above. Twins business executive Dave St. Peter remarked, in the case of a Kirby Puckett giveaway: "People in Minnesota don't riot.... But it was probably as close as we get" (Fatsis).

With the demand generated for specific giveaways, teams over the past decade have had to adapt. Bobbleheads and other giveaways have necessitated official policy to deal with the demand of fans and collectors. Teams have also, as pointed out earlier, packaged some giveaway days into ticket packs, where for the right price some level of comfort can be purchased by the ticketholder. In addition, some teams have increased production of giveaway items for larger crowds and are offering a plethora of giveaway possibilities for fans throughout the season.

The concern to avoid near-riots, like the one described in Minnesota, has pushed teams into creating formal policies to regulate the giveaway process and fans themselves. Stadium guest information guides and team websites discuss in detail the expectations and regulations for giveaways. In the case of the Phillies in the 2010 season, the team's policy was to offer only one giveaway per fan, no matter how many tickets that individual was holding. In addition the team defines an eligible fan as one who "meets advertised age limits or other requirements (i.e. All Kids 14 & Under on a kids promotion)" ("Promotions and Giveaways"). The Milwaukee Brewers' policy differs somewhat for ticketholders: "Each eligible guest shall receive one item immediately after entering the turnstile, unless specified otherwise. Those with multiple tickets must exit and re-enter receive one promotional item per additional ticket" (Milwaukee 20).

One impressively spelled-out example of promotional policies comes from the Kansas City Royals. The 373-word "Promotional Guidelines" page on their official MLB team website spells out numerous different contingencies for fans and collectors that may come up in a giveaway. The team discusses the need for a ticket to be in unadulterated form, a policy like the Brewers where fans will need to reenter with several tickets if they possess them to get multiple giveaways, age requirements, the need for fans to be cognizant of collecting their item in the "distribution area" (as they will not be given an item upon reentry back into the distribution area), and possibilities of shipping damage. Numerous other areas meant to meet any complaints or to address any previous issues abound in addition to the themes dealt with above, including a policy for younger fans: "For giveaways to children ages 14 & under, each child must have a valid ticket to be eligible to receive an item. Children 32 inches and below who do not require a ticket to enter the stadium, will be eligible to receive an item" ("Kansas City").

With such detail, one might wonder about the history of fan run-ins at the guest relations desk at Kauffman Stadium over the years. Though, as this study as suggested, the demand for these items has been such that formal rules need to be implemented for appropriate and safe distribution of free items. As money is to be made by sellers, as collections are made to grow, as online forum users will depend on these items to create a community, so must the giveaway be held with formal regard.

The Future of Baseball as Popular Culture Product

Entering the ballpark that day, I had no idea of the culture that surrounded the giveaway item I held in my hand. More than a random fun event, the giveaway has proven to be a formalized practice of the culture of MLB today. As this chapter shows, and ultimately this book will claim, scholarship on baseball needs to recognize the diverse set of influences, practices, and themes that create a remarkably important part to the whole when studying the culture of baseball today and its life as a popular culture product. It is these themes and events that occur both on and off the field that contribute to keeping the sport going amongst challenges from the economy, other sports leagues, and other entertainment venues.

The romance of the game ... the sacredness of the field ... the history of the game ... endear many, creating a space of authenticity, escape, and identity. It is off the beaten base path though, that we see the complexity and totality of the game for a whole host of audience use values. The giveaway, led by the popularity of the bobblehead, is part of the culture that surrounds the actual actions on the field. It is in this periphery where we can see numerous other facets of authenticity, escape, identity, and even profit. The giveaway has become a part of the fabric of baseball. From Bill Veeck to the Marlins' vuvuzela conundrum, the culture of the giveaway is a means, as are these other chapters, for scholars, lovers of the game, consumers, marketers, owners, casual fans, and countless others to understand the life of baseball in the modern world. Often functioning conversely as an authentic American experience and part of American identity, as well as a for-profit, complex, and formidable business model, MLB lives many lives in America and globally, pulling in as many for the ride/experience as possible. These practices, these collection plates, have kept the church of baseball's doors open, even if sometimes it may appear they are just giving it all away.

3

Everything but the Players
The Game-Used Memorabilia Market

Amongst other trends in the development of baseball stadiums in the last two decades, a key development has been a focus on access. A view of the action, a sense of proximity to the action on the field throughout the park, and a lack of massive concrete "obstructed view" pillars have all been featured concerns of teams and fans alike. The contemporary ballpark is a remarkably welcoming atmosphere, meant to make up for some of the (as some would argue) concrete monster ballparks of the '60s and '70s. As discussed in the two previous chapters on walk-on music and giveaways, MLB teams have sought to create an accessible carnival-like atmosphere of entertainment and escape. The space is yours; hopefully though, you're willing to share the space and pay for access to it.

Still, with such a sense of fun, escape, and welcome, there is a staunchly held invisible line of segregation. Though the feeling of "closeness" has perhaps increased in these new parks, and a relatively small space divides the first row of seats and the field, is it possible that this space between observer and player has never been so strikingly vast? Very visible levels of security to protect celebrity players along with the field itself, and access to both in batting practice, warm-ups, etc., are common sights in every park. Like some fans would agree, Ellen M. Iseman shared in a *New York Times* column that this has even extended itself beyond team's home stadiums. Iseman laments that the last bastion of player/game access, spring training, is gone as well: "It seems the greatest loss for spectators is their more limited contact with players, a quintessential joy of spring training." Iseman continues, "We know we will watch the Yankees play again in the Bronx. But they will be walled off by a phalanx of security guards there, farther out of reach." Security is one thing, but many aspire for better levels of access to the field and its occupants, saying it is part of the game itself.

Issues of security are joined here by a remarkably formalized economic system of access to players and to the game itself. There are many levels of access that fans can potentially pay for to get themselves past that imposing (if not physically, then ideologically) wall that separates spectator from actor, and the seat from the stage. Whether in the form of paying for a player experience like a golf outing, paying a player at a signing to autograph the "sweet spot" on a baseball, or providing a team with enough advertising dollars to guarantee an employee a first pitch, there are ways to challenge the lines that separate the game and the spectator. A specifically powerful bridge that is the focus of this chapter is the rise of authenticated memorabilia that breaks the fourth wall of MLB for many fans. This practice has become a meticulous undertaking for MLB and has come into its own in this new century of baseball. For the right price you can get closer to the field and sometimes literally in the shoes of your favorite players.

Much like the other everyday practices of MLB dealt with in this book, this chapter examines the practice of selling "game-used" and autographed memorabilia and how it contributes to the economic and popular cultural milieu that is MLB today. The practice of buying authenticated pieces of the game has taken on a new importance in the contemporary world of baseball: these are pieces that are *authentic* parts of a much larger business venture *and* popular culture product that pulls in various levels of fandom and investment into this cultural product. Fans have a chance of purchasing a piece of something that is above and beyond an economic investment or product. The successful rise of the MLB authentication program in this new century of baseball does significantly reflect on the contemporary culture of business practices that make up the MLB experience today, but the program also represents the immense need and desire for access to a game that provides a rich array of emotional and cultural linkages for those deciding to take part in the spectacle. Though, as some purists would argue, the game has never been more exclusive and elusive to fans seeking a relationship to the game, the rise of the MLB authentication program and specifically the market they have created of game-used memorabilia has successfully filled a part of this void for all levels of fans.

These Memories Are Nothing New: Memorabilia and MLB

The game has a long-storied history of signed balls, bats, and for the fortunate few, a home run or foul ball caught in the stands. What is new though are Major League Baseball's efforts to deliver memorabilia to the buying public through their authentication program that was launched in 2001. The program seeks to make those items connected to the game available for purchase, and to chronicle each item systematically to guarantee authenticity, prevent fraud, and provide a remarkable historical record of each piece's role in the action. This practice of chronicling and selling game-used and autographed items is a part of the potent memorabilia industry that surrounds MLB and other professional sports leagues.

To understand the historical context in regards to the rise of the MLB authentication program, one must dig back into the history of memorabilia a bit to make sense of it. Vice President of Operations for Field of Dreams Steve Dall, a now-partner with MLB's Authentication program, shared in an interview with us that the market for MLB memorabilia has been around "you could say forever." Indeed, one only has to check out operations like Field of Dreams or other memorabilia companies to see that right along-side autographs and game-used memorabilia associated with a player like Derek Jeter sit other items from baseball's history, such as pieces associated with Honus Wagner, Babe Ruth, etc. Especially as baseball became a product of mass media in the last century, fans have wanted to have a piece of the game or of their favorite player that connects *them* to the myth, whether through obtaining autographs, baseball cards, or game-used items.

It was in the 1980s and 1990s, though, that some significant movement occurred within the memorabilia industry that led to the current MLB authentication culture. For example, the insurance industry traces the history back to a key event for their industry in bringing the memorabilia market into a new formalized state. Robert Hyle in the *National Underwriter* states that insurers began to insure memorabilia for individuals and for memorabilia dealers increasingly in the 1980s. Tom Finkelmeier of Cornell & Finkelmeier isolates the early 80s (1982) as a time when "the hobby exploded into a $2 billion industry." The article continues, saying that the "boom in collectibles meant the need to insure them was even greater. Collectors were not the only ones who needed coverage, though. The memorabilia boom spawned a host of retail stores dealing in sports memorabilia" (Hyle). The rise of these retail outlets added another layer to this increasingly economically legitimate patchwork.

The successful founding of several major players in memorabilia retail also spoke to the boom experienced in the last several decades. For instance, Steiner Sports Memorabilia, a retail and web-based retailer, came into the market in 1987 ("Small Catalog/Web Merchant" 52). The company provides customers with in-store public signings and private signings where personal items can be sent in for an athlete to sign. Field of Dreams, the aforementioned retail and web retailer, entered the market in 1998. The company, like Steiner, also offers signings. These retail spaces, besides providing access to memorabilia, also cemented the practice of players developing "relationships" with specific companies that give these dealers exclusive access to players. Here a player may only sign "sweet spots" (the horizontal area that is the smallest between seams) on a baseball through these companies, versus signing off-sweet-spot in the stadium (if access is obtained).

These retail outlets were also joined by growing auction houses dealing in sports/MLB memorabilia. Possibly the most telling example of the expanding market and the canonization of sports memorabilia as a growing economic product, and reverence for the industry's focus, came in the form of Sotheby's dealings in these items in 1989, and at Christie's "which once sold only a few items a year, has greatly stepped up its sports offerings" (Dunkin 122). Looking into prior lots on these auction houses' sites reveals why paying attention to this market could be advantageous for such established auction houses. On Christie's site, for example, Mark McGwire's 50th home run baseball which went for $46,000 in 1998 greatly surpassed the $12,000 to $15,000 estimate ("Mark McGwire"). In 1991 Sotheby's featured the "landmark $4.5 million Copeland Collection of Important Baseball Cards and Sports Memorabilia" that included a mint-condition 1909 Honus Wagner tobacco card (Tully 190). The collection is part of the economic onslaught in the '80s and '90s that brought a formidable tone to the sports memorabilia industry, including auction houses that primarily focus on baseball.

The addition of auction houses that specialized in sports memorabilia has brought names like Leland's, Robert Edward Auctions, Ron Oser Enterprises and the now-defunct Mastro Fine Sports Auctions who consolidated with Oser Enterprises into the fray. Mastro did not close due to lack of interest, but due to a federal investigation into "'shill bidding' in which bogus bids are submitted to drive up the prices of collectibles." At the time of the investigation, Mastro was cited as reporting revenues of "$45 million in 2006" (Cohen). Later, three executives from the company morphed the holdings into Legendary Auctions. As we will see shortly, this will be far from the only instance in which the undesirable underbelly of the market allegedly showed itself. Such dedicated auction houses that focus on sports memorabilia like those mentioned before, along with more traditional names like Christie's continue to pursue this market and the continued demand for getting fans closer to the game.

The same can be said of eBay and Amazon as well. As *Time* stated in a 1999 article, the combination of high-end auctioneers and accessible forums like eBay have generated a spectrum of items for sale: "The memorabilia market runs hot and cold. In the early '90s, only truly special mementos brought big money. In today's bull market, though, collectors recently had a chance to bid via online auctioneer eBay for a McGwire jockstrap with a listed price of $1,500. Game-used bats, balls and uniforms tend to be the hottest items" (Kadlec). With such a spectrum of interests in the market, both legitimate and not-so-legitimate interests flourished, thus making forgeries a definite concern.

A concern for all of the above parties, from Sotheby's to eBay, is to tackle the concern of authenticity, as the industry is very much built on it. eBay, itself, was the target of a lawsuit in 2000 that alleged that eBay "hadn't fulfilled its obligations as an auctioneer" to "certify the authenticity of goods sold on its site" (Davis 20). For a market that seeks to get fans on the field and in the shoes of their heroes, authenticity is key. Was that ball actually struck by Ichiro at an at-bat, or are you holding an official MLB ball scuffed in the backyard of an opportunist in Kalamazoo, Michigan? The established companies above have made this a central concern. Forensic certificates of authenticity, in-store signings, and private signings have all been employed to vouch for the authentic collectible. Still, fraud abounded and became the target of investigations by the FBI via "Operation Foul Ball" and "Operation Bullpen." It was these investigations that pushed Major League Baseball, which represents a significant percentage of memorabilia market interest, into unveiling a benchmark practice for measuring authenticity in regard to baseball memorabilia. The Major League Baseball authentication program could not only ensure a sense of security with fans and dealers but also could be a remarkable revenue creator.

Looking into the Eyes of the Hologram: Major League Baseball's Authentication Program

For as long as the practice of selling baseball memorabilia has been around, the practice of selling phony items has been around as well. Though the preceding efforts to guarantee the authenticity were in practice, the number one mode of defense came in (and perhaps this speaks to the addiction of collecting) "knowing your dealer." The mid '90s saw an upswing in people concerning themselves with the memorabilia industry and its potentiality for forgeries and fakes. In 1995 Upper Deck, for instance, filed a lawsuit to "stop the flow of unauthorized sports memorabilia." Today, an official licensee of MLB's authentication program, Upper Deck named several corporations of concern, "in an attempt to force all memorabilia manufacturers to comply with California law relating to certificates of authenticity" ("Upper Deck"). The company, amongst other projects, features autographs and game-used memorabilia in their baseball cards where small bits of a ball, bat, or uniform will be framed within a baseball card. Other companies like Topps also featured such cards, including in "Sterling" packs, where guaranteed game-used memorabilia and/or autographs are included for the handsome sum of 250-plus dollars. Such cards have been popular since the late '90s.

Upper Deck's suit today seems like an admirable, yet limited undertaking when compared with the extent of fraud that was exposed in the FBI's "Operation Foul Ball" and "Operation Bullpen." These investigations that successively ran through the late 1990s determined that a massive percentage of memorabilia that was on the market at the time was fake:

> While it is impossible to definitely estimate the percentage of forged memorabilia, most industry experts concede that over half of the autographed memorabilia is forged. In fact, some cooperating subjects and memorabilia experts believe that up to 90 percent of the memorabilia on the market is forged. Industry experts estimate that the autographed memorabilia market in the United States is approximately $1 billion per year. Using these estimates, forged memorabilia comprises between $500,000,000 and $900,000,000 of the market. (Federal Bureau of Investigation)

"Operation Bullpen" was an extension of "Operation Foul Ball" conducted by the Chicago division of the FBI where "Bullpen" worked with information from Upper Deck to investigate forgeries on the market (Federal Bureau of Investigation). Both autographed and game-used memorabilia collectors and businesses were shaken by the news. Dall, of Field of Dreams, calls "Operation Bullpen" "a pivotal event in our industry as collectors then migrated to the more reputable companies" (Dall). The specific concern about baseball memorabilia had been taken to task. Major League Baseball was poised to address their corner of the memorabilia market as both an authority of authenticity and as a potential benefactor from taking on the memorabilia market that had found such popularity and formalization in the past several decades.

Major League Baseball launched the MLB Authentication Program in 2001, the first such program of any league in professional sports. "Operation Bullpen" clearly demonstrated that MLB could fill a need in regulating memorabilia and guaranteeing MLB product authenticity. According to *Sports Illustrated* the FBI determined that "up to 85 percent of memorabilia sold with the MLB [itself] emblem had been counterfeited" (Stack). Economically, it presented a way for MLB to more aggressively insert itself as an authoritative name in the sports memorabilia market that could speak to the doubts and anxieties brought up by the FBI investigations.

The launch of the program in January 2001 drew a considerable amount of attention from collectors, dealers, and the press. In a *Washington Post* article from that month, Tim Bronson, "baseball's executive vice president/business," stated that "Operation Bullpen" pushed MLB into launching the program with the intent to "protect our fans" (Sheinin). Lanny Jennings, "owner of The Batter's Box, a memorabilia store," stated in that same article that it wasn't that cut and dry in his perspective: "All this is going to do is generate more revenue for Major League Baseball and drive the prices of memorabilia to insane levels," adding that "only a 'very small' percentage of memorabilia he sees is fake" (Sheinin).

Though such concerns were voiced, the predominance of the press attention and MLB PR perspective were focused on the program, its inner-workings, and its further establishment in the memorabilia industry. A press release on *Business Wire* announced that "Major League Baseball has named MLB.com, Field of Dreams and MLB Clubhouse stores as the preferred retail outlets of the MLB Authentication Program." In addition, "MLB authenticated memorabilia can also be found in official MLB Clubhouse stores as well as retail stores across the country through the program's official licensees including Upper Deck Authenticated, Mounted Memories, Tri Star Productions, and Steiner Sports Marketing for autographs, and Legends Collectibles for game used items" (Sports and Retail). Later that year, a press release announced that "Former New York Yankees first baseman Don Mattingly has joined Major League Baseball Properties to support and promote the MLB Authentication Program," in which Mattingly stated, "This program is designed to ensure that fans receive authentic Major League Baseball autographed and game-used memorabilia, and I hope to help reinforce that message" (Major League Baseball "Former"). Attaching a major name brought attention to the program, but many MLB fans remained unaware or unknowing of the increasingly everyday practice of authenticating in MLB.

Since these initial press releases and articles, the program has solicited a stream of media attention mostly as human interest pieces, especially when it comes to the practice of collecting and inventorying pieces of game-used equipment. The *New York Times, Washington Post, Philadelphia Inquirer, Sports Illustrated,* and *Tuff Stuff,* amongst others, have chronicled the meticulous process and investment in collecting that the MLB Authentication Program helps to ensure. Many of the pieces featured in these publications deal with the program as an almost subculture living just out of sight of the fan/park attendees. The following excerpt from *Sports Illustrated* is a good representation of unearthing this unknown culture via a pitch thrown by Roy Oswalt in the NLCS to catcher Carlos Ruiz. "Ruiz hands the ball to home plate umpire Dan Iassogna, who gives the scuffed-up ball to a waiting Phillies batboy. The batboy runs back to the dugout to clean it, then hustles over to MLB authenticator Dennis Watson, who's sitting in a small field box between the first base camera pit and the front row of seats behind home plate. This is the first of dozens of baseballs Watson will receive for authentication on this night. And baseballs are only the tip of the iceberg for all the items MLB's authentication program certifies as being officially game-used" (Stack). The extent and significant orchestration that memorabilia plays in the symphony of modern baseball practices continues to be refined and further formalized.

Since its launch, the program has authenticated over 3,000,000 items with an estimated 450,000 to 600,000 items authenticated in the 2010 Season ("MLB Authentication"; Stack). The first year saw only about 500 objects authenticated (Wood). Items include autographs and game-used merchandise such as: lineup cards, locker room name placards, bases, balls, clothing, shoes, and dirt. Each piece is authenticated by a "third party authenticator at each and every game, who witnesses all items that received a signature or that were removed from the field" ("MLB Authentication"). According to an article published in 2010, authenticators at MLB games were from "Authenticators Inc." who were "current or ex-law enforcement officials chosen on an invitation-only basis" (Steinberg "Authenticating"). It appears, according to a 2006 feature in the *New York Daily News*, that representatives from "the accounting firm Deloitte & Touche" have also played a role in the program (O'Keeffe).

At each game authenticators place a hologram on the piece of game-used memorabilia that was witnessed as being used in the game. They then record the role of the item in the game. For instance, a game-used ball purchased by one of the authors of this book from the "Fan Zone" store at Miller Park, has a tamper-proof hologram attached to it (provided by a company called OpSec Security) that contains a code including a prefix of letters and series of numbers. One can then visit the MLB Authentication Website (http://www.mlb.com/mlb/authentication/index.jsp) to type in the specific code. The following then pops up in a new window underneath a MLB logo with the offered option of printing it off:

> Hologram number LH017225 was located in the MLB Authentication Database under GAME-USED BASEBALL.
> Session Product Description:
> Session Name: COL AT MIL
> Session Date: July 10, 2008
> Autographer:
> Authenticator: AUTHENTICATORS, INC.
> Additional Information: 1ST INNING DAVE BUSH PITCHING TO CLINT BARMES BALL 3 IN THE DIRT

As Brian Costa of The *Wall Street Journal* writes "Many of the items are sold to fans. Some are auctioned off for charity. In some cases, teams and players hold onto them as keepsakes. And for historic events, some go to the Hall of Fame." Hence, it seems that the authentication process is serving at least the dual purpose of guaranteeing authenticity as well as creating formal historical documents for fans and for MLB itself by chronicling the game through these artifacts.

Such minor occurrences as the ball three in the dirt become obtainable and placating answers to the absolute need for authenticity that drives the memorabilia world: a need that was sent into overdrive by "Operation Bullpen." Such is the case as well for the less pedestrian artifacts of the game that may be more coveted items for collectors, teams, players, or MLB itself. Costa's examination of the authentication program was focused through the lens of marking Alex Rodriguez's 600th career home run. The article highlights that each ball pitched to Rodriguez was be encoded after his 599th home run, ensuring an ability to check authenticity if it made its way into the hands of a fan in the stands. Along with the ball, eventually other associated items will be "tagged with high-tech holograms immediately after the game," including "His bat, his batting gloves, his jersey, his pants, his cleats, the bases he steps on during his 600th home run trot and even the dirt he steps on will instantly become pieces of memorabilia. And MLB handles every bit of it the way the FBI handles evidence" (Costa). Similar attention was paid to the event and to the process of authenticating when Rodriguez's teammate Derek Jeter hit his 3,000th hit. The practice goes well beyond these Yankees brethren to every team and involving many players.

The extent of the practice was dealt with similarly in a *Washington Post* sports article that chronicled the authentication process at Stephen Strasburg's first game. Mike Posner, the manager of the authentication program, discussed the process of authentication and the extent to which it occurred with the Major Leaguer's pitching debut. Strasburg's baseballs, bases used in the game, jersey, cap, the lineup cards, and manager cards were all marked with holograms, as buckets of dirt were also taken from the mound after the game. Some of the authenticated items were put up for sale, some authenticated for the Washington Nationals, some for the Hall of Fame, and some for Strasburg himself (Steinberg "Authenticating").

According to the *Philadelphia Inquirer*, Strasburg's desire to have items authenticated for himself is popular amongst other players as well: "Trevor Hoffman, the Milwaukee Brewers reliever who is the all-time saves leader, evidently saves more than games. Every time he adds to his record, Shelton [MLB's program manager] said, he adds to his memorabilia collection — he wants it all authenticated (Wood)." The article continues, saying that the last time authenticator Robert Bonds dealt with Hoffman, "he got his cleats done, his jersey done, and his hat" (Wood). Perhaps somewhat peculiar to some, beyond those in the stands, players absolutely look to connect themselves to the game through these artifacts as well.

With over three million pieces authenticated and counting, with formal contracts signed in the memorabilia market, and with the increasing presence in the game of the practice as evidenced by the Rodriguez, Jeter, and Strasburg cases, one could say authentication has secured an important part of the memorabilia industry and has become a growing part of MLB's portfolio. Autographed merchandise and game-used merchandise ranging from balls to bottles of bug spray are all potentially up for grabs. As fans and collectors would contend, the use of the program by the MLB for economic and historical purposes is shared with the market of collectors and dealers that complete the pathway of the life of authenticated memorabilia, encompassing a wide range of use values for these products of baseball culture. Though not universally commended by all, as one can see from a post on "Game-Used Universe" where a disgruntled author stated that the "MLB's hologram system sucks and is no better than anyone else's if not worse" ("Questions re:"). The fact is that the program has become a new, powerful standard in the memorabilia market. The MLB program has provided dealers and collectors with a program, although one that may seem like overkill or borderline obsessive to those outside of the memorabilia market, that has become a key facet in an industry built around the desire for the authentic. It has become a new standard that has gained popularity and economic success as a new cultural/economic facet of the life of contemporary MLB that has increasingly become accepted. As one post by a respondent to Steinberg's piece on Strasburg put it, "Well, considering the silliness of the memorabilia market, and the ease of pretending this or that came from here or there without any real verification, better that baseball, being the most memorabilia driven sport, take these types of extreme steps" (Steinberg).

Why the Sticker Is Going to Stick

In addition to Major League Baseball's investment into authenticated merchandise as an economic and historical concern, a plethora of interests, from retail outlets to collectors, share in a negotiated sense of meaning and purpose when it comes to figuring out the meaning of this program. This intersection of uses highlights the ability of a multiplicity of audiences to decode and use products of popular culture for their own means and outcomes. One can see the immense emotional and economic investments that individuals can make in attempts to express levels of fandom and in attempts to get closer to the product of MLB that they may hold so dear. So how has this come to pass? Though a brief chronicle of the extent of the industry and its history was presented earlier, this section will review what continues to drive the market and the place of authenticated memorabilia in the culture of MLB.

Collectors/fans take part in the process of collecting for a variance of reasons. The ability of the industry, including MLB itself, to meet these needs/uses speaks not only to contemporary marketing savvy, but also speaks of that continued need for authenticity and meaning for generations of various levels of collectors. McIntosh and Schmeichel in their article "Collectors and Collecting: A Social Psychological Perspective" offer that although some may collect to defend "the self from the threat of mortality" and that collecting "allows one to successfully navigate death anxiety" or "allows people to participate in a culture's economic script," there are reasons for collecting that extend beyond "symbolic immortality" and financial hegemony (87). For instance, these authors suggest that "collectors are drawn to collecting as a means of bolstering the self by setting up goals that are tangible, attainable, and provide the collector with concrete feedback of progress" (87). Instead of cheating death, collecting provides a sense of order, purpose, identity, and meaning.

Though it is easy to write off the passion of communities of collectors from the outside, collecting reflects a myriad of human needs and wants. Collecting, in the eyes of Long and Schiffman's work on collectors of Swatch watches, showcases that "collecting is both rational and irrational, deliberate and uncontrollable, cooperative and competitive, passive and aggressive, and tension producing and tension reducing" (496). Collectors can forge identities and a sense of purpose in their lives from collecting, just as they can become obsessive and potentially be viewed as social outcasts. Simply put, like any good hobby, collecting authenticated merchandise can also reflect "an enriching respite from the sometimes frustrating demands of everyday life" (Muensterberger 7).

The objects can become a means for social interaction and defining the self as well. *Game Used Universe*, a collecting community website, was founded "to help the collecting community become more informed, with a website that has aggregated knowledgeable, well-meaning individuals from all over the hobby who find great satisfaction in simply helping other collectors" ("Game-Used Community"). Scrolling through several of the discussion threads points out a vast potential for usage by collectors. Forums discussed what was/wasn't "important" enough to collect, why people began collecting, and even a "BEWARE Scammer alert" that used the community to send heads-up warnings for other collectors about specific dealers, etc. These spaces allowed a space for collectors to fulfill McIntosh and Schmeichel's goal-orientated perspective on collecting and reaffirmation, as well as community/identity creation for those taking an active role.

Along with celebrating/coveting the pieces themselves, authenticated objects can also be a flashpoint for personal reflection or nostalgia. For some collectors, authenticated merchandise can be a guaranteed, authentic marker of significant events. Steiner Sports president Jared Weiss contends that "It's personalized, it's unique, it's something nobody else will have. It's a great way to commemorate your kid's first game" (O'Keeffe). Memories of a specific game, event, or an associated event connected to the game are, for some collectors, triggered/basked in via these objects. As one post noted on *Game Used Universe*, "In a way, we don't collect 'stuff.' We collect memories" ("Important"). Steve Dall from Field of Dreams agrees with such sentiment:

> I really believe that baseball is a game of history and folks love that history. Old baseball, pre-1970 baseball, has an amazing effect on the collector. It really is a whole different animal in the sense that folks want something that is A: real, B: rare, C: that takes them back. We saw a huge surge of this as the "big 3" passed away.... Mantle, Williams and DiMaggio. As they passed, people really sought their game-used product [Dall].

Indeed, if the piece of memorabilia conflicts at all with romantic visions of the past for fans, the objects can become unwanted reflections of humanity in a game built upon a mythical status. For instance, Gallery of History, a Las Vegas auction house, featured "Mantle signed baseballs inscribed, F— YOU!, WILLIE MAYS SUCKS!, AND MARILYN MONROE TOLD ME JOE D. SUCKS!... I AGREE" (Cook and O'Brien). The balls did not sell, though they were deemed authentic. Perhaps they were *too* authentic to match the myth of Mantle in baseball's history, or they just didn't find the right buyer yet.

As it is a mythical entity in the American experience, MLB memorabilia collectors may have a leg up on general social acceptance, as they are dealing with a "national pastime" and one that, like any other level of collecting, reflects a broad range of many fans, from the casual to the religiously dedicated. Those taking part in collecting authenticated MLB memorabilia are able with little effort to smash down the immense metaphorical wall between audience and actor, and between consumption and culture (that these boundaries may very much still exist). The seriousness of this disconnect becomes apparent when one begins to talk with fans.

A 2005 *Sports Illustrated* piece that chronicled two dedicated collectors included such quotes of damning isolationism as: "Basketball is the worst for getting autographs, but baseball is a close second" and in reference to Ken Griffey, Jr. "You got a better chance of getting Bin Laden." One autograph seeker's comment spoke poignantly about the division between field and spectator: "It's so hard to get autographs at Wrigley these days. They should just put in a moat between the stands and the players" (McCallum). Authenticated memorabilia differentiates collectors from the masses that surround them, and brings them closer to a normally very segregated and mediated world of sport in contemporary life. Brandon Steiner, of Steiner Sports, recognizes that this want for connection is a powerful motive that the memorabilia industry can answer: "People want something that will help them connect to their favorite players and teams. They want something that will feel closer to the great moments in sports" (O'Keefe).

The items, because of their ability to link collector and the game/players, can become infused with a sense of the sacred. They also can provide interpersonal connection to the events that take place on the field and in the realm of the sport celebrity today. As McIntosh and Schmeichel contend, "As the acquisition is incorporated into the collector's self it is imparted with a sense of sacredness" where a "magical connection" can occur in the eyes of the owner between themselves and the original handler/signer of the object (92). As John Lauer discusses in his study on autograph collectors in nineteenth-century America, the history and contemporary practice of collecting autographs reaffirms this "magical connection" that is created by collectors through their objects. The signature for collectors fulfills a need for authenticity that is as apparent today, as it was with the collectors Lauer focused on: the collectors of signatures from the signers of the Declaration of Independence (145).

Leland's chairman, Joshua Evans, explains, "The closer you get to the player, the better. Lots of use is desirable. Our great jerseys have never been cleaned and are all sweaty and dirty" (Seideman and Dickerson 24). According to Lauer, an autographed object becomes a connection to a specific time, place, and person: "Strictly speaking, it is not the seal or signature that is of the essence, but the action of the living actor to which it refers" (146). As those nineteenth-century collectors were searching for an "authenticity and closeness to the *real*," so too are collectors of authenticated MLB memorabilia (Lauer 157). Such connections provide a way for collectors to "identify with their heroes by collecting associated memorabilia" whether it be through autographs or game-used memorabilia (Mulligan and Grube 75). The demand for a connection to the game and a lament for this loss of access to players have produced a product of Major League Baseball that fills in this gap. On *Game Used Universe* a thread on photo-matched pieces of memorabilia appeared and became an online gallery of fans sharing their joy in finding photos of specific players wearing/using the game-used and sometimes now-signed memorabilia they had purchased. Essentially, these photos took the level of connection to the game even further for some collectors, as they now possessed a part of the visual historical baseball document in front of them. One post excitedly stated, "It's not just any picture of them wearing it, but the actual picture of them wearing them [cleats]. Here's my Rafael Furcal game worn game winning cleats from May 2, 2003. I was lucky enough to find a pic of him from that night on Getty Images" ("Post Your"). This collector is provided with a new layer of authenticity with visual proof of the item in action.

Much like nineteenth century collectors of Declaration signers, baseball "fans desire the items in order to bask in reflected glory" of a very exclusive space that was/is relegated to a select few (Mulligan and Grube 77). Both casual fans and dedicated collectors can buy a piece of the game, a connection to the game that extends itself for those looking for feedback in a relationship to a formal and successful popular culture product. As Brandon Steiner of Steiner Sports sees it, "Following a team through the course of a season is a commitment — it's like having a girlfriend. People want something to show for it" (O'Keeffe). Perhaps speaking to Steiner's idea, it is also quite common for collectors to pick up merchandise from *both* wins and losses. Glory is good, but so is being part of the continued struggle of the player or team to achieve said glory. An artifact can represent this trajectory. Team identification, specific game identification, as well as player identification pushes the potential collector to obtain a part of the reflected effort and even perhaps glory of the game. One collector shared: "I collect game-used baseballs, and their worth on the secondary market doesn't matter to me in the least bit. I was able to pick up 4 baseballs from Jeff Bagwell's 2000th hit game.... I would never sell them, because they are meaningful to me, and Bagwell never got to 2,500 or 3,000 hits, so this is a big milestone relative to his career" ("Important").

Amidst the wellspring of emotional investment described above, collectors can also be in it for the potential payout. Though the research reflects an overwhelming amount of emotional investment, collectors can be partially or totally motivated by financial interest. As stated in a *Time* article in 1999, "Big Mac and Sammy have made baseball memorabilia hot again. Here's how to play it smart." The names contained within the title themselves indicate that the article's claim that "the memorabilia market runs hot and cold" is all too true (Kadlec 74). Though a hope for payout may be there, it appears that very few fans in the research have built their retirement portfolios solely out of this single investment strategy. Still, the fact is that it is an industry that has real economic impact and can be a potential investment as it can be a hobby. Yet, for the collector, the research dictates that the discussion of investment is significantly focused on as an emotional one. As Dall views it:

> I truly believe that emotion motivates collectors. I am a collector as well, so I am comfortable saying that "we" purchase based on emotion, because we become attached to the memorabilia of our heroes. We live vicariously through our sports memories ... our first game of catch, our first baseball game, the smells, what we ate, filling out our first scorecard ... you remember everything when it comes to sports [Dall].

Rounding for Home

The MLB authentication program speaks volumes about the multifaceted economic and cultural product that is MLB today. Providing pieces of the game for casual fans and dedicated collectors/fans, MLB has found a way to fill in the aforementioned fan's idea of a "moat" separating the game and the spectator. MLB not only represents the successful marketing of an economic giant, but also represents the remarkable usability of the game as a springboard for various uses, including creating individual identities, passionate investment, welcome distraction, economic investment, or to guarantee an authentic item in everyday life. It is also powerful in its ability to create social outlets, personal and collective historical markers, cultural capital/knowledge, and tangible goals to define and achieve. Perhaps too, for those making sense of collecting such objects, it could also represent a means to attempt to cheat death, and to rationally or irrationally cooperate/compete, to be passive/aggressive, or to tear down or build tension (McIntosh and Schmeichel 87; Long and Schiffman 496). Whatever role the MLB authentication program is playing in a collector's life, study of the program should reveal to all invested in baseball in some way or another that each time an umpire tosses a ball towards a batboy or dugout, or a player signing is watched over by an authenticator, there is a long narrative ahead for these pieces of the game. It is the beginning of a tale that could link potential generations of fans to an authentic part of the action on the other side of the ballpark divide.

4

Making the Mark
The Life of MLB Logos

Much like the game itself, baseball parks, players, symbols, and logos in Major League Baseball can take on mythical proportions. Like a symbol connoting a major entertainment or oil company, the symbols and logos in MLB are icons capable of packaging complex business entities into commodities with personalities associated with human characteristics like trust, daring, strength, and efficiency. They can also take on a feeling of collective or personal ownership. Though a fan may only pay into the business, these visuals are an important part in creating central concepts of identity and team. Modern MLB baseball fans find themselves significantly invested in these logos that differentiate not only different franchises but differentiate team cultures, histories, narratives, and individual fan identities and experiences. The church of baseball, as many churches do, invests greatly in their visual symbols and infuses them with meaning and attachment that can order and signify the experience of their respective houses of worship.

These visuals are contested sights where emotion, nostalgia, and community demands meet with branding, design, and merchandising demands. There is ownership and then there is *ownership*. Proper licensing is joined with a voracious industry of non-official/illegal uses of logos, from homemade yard signs to bootleg merchandise sold by street vendors. Though MLB and its teams aggressively protect their brand, as a popular culture product like Star Wars or the newest remastered release of a Beatles album, baseball takes on a *de facto* (though still illegal in numerous instances) sense of public ownership as a part of now common cultural reference and practice in everyday life. It is through the successful official marketing of such brands/entities that these products become part of a common vernacular.

This chapter delves into the life of the MLB team logo in order to better understand its function in propelling the popular culture product that is the big leagues. It is these logos that give a face and a common referent that can become the signifier of a sports tradition. Logos can also be resisted, admonished, and overtly rejected as insufficient visual representations of fans' chosen teams. Somewhere between the sacred and the profane, each of these logos becomes part of the narrative, culture, and business of baseball.

The Logo

Studied aesthetically, psychologically, culturally, and economically, logos are "visual signs that stand for a brand in some way" that represent a "primary marketing strategy since the turn of the twentieth century" (Danesi 78–79). These icons have become not only potent economic concerns, but also sometimes dominant and omnipresent cultural markers. The practice of baseball has reflected the importance of logos throughout its history and has used them to create, maintain, and repackage both amateur and professional teams. Professional teams as we have come to know them today feature logos on many uniforms, caps, letterheads, and merchandise. In fact, the "the first openly professional ball club (that is, the entire starting roster, or 'picked nine,' that received salaries)" featured a prominent old English "C" on their uniforms (Katz 18).

This letter logo, as it did in 1869, persists to be an effective visual representation of a baseball brand. This variety of logo, for example, seems to still speak to the ability of the logo to blend "the linguistic (the brand name) with the visual (the stylized representation of the name or parts of the name) is highly effective since it taps into two forms of memory-the verbal and the eidetic" (Danesi 86). One only has to look at the continued use of the old English "D" by the Detroit Tigers or the more updated "W" of the Washington Nationals that are used as primary cap logos, to see that the historical *and* economic viability of this and many other varieties of logos in baseball continues unfettered. So, whether we are talking about the iconic Brooklyn Dodgers "B" or the cartoon depiction of a bird swinging a bat that was the prominent logo of the Baltimore Orioles from 1966 to 1989 ("Orioles"), the logo creates a common vernacular recognized wherever MLB reaches around the globe.

Major League Baseball teams and MLB itself have experimented with numerous different kinds of logos to push professional baseball deep into the public's consciousness. As a standard business practice, the experimentation and life of logos in baseball over the past century has yielded a great deal of knowledge about the creation of successful logos and their important role in marketing and bringing a brand to life. These developments and lessons can be seen in the evolution of MLB's family of team logos and the breadth of the logos used.

MLB logos are truly a *family* of logos. Aside from the fact that each team has a logo to differentiate themselves from the other teams, there are also numerous logos employed by each team. MLB teams commonly have primary logos, secondary logos, as well as primary and secondary cap logos. For instance, the St. Louis Cardinals, a team with a lengthy history in MLB, employs a primary logo that depicts a single Cardinal bird perched upon a bat with "Cardinals" written out underneath ("Team-by-Team"). The team also utilizes an alphabetic logo of an interlocking "S" "T" and "L," or hats depicting the perched bird without lettering. In addition, one can also find other team uses, licensed merchandise uses, and stadium uses of other alternate logos. Retro logos from throughout the team's history, like the iconic cardinal perched in front of a baseball surrounded by "St. Louis Cardinals" written around the ball (approximately '70s–'90s) or the depiction of a cardinal bird holding a bat in the batting stance (approximately '50s '60s), can all be found in official merchandise and via team usage (Creamer). These join several other logos that are used amongst other trademarked designs meant to depict/represent the team both on and off of the field.

Due to the multiplicity of logos used in MLB today, this chapter examines these families of logos. One can just as easily find the interconnecting "NY" for the Yankees on a t-shirt as one could find the primary logo featuring the Uncle Sam hat on top of a bat with a baseball as backing. This multiplicity of logos becomes recognized symbolic shorthand for the entities that they represent, whether in primary, secondary, or "throwback" form, or through any other alternate logos associated with the team.

The Life of Logos

At a *very* fundamental level, logos are a means of representing a brand's name, image, and creating a culture around a non-living, legally created entity. This chapter works with a basic, loose concept of logo proposed by Marcel Dansei, though one only has to look at the popular press or even to sources on design to see that terminology can differ, based upon the source and discipline using the concept. "Logos" will refer to the collection of common MLB forms used to visually represent respective teams. Logos can be composed of stylized lettering featuring a full name or first letters of teams/cities (sometimes called a "logotype"), a combination mark of icon/lettering, or only an icon (sometimes referred to as "symbol" or "graphic"). These divisions become somewhat muddied when we look into the vast official and nonofficial usages. Like the 1869 Cincinnati Red Stockings that used of the Old English "C," baseball teams today seek to create an identity and culture around their teams; these visual representations solidify the identity and become, as Danesi points out in companies like NBC or IBM, "equivalent to the logos that represent them" (78). The logo takes a legal and economic construct and gives it a visual life: a base of identity and culture. They are there to fulfill specific responsibilities: "Henderson and Cote (1998) observe that logos can only have added value if two preconditions are fulfilled. First, stakeholders must remember seeing the logo (correct recognition). Second, logos must remind stakeholders of the brand or company name (recall). Ultimately, companies want their name recalled, so the logo serves as shorthand for the company" (Van Riel). According to Green and Loveluck's "Understanding a Corporate Symbol," such associations are important for the business both internally and externally, since logos, they argue, "serve as a focus for the members of the organization" and "indicate to external audiences (customers, suppliers, and financial groups) the nature of that new identity" (37).

Major League Baseball and its teams, as both an economic industry and a cultural industry, realize that logos differentiate their teams from each other, from other levels of play, and create potential referents of identity, history, nostalgia, and the culture of the team. As Coca-Cola and other companies "seek to embody corporate values in their designs" so do MLB teams and the organization itself (Green and Loveluck 38). Sometimes these logos can aptly create a stamp of identity and recognition that very much rests at the heart of the company or organization.

When one sees the logos associated with teams like the Yankees, Red Sox, or Dodgers, certain associations, values, and even a personality are created in those immersed in baseball culture, and even those merely on its periphery.

Due to the weight that is placed on logos and the central role they play in company culture and everyday life, companies/organizations are willing to spend the money needed to create the recognition and culture they seek. The development of a logo is not an inexpensive undertaking, as logos are entrusted with doing so much. In addition to teams featuring logos on merchandise, they also show up in the media as well as "packaging, letterhead, business cards, and signs and in print advertisements, annual reports, and product designs" (Henderson and Cote 14).

Far from conjecture, the use and reception of logos is one that companies/organizations are happy to invest in and research prolifically. Van Reil, building off of the work of Green and Lovelock, Henderson and Cote, and Maathuis contends that there is a solid base of "theoretical and empirical evidence that corporate logos can have added value for companies, not only because it is the only consistent element in the corporate identity-mix, simplifying identification of own employees with their company and providing a tool for external audiences to recognise and appreciate an organisation." To develop a logo in Major League Baseball or elsewhere constitutes a science to meet and embrace these expectations through logo design.

The study of and creation of logos can be dealt with in terms of considering perception management: "Intrinsic properties of a logo are properties resulting directly from a confrontation with the logo itself divided into: a perception of the graphical parts" and "perceptions of the referential parts (what does the logo represent?)" (Van Riel). One needs to keep in mind extrinsic properties as well. These are "associations with the company behind the logo" (Van Riel). The culture of a team has a great deal to do with the community created regionally and elsewhere in situating and supporting that team in MLB.

Graphically, we can look to the study of logos to better understand the intrinsic possibilities of design and the practices used by MLB to create and maintain itself as an entity, as well as within each of its teams. According to a study published in the *Journal of Marketing*, better understanding how to solicit "positive affective reactions" as the "affect can transfer from the logo to the product or company" is essential to understanding the realm of logo use and interpretation (Henderson and Cote

15). MLB as a unit and individual teams themselves represent a plethora of approaches taking place that differentiate teams from each other, and indeed, using differing logos to connote different meanings and associations *within* the team itself. Still, there are reigning standards, conventions, and formulas meant to comfort audiences by logos "evoking a familiar meaning or from the design being similar to well-known symbols." To assist companies/teams/MLB in creating meaningful and usable linkages with their customers, they use Gestalt psychology which "suggests that 'good' design is determined by culturally held beliefs. Designs thought to possess 'good form' typically are liked more than other designs" (Henderson and Cote 18). Hence, the prior establishment and success of other logos can pave the way for accessible new ones.

This may explain why a predominance of the logos used by teams often utilize similar conventions that other teams and even other eras of baseball use/have used. When conventions are not followed, when color schemes are experimented with, when established logos are retired and are replaced, "bad design" can become a legacy that will follow a club forever: a dark mark. Dominant color palettes like red, white, and blue, and specific design styles are prevalent throughout the history of professional baseball. George H. Sage remarks in the *Sociology of Sport Journal* that this is not merely a case of aesthetics. The selection of a specific color pallet of red, white and blue will "encourage consumers not only to purchase the licensed merchandise but also to think of pro sports as emblematic of Americanism and patriotism, which are deeply felt, extremely popular cultural values" (4). The national pastime for that reason better understands that such linkages to nationalism in this instance can help a logo/team succeed or fail. MLB and its teams are very much concerned with putting their pulse on the creation of effective logos to reach fans through such understood associations and methodologies.

The "letter logo" previously mentioned has been popular throughout the history of professional baseball, and is one that can speak to the pull of tradition and familiarity. From the Red Stockings of 1869 to the primary cap logo of the Boston Red Sox today, logos featuring written script bring a sense of history and familiarity of the game into individual organizations (or at least the hope thereof). The elongated career of the Tigers "D," the iconic interlocking "N" and "Y" of the Yankees, as well as the "SOX" present today in the White Sox family of logos (it's been offered in variations throughout the twentieth century), amongst many other such logos throughout the history of baseball, laid the groundwork for the Arizona Diamondbacks "A" and the haloed "A" of the Angels. Frequently used as primary cap logos, these designs will also sometimes function as teams' primary logos as well.

Teams prominently also feature logos where lettering is used in conjunction with an icon. For instance, in 2011, the Mets, Yankees, Rangers, Giants, Twins, Brewers, Mariners (behind its compass rose) and the Marlins (behind the marlin icon) are all examples of prominent featured logos that are structured on or around representations of baseballs. Other teams utilize icons along with lettering where the icons are meant to refer back to the team name thematically; the tomahawk of the Braves, and the compass rose of the Mariners are both examples of teams incorporating associated icons that describe location, team identities, etc. Script is used along visual icons of the Orioles, Marlins, Cardinals, and Blue Jays to create differing kinds of cognitive links to the brand/team.

One variety of logo that has somewhat fallen out of favor in recent years has been the use of cartoon logos, with more realistic icons gaining favor. In a piece written for *ESPN.com*, logo designer Dan Simon explains the reason for this trend: "When sports branding became an industry and mascot depiction became more graphic, teams and schools moved away from those cartoon renderings in favor of more iconic executions, which are visually more 'professional'" (qtd. in Caple). Though "cartoon" perhaps conjures up notions of fun and frivolity, examples like the Cleveland Indians' Chief Wahoo have the possibility of becoming both treasured icons and deplorable visions of race/ethnicity. Still, there is some use of icon-only logos, including Boston's "hanging socks" logo.

Now somewhat out of favor as primary logos, many teams prominently feature cartoon logos on various kinds of merchandise, not affiliated with "official" on-field action. Throwback merchandise sometimes features former cartoon icons like the swinging Baltimore Oriole or the swinging friar that still adorns Padres merchandise. Contemporary mascots are also used as marketable logos for teams, but are generally avoided as primary logos for teams. The Philly Phanatic, Fredbird in St. Louis, or Bernie Brewer also become important members of a team's family of logos that can attract a different sense of aesthetic in fans and differing connotations when it comes to their relationships to the team. Though, as one study suggests, "logos using characters tend to be well recognized but can hurt image" (Henderson and Cote 27). Still, the revenue created by targeting a mascot and/or cartoon character, especially to children, can pay big dividends.

Since baseball is a sport that very much reaches different audiences, including international ones, MLB teams also use the strength of these multiple logos to reach numerous audiences. Though the Philly Phanatic may represent very different associations than the team's "P" or the cracked-bell logo, graphics and typefaces of numerous varieties help to reach these audiences, provide multiple opportunities for merchandising, and even create different aspects of personality for the team, league, and game.

Beyond Recognition: Team and League Use of Logos

MLB and its teams are the brands positioned into popular culture and everyday life. These brands seek to package a product and create a profit, whether it be through the MLB "batter" logo or the haloed "A" of the Angels. Licensed and available on items from baby clothing to caskets, logos become part of local, state, regional, national, and even international popular culture. The power of these logos to transcend from the business world to the cultural world makes them the especially powerful, profitable entities they are today. As we will see, this transcendence also creates a host of problems for those individuals protecting their economic interests and intellectual property. Fan usage, a usage that can attempt to claim these logos not as protected visual icons but as common cultural referents, is an actuality these brands must contend with frequently.

Walking through any of the countless fan shops in MLB parks, not to mention a plethora of retail outlets outside of the confines of the stadium, one may assume that merchandising is *the* primary concern of MLB and its teams. It is a just assumption, but one that demands further qualification. MLB is a single league entity that pools merchandising profits into one fund that is distributed equally amongst teams. Hence, large-market teams like the Yankees, no matter how much merchandise they may sell nationally/internationally, make the same amount of revenue as smaller-market teams like the Royals, who may not be selling nearly as many licensed products comparatively (Mihoces). It should be noted that each team is able to lay complete claim (without putting in towards shared revenues) to the profits made from the sales of merchandise within a certain sphere surrounding the team's main location at select outlets (Irwin, Sutton, and McCarthy 220). The business of merchandising is a brisk one with sales in the billions for MLB alone.

Aside from the collective good and the hope for a universal increase in revenue, teams also are interested in merchandising their specific team, designs, and logos to increase brand awareness and to create ties to their respective teams (it also doesn't hurt to increase those local sales that do go to teams). To create a team culture, as was pointed out in the earlier giveaways chapter, is to connect this product of popular culture with essential facets of identity for those taking part. Teams build on senses of nationalism, regionalism, community, and collective celebration to assist in building relationships with these products of popular culture. Such emphasis can increase the numbers through the turnstiles in the ballpark itself, build economically beneficial relationships with the city in which they are located, increase media attention, and keep their brand moving. Brendan Byrne, identified as a "director of business development for Sean Michael Edwards Design, a new York firm that has done many pro and college logos," states: "Each team is a brand.... They want to make sure they're in the market, in the game.... They ask 'How does my product compare to others on the shelf? Well, mine is old and tired. The others are young and marketed well. Boy, I'd better get off my fanny'" (Mihoces). Mihoces' article reveals that MLB Properties can assist teams, their creative staff, and outside design firms in creating the most effective family of logos for their team's needs.

Teams can also capitalize on and continue to build their own sense of narrative history through logos. Much like the Hall of Fame can construct the narrative of MLB and baseball, a team's strategic use of logos and design can create individual team histories within the larger project of MLB. This, of course, is motivated by nostalgia, pride, *and* merchandising. To come back to a phrase turned earlier, the use of older logos and designs on merchandise "demands further qualification." Running "turn back the clock" games or "retro" games (amongst other references employed) and stocking the merchandise featuring these old logos gives MLB and its teams an opportunity to infuse further merchandising possibilities into the market. The use of these logos on hats, shirts, etc. also assists in creating a sense of history, and perhaps as we will see in the examination of the audience/fan usage of these past designs, a remarkably potent force in the creation of a sense of history and nostalgia. As the

Hall of Fame supports the present world of the MLB through the preservation of the past, the use of retired logos, along with practices like the display of retired numbers and team relics displayed throughout stadium concourses and team museums, creates emotional and lucrative connections to the past.

A 2008 feature in the Boston Globe highlights the ability of teams to build on a sense of history via a newly introduced change in the Red Sox' new, old uniform, where an earlier design was reintroduced to contemporary fans as a secondary logo. In the article Silva assertively brings in the reality of merchandising immediately, describing it as a "marketing-driven event in the midst of the holiday season, the Red Sox Thursday night unveiled new team logos, uniforms, and caps that will make their debut on the field at the start of the 2009 season." The demand and success of the "hanging sox" logo is cited as being inspired by a "turn back the clock" game. Originally appearing in 1931 the use of the logo by the team now "reflect[s] the team's decision to make changes in design that return select visual brand elements and team appearance to the core traditions of the organization" (Silva). Red Sox COO Mike Dee explains the move to the new logo, saying that it possesses "an iconic value that transcends anything else in our assortment of brands and logos," and "to have it be defined and standing alone is certainly the right thing to do" (qtd. in Silva).

The Milwaukee Brewers have played with this sense of nostalgia and history in promotional events with their fans, including an event where the team set up a "giant, yet informal focus group for the Brewers, who want to know if fans prefer the old logo to the current one" (Tarnoff). Fans making their way into the game during the event in 2005 "voted" by obtaining giveaway shirts that displayed either the Brewers' "blue and gold, intertwined 'm' and 'b' logo" or "the cursive 'M' atop a sprig of barley" (Tarnoff). Officially meant to garner fan insight, the promotion also worked out well as a media event that was astutely suited for the game broadcast itself thanks to the oceans of logo-clad fans, as well as acting as a public interest piece in other media outlets. Though "the old logo sells very well," the fact is that "overall, items with the current logo actually sell better" (qtd. in Tarnoff). The Brewers have achieved in this process an ideal mixture of merchandising interest and specifically vested team interests, with both benefiting from the "debate." The event speaks to the realities of merchandising and packaging for and within MLB. It also helps in fulfilling a needed sense of community and history that benefits the team as they maintain a consumer community culture around the team. As the next section will argue, it can also be of great benefit to the fans finding connection, identity, and passion with the brands and logos of MLB.

From Causal to Fanatical: Reception of Logos

Though very easy to dismiss as visual representations of business entities, logos live a diverse and potent life beyond and above the teams they represent in MLB. As William Shelton observes in his "Higher Education, Higher Values: The Anatomy of a Logo Decision," a piece written to explore the problematic use of "Native American names, logos, or mascots" in Michigan: "Symbols promote and perpetuate values, define those who use them, and create their future as well as reflect their past." (37) The use of such referents can facilitate numerous uses and interpretations that are as diverse as those groups consuming them.

As research on the controversy surrounding Native American logos suggests, creating a "shorthand" for something via a logo creates a distinct ability to summon associations: the good, the bad, and the in-between. The appearance of a Red Sox logo to a Yankees fan can create instant animosity; the use of a Cubs logo can create associations of history, tradition, and possibly even some rough luck when considering World Series victories. Others on the South Side of Chicago might just see a rival to beat when they see a Cubs' family of logos. To understand the usage of logos by fans, let's return to the theme of Native American names and images used as team identities and within their logos.

There is significant work dedicated to the subject of Native American logos/names. This chapter will only touch upon this briefly in context to examining the spectrum of uses for logos by fans and general audiences. It may be opportune to start here though as a part to the whole. Native American names in baseball were prominently featured during the last few decades. The Atlanta Braves have broadcast their fans doing the "tomahawk chop," a weapon featured in their primary logo, on the Turner Network. The use of Chief Wahoo by the Cleveland Indians speaks to the focus on identity and values that Shelton discusses as well.

Fans, in defense of the imagery, have cited the history of the team in the case of the Cleveland Indians. It is a symbol of a team connected to the city, with names like Bob Feller to Grady Sizemore associated with the team. The prevalence, use, and the history of the Indians and Chief Wahoo, contend some fans, is one that trumps any associations other than the team itself and its own culture and history. Fans have cited that they have "nostalgic connections to the Chief, and talk about their remembrances of him growing up as an Indians fan" (Liscio). Yet, this sense of history and team narrative means little to critics of the logo itself. In Caple's piece for ESPN, that was discussed earlier in reference to the fall of "cartoon" logos, he rates Chief Wahoo as the worst logo in the MLB: "And sometimes even cartoons are just wildly inappropriate. People defend Chief Wahoo on the basis of tradition, but what kind of defense is that? *Yes, it's incredibly offensive, but we've been offending people with it for sooooooo long we can't stop now.* Do you think any responsible team or business would produce this logo today? Of course not." He also mentions that the Atlanta Braves logo "certainly beats the old logo of a Native American warrior screaming so demonstrably it was as if he just received his season-ticket renewal bill." Caple's joking aside, the two polarities between the interpretations above indicate an inherent capability of audiences to use logos to discern for themselves the "true" meaning locked behind each of them.

Baseball's use of these logos/names, as has been the case in the Native American logo debate for several decades now, fulfills numerous functions. In the case of Shelton's work on Native American iconography at Eastern Michigan University (EMU), the logo/name served as "the basis of their power as well as the root of our [Eastern Michigan University and their concern over changing their 'Huron" logo and identity] dilemma. If these symbols carried similar meaning for all, there would have been no controversy." He explains the logo, in the case of EMU, "invited a range of social and cultural connotations, and therefore were particularly subject to changing social values, sensibilities, and awareness" (37). Such concerns that involve audience use, interpretation, and perceived ownership surround a multitude of sports, where fans become active community members. EMU's concerns and the debates that ensued about the meaning and potency of logos are many sports teams' concerns, including in the arena of MLB.

The debate surrounding Native American names and logos does not stand alone, however, in highlighting audience/fan consumption and interpretation of these logos in everyday life and in the ballparks themselves. A whole host of issues including the creation of real or imagined communities, in/out group status, relation to teams and players, a need for purity, and a continued demand for nostalgia, permeates the active pathways these logos traverse on a daily basis. Keeping in mind the parameters of encoding and decoding that MLB and its clubs partake in to further their goals as an economic entity and to create the "community" of the team, the following allows insight into the intended meanings and usages constructed by MLB and its teams. These encodings can be successfully decoded in the way MLB would hope, but the decoding of logos presents a whole host of appropriations, against-the-grain readings, and sometimes a complete bastardization of the meaning/values intended. Sometimes these intended meanings are the *last* thing on the minds of fans that invest into the game as a cultural event.

In a piece done for *Brandweek* concerning a MLB sponsorship deal featuring the film *Spiderman 2*, Ed Tazzia scorns angered fans that damn signs of "business" in the game (in this case, ads for the film plastered on bases) as a travesty to the purity of the game. Tazzia fumes: "Whose teams do you think these are anyway? The public is under a misimpression that just because a team wears a town's name on its jerseys, they somehow belong to local fans. While a quaint idea that all club owners try to use to their advantage, the fact is that a handful of investors own most of these clubs." Tazzia continues with the sobering message: "Sports are just another form of media content and if that content can attract a consumer following, then its fair game to slap a sponsor's logo on it and try to make a buck."

Such a top-down notion of control is a central concern in terms of understanding the life and power of logos. Still, uses of logos exist beyond official and definitive frameworks, and can be quite profitable for the teams, too. MLB, its teams, and even its logos operate as symbols of shared and customizable reference, as say, religious and nationalistic icons are so wont to do. Users/consumers of these logos, sometimes in ways that could technically land them in prison for copyright infringement, utilize logos for their own everyday individual wants and needs. Official sites, such as individual team's websites through MLB.com, along with not-so-official sites, including countless fan discussion boards, are active primary resources that can be dredged to get a sense of this spectrum of uses. These are a more lasting reference/record that formally documents the countless discussions so prevalent in the ballparks, bars, and living rooms worldwide. These sources are as important as formal accounts by authors discussing these logos in popular and even academic publications. These "informal" sources demonstrate the usability and interpretation of logos by the very fans that also so prolifically and economically ensure MLB's successful use of logos.

To begin, we'll first examine some of the more formal channels of interpretations and move to the realm of fan interpretation. Some of these more formal sources that look at audience usage, such as Sage's "Patriotic Images and Capitalist Profit," have been dealt with earlier in examining logos as a business and cultural product. Journalistically, attention paid to design, including uniform design and logos, are significant news items. Local and national news sources are assured to be places of prediction, information, and debate when it comes to Major League teams' operations on and off the field. These updates and discussions can occur routinely during the season, as they can often occur during the off-season.

Depending on the section of the newspaper or website that one is looking at, information on these concerns can be presented in several fashions. In the case of the previously mentioned *Boston Globe* piece, this off-season piece very much read as an official sounding press release chronicling an upcoming change in logos and uniform design. The article alerts the reader that "it's still not clear how many new faces will be on the Red Sox roster next season, but we now know what they'll be wearing" (Silva). In articles for the *Dallas Morning News* and *Washington Times*, logos and design are dealt with, in part, as consumer updates. In 2002, the *News* forewarns that "Club officials [Texas Rangers] on Saturday confirmed the process [changing their logo], which could alter the team's uniform and merchandise for the third time since the conclusion of the 1999 season" (Grant). The *Times* focuses on such news in a similar way with the comment, "The Expos were rechristened the Washington Nationals yesterday with a few glitches and a tussle — but just in time for the Christmas shopping season" (Fisher "Baseball"). Opposed to considering the teams' fans passive dupes, it appears that such publications understand the realities of the merchandising going on, and realize that readers appreciate being in the know on how these decisions are made, the extent of the industry, and a want to understand the business that makes the culture for the average MLB fan, or just a momentarily interested reader.

Even with such comments focusing on marketing and merchandising, news pieces will also present these team image concerns as general information and interest pieces. As this chapter is arguing, it appears that such publications are aware that interest extends beyond "buying in" to merchandise. Articles are written to inform readers about a cultural event ... a cultural practice that is prevalent and potent in the everyday life of many of their readers. Within both of the aforementioned articles, the authors also understand the need for context, narrative, and behind-the-scenes access. Fisher describes the appearance of logos and uniforms while discussing the process behind selecting and utilizing logos, one that involves teams but also MLB itself. It is an article that shed light onto the process of design and explains how these common references become *so* common.

As this chapter has demonstrated, logos have also been the focus of academic interpretation as well. MLB logos themselves are not extensively written on, but a great deal of effort is dedicated to studying logos as part of design, economics, and semiotic inquiry. Work done on understanding sports logos specifically as cultural concerns is a bit less prevalent in the academy. Though works focusing on fandom may be positive, it is more likely that one will see works that look into the economic exploitation of fans via a purchased culture. Ron Bishop in *Social Semiotics* argues that "now content to consume variations on a team's logo and colors, fans have been to some degree reconstituted as a 'series of identical beings'" (24). This is because "the teams and their licensees today have the more active meaning-making role; in part, because fans have become so disenchanted with the arrogance and greed they see in today's professional athlete" (Bishop 23–24). Consumption is the closest relationship a fan can have with a team: "Alliances to teams are now built on team colors or on a distant team's reputation and performance instead of any kind of personally forged link to the team or its players" (Bishop 25).

Such criticisms of rampant consumption might make sense in an age where MLB does have such an extensive international business model and presence. Still, MLB has a long history of using logos and merchandising, though admittedly, not to the extent it is done today. To test the relationship of fans to the game itself and their investments in logos, it would be worthwhile to check in with the fans. This is a group that can actually be left behind in a surprising amount of work done on MLB.

To begin, fans do seem quite keenly aware of the industry behind their respective teams. In fact, fans are quite capable of being critical of teams, merchandising trends, and costs. "obsessedwithbrewcrew," a member responsible for 2454 posts on "brewersfan.net," astutely points out the profitability of the teams using multiple logos: "The Brewers marketing department must love the continued discussion about the logo. If they change back to the old logo, there's no going back. Better to keep both logos and feed the debate with little modifications every few years. I certainly own more Brewers stuff than I would if they only had one color scheme/logo."

Much like authors in academic or journalistic settings, fans are quite capable of calling out the strategic use of logos to move merchandise. After all, they are the ones on the front lines deciding if they should be investing in items featuring team logos/representations. Still, this does not seem to deter many MLB fans that are out there. Opposed to reflecting manipulation and secondary investment, with their dwindling passions pushed aside by the MLB machine, fans spend seemingly a great deal of time discussing their personal investments, praises/damnations of MLB logos in discussions about their respective teams. There is connection, emotional investment, aesthetic interpretation, and even a sense of ownership that does challenge the notion that these teams do not "somehow belong to the local fans," even if those fans are not happy with official team decisions and plans.

For example, fans discussed the merits and demerits of the Houston Astros' "brick and tan star above Astros script in black" logo on a website dedicated to logos. The aesthetic qualities of the design were discussed as were fans connections to the team. "rocketman10" lamented, "Don't you hate when your hometeam has a horrible logo and you are too embarresed [sic] to wear it? enough said." "RocketDude" agreed several months later: "As an Astros fan, I have never worn anything with this logo on it — it is embarrassing. I wear the old school orange and blue all the time when I go to games. The late 90's gold star was the best logo they have ever put on their caps. I wear one of those around H-town often. It's time to change these horrendous uniforms and logos the astros have now." It wasn't all bad, though; "MikeBunds2001" reasoned that "Because the 'Stros made the world series in this logo, they should never change it or the uniforms" (Creamer "Houston").

The last comment is one that points to specific memories and/or associations with these logos. Comments abounded on teams' official sites and on many fan pages discussing ways in which fans celebrated or lamented moments in team histories based upon seeing logos. One discussion post by "Chisox73" stated that an older logo for the Brewers reminded him/her of great seasons past: "I love both those Brewer logos. The old glove logo brings back memories of winning baseball teams in Brew Town" (Chisox73). A St. Louis fan's comment simply referred to the Cardinals' logo from 1967–1997 as simply connoting "Gibson, Brock, Smith, Whiteyball, Mc Gee" (Creamer "St. Louis"). Nicholas Dawidoff warns that as teams actively use throwback logos and uniforms, such nostalgia can flatten "the past and makes it generic rather than personal. It turns real memories into folklore; genuine stories into a design style" (24). Some of this nostalgia Dawidoff says, as Bishop would agree, comes from the fact that "many fans today seem disaffected with contemporary Major Leaguers who routinely command multi-million-dollar contracts" (22). Empty signification and commodified history obviously are a concern for cultural critics seeing the machine of baseball overtaking the *practice* of baseball.

Fans generally knowingly understand that business concerns are at the helm of MLB teams; they *feel* the prices in the company store or when picking up a licensed gift for a friend at a local department store. It is the testimonies of the fans above that clearly point out that logos, though consumed, are much more than commodifiable signifiers. The logos can be a hindrance in publically supporting the team, they can be proud signifiers of communities, and they can be wellsprings of memory and nostalgia. As one fan explained their affection for the Rockies logos, it "reminds me of me and my wife's first ever vacation together" (Stars_Rangers_82). The reasons are many, but certainly extend beyond endlessly gulping down continuous supplies of merchandise. There can be a discussion of merely style amongst fans, though these discussions would have no meaning unless there was a connection of fans to the team, and even to the players that compose that team. One only has to take a glance at a local department store to see the plethora of player jerseys and t-shirts. Kohl's, alone, was offering seven different Albert Pujols shirts/jerseys themselves in the men's section of their website in the mid-summer of 2011 (*Kohl's*). Though greed and the age of free agency can instill some anxiety in someone considering forking over a good deal of cash for a replica player jersey, the connection, even if momentary, can situate a person within a team and a specific time.

In fact, fan usage can overtly conflict with MLB's primary concern of defending their legally protected brands, especially through the close vigilance needed to protect the face of these brands: logos. In a 2002 *USA Today* piece, a devoted Astros fan received a letter from MLB's legal department saying that his website was breaking copyright by displaying "photographs of players in Astros uniforms" (Beaton). As fans like that website's creator can attest, these logos are of primary concern for fans too, as they are central aspects of their connection to their respective teams. Perhaps this may even explain why some fans may feel justified in purchasing much cheaper bootlegged team merchandise or why a fan may feel their use of a team logo, even though not legally permitted, is okay. Culture and business clash in these instances where a cultural product, a product of people's everyday lives, breaks the wall of sacredness and identity in favor of legal and financial rights.

Future Life of Logos

The success of MLB logos is dependent on production and consumption. The well-orchestrated employment and selling of MLB logos is built upon creating identification and connection to teams of the present and of the past with fans. Endless empty consumption, fueling false senses of nostalgia, and postmodern drudgery are all possible outcomes of the employment and life of logos. This would be the case completely if fans relinquished their own personal and collective ownerships of these icons.

Symbolic shorthand for geography, community, and personal and shared history, the MLB logo is a contested ground. It is a contested ground where fans refuse, even under the duress of the law, to let the logo mean only consumption. It is business and it is culture meeting in brightly colored omnipresent icons of baseball's presence in everyday life.

These visual incarnations of an economic and cultural entity bespeak of consumption and identity. Beyond the official uses of birds, bats, baseballs, and various styles of lettering ... fans, at the moment of reception and use, are the ones that actually give these teams life and create the true communities that are hoped for by marketers and owners alike. Though points of consternation and conflict occur, logos are a common referent that link disparate and global groups of people under the experience of an extended identity and potentially family, even if it is at a cost. The following chapters will further extend the conversation to how MLB reaches these groups and opens up these use values to millions more.

5

From Pastime to Obsession

Major League Baseball and Its Media Strategy

Media and baseball are inseparable. Major League Baseball and media of various types have had an inseparable and codependent relationship since MLB's foundational era. Ever since radio began pitch-by-pitch and play-by-play reports from ballparks for fans at home and at work in the early 1920s, MLB has utilized the power of live media to attract more fans, disseminate its myths and legacy, keep fans entertained, and generate more revenue. Ballgames are, in essence, MLB's "private property" that can generate an incredible amount of profit. In other words, MLB games and its properties are "prime estate" just like real estate in Tokyo or Paris (Hiestand "MLB"). MLB has well taken advantage of its assets. Of course, baseball news had existed in print publications or via telegraph reports for decades prior to the popularization of radio. The value of baseball, however, increased significantly with radio broadcasts. Being at the ballpark became no longer the only way to enjoy the game live. Sometimes, being at home may offer more entertainment than being at the game. Media have turned the American pastime into a capital-generating enterprise and American obsession.

Modern media and professional baseball developed together. As media developed as an entertainment form, baseball took advantage of it as its outlet. After the prosperous days of radio in the 1920s and 1930s, television became a focal means of MLB live reporting. The popularization of cable television in the 1970s onward also changed the dynamics of MLB's use of media. In the late twentieth century, the Internet became one of the main drivers of MLB's media strategy. More recently, mobile devices have been added to this list. Because of this, as George Castle argues, "we talk about baseball 24/7/52/365" (vii).

America's national pastime is a national obsession because of media. Baseball no longer was a way for a family to spend an evening at a local ballpark. It has become omnipresent. With radio, fans of the early twentieth century could keep updated with what was happening at the game without leaving the house. Television allowed fans to watch games in their living room. With the Internet, the latest information on baseball is available to fans constantly. Fans are frequently updated with the progress of games. They do not need to seek information. News comes to them. Once the season ends, media feed them with speculations and predictions for the next season. Rumors about free agents, possible talents from abroad, and many other off-the-field topics keep fans entertained, informed, and connected to their teams.

It is a cliché to say that the Internet has changed our lives. Despite the mundaneness of this statement, there is some truth to it. The Internet has allowed MLB to expand its business scope. Major League Baseball Advanced Media (MLBAM) is primarily responsible for this shift. Its foremost responsibility exists in maintaining a well-organized and frequently-updated website for MLB. However, that is only one part of MLBAM's scope of business. It also caters to websites that belong to other sports, leagues, and non-baseball athletes and celebrities. Examining the history and status quo of MLB's media strategy reveals that media play an increasingly significant role in MLB's global and domestic agenda, especially because they are the main linkage between the League and its fans. Fans interact with MLB while sitting in their living rooms or through their fingertips, not just at a ballpark.

It is also important to note that MLB's media strategy is an immense topic that deserves a book of its own, if not an encyclopedia. Aiming to be comprehensive in a chapter like this is an ambitious but unfeasible task. Brian Hutton's literature review in his work on Major League Baseball and media alone shows the vast scholarship that exists on this topic. The purpose of this chapter, therefore, is limited to considering how the relationship between MLB and media has changed and expanded over time, what some of the key events and moments were in the history, what kind of media expansions that MLB has gone through particularly during the last few decades, and other selective issues concerning baseball and the media. Hutton claims that baseball has had a "long, dysfunctional history with broadcasters" (i). This chapter will examine this allegedly "dysfunctional," arguably entrepreneurial, history as a legal anti-trust exempt monopoly, in order to add to and stimulate intellectual understanding about this enterprise.

MLB on Radio

While newspaper and other print media have reported games since MLB's foundational years, it was the arrival of radio that enabled instantaneous sharing of game information with fans that were not at the ballpark. Its history is approximately ninety years old. The first baseball game to be broadcast over radio was the game between the Pittsburgh Pirates and Philadelphia Phillies on August 5, 1921. Harold Arlin, a twenty-six-year-old nighttime studio announcer—during the day he worked as a Westinghouse foreman—reported pitch-by-pitch on KDKA, America's first commercial radio station. Arlin remembers that his idea was more of a "one-shot project" and he did not believe that baseball would remain popular on radio (Vecsey *Baseball* 97; McCoy). Considering how baseball has developed since then, this view seems very pessimistic.

Arlin's somewhat pessimistic prediction was soon proven wrong. Two months after this first baseball broadcasting, the Giants and the Yankees met in the 1921 World Series. In addition to KDKA, WJZ from Newark, New Jersey, and WBZ from Springfield, Massachusetts provided live radiocasts of the World Series to their audience. By the end of the decade, baseball expanded as a significant part of radio programming, which changed the demographic composition of its fans:

> The early broadcasters brought the game to the far corners of America.... Fans in Arkansas and Georgia became fans of the St. Louis Cardinals via station KMOX. In dense valleys of Appalachia, fans picked up the games over WLIW in Cincinnati or KDKA in Pittsburgh. In rural sections of upstate New York, you could pick up games on several New York stations— or from Boston, Cleveland, [or] Detroit [Vecsey *Baseball* 99].

Radio contributed to the expansion of baseball teams' fan base outside of the regular market of stadium-visiting fans. It marked one of the early examples of live baseball outside of a ballpark.

This expansion, however, was not always free of resistance. While many American cities had radio stations airing baseball games in the 1930s, New York City was an exception. It delayed the inclusion of radio to its baseball community until the late 1930s for a very simple reason. Teams feared that the ticket sales might go down if games were available on the radio. In today's professional sports, the same fear continues to exist. It is not only MLB but also the NFL and NHL that have blackout days. The fear about declining ticket sales because of media is not a recent phenomenon. Even for team owners, managers, and investors in the early twentieth century, media causes a sense of fear about losing potential ticket sales (Vecsey *Baseball* 102).

Decades later, dynamics have changed. MLB no longer sees media as a threat today. Media represent where MLB generates revenue. For example, while the general importance of radio as a source of information and news is on a sharp decline (Purcell, et al.), MLB continues to invest in its radio content, called "MLB.com Gameday Audio." As the name suggests, this audio service is an extension of "MLB.com Gameday," a free content service that provides up-to-date game status for all MLB games. The audio program is available for $19.99 for a season and is supported not only on a web browser but also on Blackberry, iPhone, and other mobile devices. The League also markets its audio content by emphasizing that there are no blackout days. This service features pre- and post-game programs, full game archives, and other fan experiences.

This investment in radio by MLB is particularly remarkable for two reasons. First, it is where old media meet new media. This audio service offers a very different radio experience compared to traditional radio in a living room or in a car. Second, despite the wide audience digital radio can capture both nationally and globally, the programs are made possible with a strong focus on local producers and programming. Radio is where new and old, as well as local and global, meet.

MLB and Television

Discussing MLB.TV requires an understanding of its historical context. As the collaborative relationship between MLB and radio developed between the 1920s and through the end of the century, the arrival of television in many households during the mid-century also changed the ecology of baseball media. As the expression "electronic hearth" suggests, a television set became a place around which family members gathered, sometimes to discuss but other times to share entertainment. Just as radio developed with the American obsession about its national pastime, television developed with the sport. The nurturing of baseball on television took place in at least three ways. The first was network stations, especially during television's early period in the mid-twentieth century. The second was the rise of cable television. ESPN, FOX, TBS, and other channels affected the way the sport entered American households. The last was the presence of superstations. This section will explore the implications of each of these phases.

It is important to remember that the prosperous days of television as an outlet for MLB did not arrive till the mid-century. Although 1939 marked the year of the first ballgames on television, it was not until the mid–1950s and later when television truly because a means for fans to enjoy baseball. The first baseball game to be televised on air was not an MLB game on TV, but rather a game between Princeton University and Columbia University on May 17, 1939. NBC, the broadcaster that aired this collegiate game, became the first station to televise an MLB game on August 26, 1939, when it aired the game between the Cincinnati Reds and the Brooklyn Dodgers. Vecsey quotes a *New York Times* article that depicted this monumental event by stating, "Television set owners as far as fifty miles away viewed the action and heard the roar of the crowd" (*Baseball* 102). Television, during this period, was yet to be a popular form of entertainment. In 1940, while approximately 28.5 million households out of the 34.8 million total possessed a radio, there were only 10,000 television sets in the U.S., with half of these sets expected to be in New York (Bogart 8–11). Enjoying an MLB game on television was by no means a common way of appreciating the sport. Well into the 1940s, radio continued to be the sole means for many fans to remotely enjoy the game.

Television became increasingly vital as a means of broadcasting media in the mid–twentieth century, when it penetrated the American market. For example, only 12 percent of American households owned a television in 1949 as NBC offered the first live network coverage of the World Series. Four years later, however, fifteen out of sixteen MLB teams had signed a contract with local television stations. ABC started featuring a select game of the week for the first time in 1953. By 1955, 67 percent of U.S. households had a television. The number went up to 87 percent by the end of the decade. It was just not the idea of television sets but that of network television that became significantly important during this period (Lee and Chun).

Once television secured its role in American households, it expectedly featured numerous baseball games. Initially, there were only a few channels available to American audiences. During the 1950s and 1960s, three major networks—ABC, NBC, and CBS—broadcast different MLB games. Unlike today, fans did not expect to be able to watch any game they wanted to. Although the number of games each station played per week varied from year to year, these three channels were the primary players in the MLB television industry well into the 1970s. Following this period, ABC and NBC would alternate coverage between 1976 and 1989. The dynamic changed when ESPN entered the competition. Although the cost of securing a contract with MLB had become higher year by year before 1989, the overall trend was intensified in the 1990s.

Between 1990 and 2010, there were only a few television institutions that secured broadcasting contracts with MLB. This is to say that despite its large presence, baseball on television only is a closed industry with a few players. But there is a lot of capital involved. Baseball is an expensive business. When ESPN signed its contract with MLB in 1990 for four years, the contract cost $400 million. MLB also made $1.06 billion dollars in the same year by signing another four-year contract with CBS. Once these contracts expired, ABC and NBC signed a revenue sharing contract for six years whereas ESPN signed another six-year contract for $225 million. This contract with ESPN, however, was voided after a year, only to be replaced by another five-year contract, valid through 2000. MLB maintained three contracts during the 1996 to 2000 period. The contract with ESPN earned them $435 million. That with FOX generated an income of $575 million, while NBC paid MLB $400 million. For a four-year contract spanning from 1997 to 2000, FOX spent $162 million for the broadcasting rights. Once these contracts expired, ESPN renewed its contract six more years by investing $851 million in 2000. FOX followed suit a year later with a $2.5 billion contract valid through 2006 (Lee and Chun).

The partnership between 1994 and 1999 among ABC, NBC, and MLB was a unique one that deserves elaboration. It was a business alliance that was expected to stay for six years. Named "The Baseball Network," this project was a way for MLB to produce its own media content with the following business strategy.

As a media entity, TBN [The Baseball Network] was charged with generating revenue for MLB by selling advertising time and promotional rights. Rather than take a projected 55 percent cut in rights fees and receive a typical rights fee from the networks, MLB agreed to accept 88 percent of the net revenue generated by TBN from sale of advertising and corporate sponsorship. Consequently, MLB shared the financial risk with the networks. It was thought that if its advertising rates were reasonable, TBN would help the networks, MLB, corporate sponsors, and players market the sport. The networks stood to benefit because they reduced the risk associated with purchasing broadcast rights outright.... MLB and its players liked the new arrangement because the recently expanded play-off format would further line their already bulging pockets. Finally, the advertisers were excited about the arrangement with TBN because the new package included several changes intended to boost ratings, especially among younger viewers. Since this type of partnership appeared to please all parties involved, many thought other major sport leagues and their affiliated networks would eventually adopt it, thus furthering the growth of sport sponsorship and advertising (Lee and Chun).

What happened in the 1990s and 2000s, especially TBN's attempt to produce its own content, suggested a new form of MLB involvement in media. Prior to this period, MLB and media corporations were highly independent from each other. On the one hand, MLB organized games. The league's involvement in broadcasting was limited. On the other hand, media corporations reported these games, sometimes live and sometimes recorded. The relationship was contractual. What TBN showed was that MLB could be actively involved in the generation of media content not simply to market MLB but also to make substantial revenue through its media strategy.

The rise of cable television during the 1970s and later decades was another contributor to the increasing presence of MLB on television. It is also remarkable that cable channels are far from simple televisual entertainment providers. They have marked various key moments in recent MLB history and integrated numerous outlets. ESPN and FOX are leading players in the cable field. As stated earlier, ESPN's contract with MLB started in 1990. Its first *Baseball Tonight* telecast took place on March 19, 1990. About a month later, on April 9, it aired its first MLB regular season game, between Baltimore and Kansas City. On October 6, 1996, ESPN became the first cable television station to televise a post-season game, a match-up between Cleveland and Baltimore. The channel also featured some international firsts. On March 28, 1999, the first MLB game in Cuba since 1959 was put on air when the Baltimore Orioles played the Cuban National Team. In April 2001, ESPN showed MLB's first game in Puerto Rico, a game between Texas and Toronto ("ESPN's 20th").

ESPN's most recent contract with MLB that runs through 2013

offers diverse options to its customers. It airs television content on ESPN, ESPN2, ESPNHD, and ESPN2HD. ESPN's MLB coverage is extensive. In addition to these four cable channels on television, it offers programs on ESPN 3D, regional channels, and other television outlets. It also includes in its portfolio ESPN Radio, *ESPN.com*, *ESPN3.com*, *ESPN The Magazine*, ESPN mobile services, and other non-conventional media outlets ("ESPN Fact Sheet"). Due partially to these synergetic efforts, the viewership of MLB on ESPN is on the increase. The firm reported in 2010 that its *Baseball Tonight* had on average 713,000 viewers for four nights on game nights during the MLB Division Series. It was 61 percent more than the figure from the previous year. Similarly, its *SportsCenter* also recorded a 14 percent increase in its viewership compared to the previous year (Smeltz).

After entering the competition in 1996, FOX has been successful along with its affiliate and sister stations. Similar to ESPN, FOX is rich in digital content that is not confined to the traditional sense of cable programs. Popular games such as the ones that involve the Boston Red Sox or the New York Yankees continue to attract over three million viewers, if not more ("Primetime"). During the early weeks of the 2011 season, FOX reported the highest ratings in almost three years ("FOX Hits"). Furthermore, one of FOX's executives is a strong advocate of turning MLB games into more television-viewer-friendly programs. Ed Goren, a founding executive, now a vice chairman, once suggested that MLB should allow cameras to be affixed to catcher masks or to be buried near home plate. He also suggested that MLB should permit television stations to interview players and managers during the game (Hiestand "Baseball"). Fox's involvement in MLB becomes ever more apparent after examining Fox Sports Network's extensive coverage. From Detroit to Tampa Bay, Houston, and Cincinnati, FSN has exclusive or non-exclusive coverage of its local MLB team games. For Braves fans, an easy way to catch an Atlanta game would be to tune in to Fox Sports South. Similarly, Fox Sports Southwest would be a prime destination for Texas Rangers fans.

The nature of FOX's involvement in MLB broadcasting becomes clearer when put in context with the contract between MLB and Turner Broadcasting System, or TBS. When MLB renewed its contract with FOX in 2006 for it to take effect between 2007 and 2013, the document also stipulated how to balance cable television rights between FOX and TBS. According to the agreement among the three parties, FOX kept its exclusive annual rights to the All-Star Game and the World Series. It also broadcasts the American League Championship Series on the odd years, or 2007, 2009, 2011, and 2013, and the National League Championship Series on the even years. While FOX had eighteen weeks of coverage for *FOX Saturday Baseball Game of the Week* in its previous contract, the new contracted granted them eight additional weeks. On the other hand, TBS's contract stated that it would broadcast all regular season tie-breaker games, all Division Series games, and the *All-Start Game Selection Show*, which used to belong to ESPN. On twenty-six Sundays, it would also have a right to broadcast a game ("MLB, FOX, and Turner").

Just as network and cable channels determined how baseball developed in relation to the televisual medium, superstations also affected how baseball fans, especially local audiences, appreciated the game. The Federal Communications Commission defines the superstations as "a television broadcast station, other than a network station, licensed by the FCC that is secondarily transmitted by a satellite carrier. " In many ways, because of the rise of digital and modern technology, and also because of conflicts with other stations, many channels that were once considered as "superstations" no longer fall under this category, frequently after becoming a regular cable station. To discuss this change or definitional difference is not within the scope this chapter. For the purpose of this chapter, the term is used flexibly, to include some of the regional cable television networks.

For many fans, superstations are frequently the "go-to channel" to watch their local favorite team. While many of these channels are quite independent from their local MLB teams, this is not the case with the New England Sports Network. Established in 1984, its affiliation to the Boston Red Sox is clear, since 80 percent of the corporation is owned by Fenway Sports Group, whose parent companies are the Boston Red Sox and Liverpool F. C. of England. The rest of the company is owned by Delaware North Companies, the owner of the Boston Bruins hockey team. Taking advantage of its strong connection to Boston's two highly popular professional sport teams, NESN has regularly been recognized as the most successful "regional sports network" in the U.S. and became "the first regional sports network in the country to originate every game and studio show in high definition." Although the involvement by an MLB team to this extent is unique, the Red Sox's interest in the media industry is noteworthy. Additionally, as explained elsewhere in this book, the Red

Sox generate a substantial amount of advertisement revenue through NESN (NESN; Adams 57; Vrooman 31).

For the fans that want to have a channel dedicated to MLB, MLB Network is an optimal television station. This is MLB's own television station launched in 2009. MLB owns 66.7 percent of the company whereas Comcast, Time Warner, COX Communications, and other cable stations own the rest. This development in 2009 was long expected in many ways. For example, the NBA launched its own television station in 1999, and the NFL started its station in 2003. The NHL was two years ahead of MLB. Despite this late start, "MLB Tonight," "Hot Stove," and other programs that are put on air twenty-four hours a day have kept fans entertained. The projected profit by 2015 is $100 million (Brown "MLBAM"; Brown "Understanding"; Furuuchi 23–24).

All of these examples involving radio and various forms of television suggest that MLB developed as media technology developed. MLB utilized the latest means of information and entertainment distribution to attract and maintain fans, and generate revenue for the league. Each team has its own history, episodes, and legends about its relationship to media. It may have a legendary anchor who reported the game for decades. Fans may share a special game that they watched on television with friends that they continue to talk about for years to come. Despite the differences, the mid–twentieth century witnessed a national trend of experiencing MLB not just at ballparks but also via media. A new phase of this trend transpired at the end of the century with the digital revolution.

Baseball 2.0: MLBAM Behind the Curtains

Baseball commissioner Bud Selig once admitted that he was a technophobe. He stated, "As proud as I am, believe it or not, I don't use a computer.... My five granddaughters are stunned that I'm computer illiterate. If I go online, I drive people crazy" (Sandomir "Baseball's"). This quote, uttered back in 2006, cannot be more opposite from MLB's aggressive online marketing tactics in 2011.

While the MLB viewership is strong on television, MLB also reaches its fans through its official website, MLB.com. Launched in 1995, the website's main features include informational content such as news updates, score and statistic updates, schedules, and standings. MLB's digital strategy is not only informational but also commercial, allowing visitors to pay subscription fees to access the site's content or to buy MLB merchandise. Its popularity is on the rise. In 2007, MLB.com registered approximately 500 million visitors, an increase from about 400 million the year prior. Approximately 30 million tickets are sold on the website (Walker "MLB").

This heavily successful website also is the gateway to MLB. TV, a subscription-based service to watch streamed live games. For mobile devices, the site offers "MLB.com at Bat," an application that shows the digital scoreboards and other information to keep subscribers up to date on their iPhone, BlackBerry, and other mobile devices. Similarly, this website is where fans enjoy "MLB.com Fantasy," a fantasy baseball game online. Examining this highly successful website that is a very strong revenue generator for MLB and its teams reveals some of the new media strategies that MLB has engaged in.

The wirepuller behind the scene for MLB.com is Major League Baseball Advanced Media (MLBAM). This winner of the 2010 "Best in Digital Sports Media" award is a "separate, for-profit" private company owned by the MLB club owners ("Cowboys"; Brown "MLB Advanced"). The company was established in June 2000 when thirty MLB teams invested a total of approximately 300 million dollars (Furuuchi 22). MLB explains that MLBAM "is the interactive media and Internet Company of Major League Baseball. MLBAM manages the official league site, *www.MLB. com*, each of the 30 individual Club sites, and delivers live online streaming audio and video of every game as well as the most complete real-time baseball information and interactivity on the Internet and wireless devices" ("MLB Advanced Media").

Since MLB's expansion frequently takes place digitally even to fans that seldom have access to televisiual reports in foreign countries and other domestic areas where they cannot visit their favorite team's games, MLBAM's involvement in the MLB business is a key to the success of the League. Bob Bowman explained in 2003 that as more and more "homes [are] on broadband, and nearly everyone at work, that is a big enough sandbox for us to play in" (Hansell). MLBAM is the branch of MLB that produces more than 12,000 digital live events per year. Much of the content is available outside of MLB.com, including *ESPN3.com*. During the regular season, MLBAM generates 500 new videos every day (Spangler). Jorge Ortiz agrees in his article in *USA Today* stating, "[MLBAM] has created a cash cow that has been instrumental in boosting the industry's annual revenues past $6 billion and inflating franchise values" ("MLB's").

MLB.com is a major portal website for many baseball fans. Bob Bowman explained in 2008 that over 10 million viewers visited their website on a regular day during a season. This means that the website attracts more visitors in a day than many websites do in a year. Additionally, MLB.com streams around 3 million videos per day. Interestingly enough, it is not always the eye-pleasing video and flash content that attracts MLB fans. In the midst of the steroid and other performance-enhancing medicine scandal in 2007, over 2.2 million fans downloaded the 400-page "Mitchell Report," or the outcome of the twenty-one-month-long-investigation officially entitled "Report to the Commissioner of Baseball of an Independent Investigation into the Illegal Use of Steroids and Other Performance Enhancing Substances by Players in Major League Baseball." This shows that the website is the source of both information and entertainment for millions of baseball fans daily (Brown "Interview").

The financial expansion that MLBAM demonstrated during its first decade of existence was exceptional. Just as most new companies experience, the first few years for MLBAM were not profitable. It recorded losses for the first two years when it made revenue of $36 million in 2001 and $50 million in 2002 (Ortiz "MLB's"). Most of the revenue came from commissions and online ticketing fees. There was very little income made through the company's online media content (Fisher "Ten Years Later"). After the third year, however, MLBAM became profitable with the income of $91 million. The growth has been steady. In 2005, it recorded $236 million in revenue and $380 million two years later (Ortiz "MLB's"). MLBAM's president and chief executive, Bob Bowman, once speculated that the company would generate $685 million in revenue. Ten years after the launching of the firm, his forecast is yet to come true. MLBAM, however, is almost a $500-million company. One half of the fans that visited an MLB game in 2010 purchased their tickets online.

MLBAM has established numerous means to generate profit. Its website records approximately 50 million hits per month, making them very close to becoming one of the top 100 websites in the entire digital world. It sells diverse services and merchandise that profits teams. For example, subscribers may pay over $100 to access MLB.com's video content. As quoted in a 2002 article in *Newsweek*, Bowman explained, "To be successful economically, subscription services have to be the engine.... It's happening, and will continue to happen." In 2010, more than 500,000 subscriptions to MLB. TV were created, each featuring a $120 service for an out-of-market live game package. As mentioned earlier, MLBAM's audio content costs about $20 for a season. More than a million fans subscribe to MLB's mobile services including news, ringtones, and cellphone wallpapers. Although "MLB.com at Bat" ended in 2010, about 500,000 fans downloaded this $14.99 application in 2010 alone. MLBAM's merchandise sales ranging from mass-produced hats and jerseys to autographed or authenticated memorabilia are greater than $80 million per year. For example, within a day after the Boston Red Sox won the World Series in 2004, fans bought $5 million worth of Red Sox merchandise. MLB.com sells tickets for games. MLBAM once operated the official website for the National Baseball Hall of Fame and Museum. Before the collaboration between two parties, Brad Horn explained in his interview with Erich Fisher from *Sports Business Journal Daily* that "MLB Advanced Media has had great success and shown us a model that is very conducive to the way we conduct business.... This will help us better fulfill our mission and go a long way to extending us beyond Cooperstown and beyond our peak season." Last but not least, the website contributes to the bottom line through advertisements, with 15 percent of MLB's revenue now coming from advertisements. These diversified income sources make sure that fans spend money in different portals, all of which eventually brings revenue to the same source (Fisher "MLBAM"; Fisher "Ten Years Later"; Levy; Sandomir "Baseball's"; Schwartz).

    The success of MLBAM results in revenue for all thirty MLB teams, which share an equal amount of profit regardless of the performance or the size of the team. It has been the case with ABC's "Game of the Week" starting in 1965 (Hutton 34). In other words, the Yankees and the Red Sox may attract more online fans than less popular teams, but as far as MLBAM revenue is concerned, however, "the mighty New York Yankee's share of the pie is no bigger than that of the [at the time] hapless Tampa Bay Devil Rays" (Levy). By mid–2007, teams had invested about $75 million in MLBAM, or at least $2.6 million per team. By the end of the year, however, the clubs were fully reimbursed for their investment. When there was a speculation that MLBAM might go public in 2004, the estimated initial public offering capitalization value was approximately $2.0 to $2.5 billion. The number is well above $5 billion today, or $150 million per team (Levy; Ortiz "MLB's").

    MLBAM has also maintained a productive relationship with the

Major League Baseball's Players Association. In January 2005, MLBAM signed a deal with the Players Association that shifted the dynamics of property rights. An article in the *Washington Post* concisely explains the change brought about by this collaboration: "Typically, sites such as ESPN and Yahoo! purchase rights to use players' names and uniform numbers from the union. Under the deal, sites will now purchase those rights from MLBAM and will package them with video highlights, images of uniforms, team logos and other intellectual properties owned by the league" ("MLB, Players"). This $50 million agreement for five years aimed to improve MLB's presence online. Being specialized in digital and online content, MLBAM was an optimal branch of MLB to be in charge of this business that could generate synergy. A *Washington Post* article elaborates that the deal would allow "more joint projects involving online baseball games, fantasy baseball, merchandise and memorabilia. The deal also allows MLB to market and sell products linked to wireless communication devices such as cell phones" ("MLB, Players"; Wingfield).

This deal from 2005 was particularly significant because of its impact to fantasy baseball. Although it caused legal ramifications to both MLB and MLBAM, the latter party was fully aware of the popularity of fantasy baseball. The agreement centralized the intellectual property rights at MLBAM and allowed any interested party to negotiate solely with MLBAM. Additionally, MLBAM offers its own fantasy baseball on MLB's official website, MLB.com. Bob Bowman explains that although few fans have time to play fantasy baseball for twenty minutes a day, they can spend a few minutes a day to play the game. He told Tim Lemke from the *Washington Times* that "these games only take a minute or two. They take up a lot less time and are a lot more fun" (Lemke "Bite-Sized"). This ease of playing fantasy baseball was an appeal to many fans.

Bowman estimated that there were about 750,000 people that played "non-traditional" or online fantasy baseball on MLB.com in 2007. The number was expected to rise by one-third in the following year, if not double. This rise represented not necessarily an increasing attention to fantasy baseball in general, but rather an available format for which many fans felt they could afford the time. As Bowman explains "Fantasy fans are better baseball fans.... The more people playing fantasy, the better off we are. We've tried to come up with games that require a little less effort to play and a lot less time" (Lemke "Bite-Sized").

MLBAM's Expansion to Non-Baseball Markets

MLBAM's expansion has taken shape not only through developing its MLB content but also through venturing into non–MLB and even non-baseball markets. As mentioned above, MLBAM offers MLB.com, MLB Gameday, streaming video and audio content, wallpaper and ringtones for cell phones, and other MLB-related services. Additionally, it maintains websites for the MLB Player Alumni, World Baseball Classic, Minor League Baseball, the Australian Baseball League, College Baseball Hall of Fame, and other baseball-related websites. Alex Rodriguez and Derek Jeter are just two players out of many to have their personal website run by MLBAM. During the 2006 World Baseball Classic, 40,000 fans paid $9.95 to watch games on the MLBAM-managed website. But MLBAM's reach goes even further. Non-baseball websites run by MLBAM includes Tiger Woods' personal and official website. Until 2009, MLBAM also ran the official website for Major League Soccer. Furthermore, MLBAM runs or owns websites of Bob Marley, Bon Jovi, Scott Stapp, and other singers (Brown "MLBAM"; Mickle; "MLB Advanced Media Plays"; Sandomir "Baseball's").

MLBAM's involvement in non–MLB sports is nothing new. It has been a core of the company's synergy project. During NCAA March Madness of 2006, the basketball tournament games were streamed online on cbs.sportsline.com, cstv.com, and ncaasports.com through MLBAM's broadband network.

Bowman elaborated on this collaboration with NCAA March Madness by stating that "better content helps our business.... If people watch March Madness, they'll watch baseball. They know we're out there" (Sandomir "Baseball's").

Another example of synergy materialized in 2005 when MLBAM acquired tickets.com and in 2010 when it launched Priceless Perks. The acquisition of tickets.com was an unprecedented business deal in the sport industry. Before this $66 million deal, no professional sports league had purchased a publicly traded company. Today, one-third to one-half of all the MLB game ticket buyers purchase their tickets online. Furthermore, after the collaboration between MLB and MasterCard, MasterCard cardholders have been able to enjoy special savings and experiences upon the purchase of MLB tickets and merchandise. This business alliance allows a 20 percent discount on general merchandise purchases and special MasterCard ticket offers (Fisher "MLB Pays"; "MasterCard").

In 2010 another significant business deal for MLBAM was its collaboration with ESPN. As mentioned earlier, MLB and ESPN have had a long relationship that has generated big revenue. In March 2010, these two companies announced that *ESPN3.com*, the successor of *ESPN360.com*, would feature technological infrastructure and operational support provided by MLBAM. MLB's media branch had already proven its effectiveness in offering various media content, customizable widgets, schedules, scores, and so on. ESPN, on the other hand, had rich sport content that MLBAM considered profitable. ("ESPN360.com"; Fisher "Ten Years Later")

This announcement was particularly consequential because 2010 was the year for the FIFA World Cup in South Africa. As Ronald Grover's article in *Bloomberg Businessweek* suggests, "The World Cup Online, Brought to you by Major League Baseball" was a counterintuitive idea. But for MLBAM that had streamed videos from March Madness to the Masters golf tournament for CBS, it was a natural business decision. MLBAM's senior vice president for multimedia and distribution explained that his firm had the capacity for 2 million concurrent streams while the expected amount was above 1 million. This technological superiority was one of the strengths of MLBAM. As former president of CBS Sports, Neal Pilson, commented, "MLBAM has become the technology leader in the sports industry.... They have the latest and best technology, the most experienced manpower, and huge excess capacity" (Grotticelli; Grover "Watching"; Grover "The World Cup"; Stone).

As its name shows, MLBAM is fundamentally a media branch for MLB. It is owned by the League's teams. Its business operation, however, also shows that it is a for-profit entity that is willing to expand outside of its traditional baseball market in order to generate profit and bring more income to the teams. Rarely do we find a quote by an MLBAM representative striving to popularize non-baseball sports. What we find, instead, is a series of discussions as to how best to take advantage of MLBAM's superior media technology in order to maximize its financial potential and to bring more fans to baseball. This is a stark contrast to, for example, the National Baseball Hall of Fame which exists purely on a non-profit basis.

MLBAM continues to evolve. Bob Bowman explains that the company plans to invest $20 million per year in technology, about 5 percent of its annual revenue (Van Riper). Joe Inzerillo, MLBAM's senior vice president for multimedia and distribution, states that its investment in "adoptive bit rate technology" would optimize the viewing experience of MLB media content for fans. Additionally, increasing investments in technology for mobile devices will maintain and attract more fans and improve their baseball experience (Dachman).

Internet Media Drive Contemporary Baseball

The relationship between Major League Baseball and broadcasting and narrowcasting media has not always been rosy. In some instances, Hutton's assessment of it being "dysfunctional" was an accurate way of depicting the conflicting interests among interested parties, including maximizing the number of fans watching games on television while coping with the fear that fans would not physically attend games. In many other instances, however, media and MLB developed collaboratively. The development of radio and television reflects that of MLB. The game frequently existed at the forefront of the media industry. The same has been true with the more modern digital media. While the audience study, examination of social media, and many other topics are outside of the scope of this book, this chapter has shown that MLBAM drives contemporary baseball.

Major League Baseball does not happen only inside of a ballpark or a training facility. It also exists in front of a television set in a suburban living room, at the desk of an office worker who sneakily checks the latest about his or her favorite team during a day game, at the finger tip of an urban commuter holding a smartphone, and in many other places. With the rise of radio and television, live baseball left ballparks and entered our living rooms. With the Internet, it has become portable and a matter of 24/7 access. Along with walk-on music, game-day giveaways, and many other facets of MLB, media have turned baseball into an environment. It is not just an object of consumption, or to some, that of obsession. It is an environment in which millions of MLB fans live and which they experience the culture of baseball. Media have turned America's favorite pastime to its favorite obsession.

6

Telling the Story
Creating the History of Baseball

In a study of Major League Baseball and its life as a contemporary popular culture practice and as a business venture, one should take the time look not only into the present, but also into the construction of the past. MLB can live not only through shaping the experience of the present for its fans, but can also shape its narrative in constructing its history. The ability to shape/construct history can be a potent cultural text as well as product to be commodified and purchased. Major League teams each possess the ability to create a sense of history in their respective stadiums. Whether it is through walls adorned with photos from the team's past, memorabilia from great games in team history, marked areas of the ballpark itself (such as the red seat in Fenway Park to commemorate Ted Williams' epic long-shot home run), or even team halls of fame such as Monument Park, commemorating great Yankees players in Yankee Stadium, teams seek to create, manage, and market a sense of history and identity as an organization.

Above these local efforts, or MLB efforts such as MLB Productions, the epicenter of baseball history and more specifically MLB history rests in a small village in the state of New York: Cooperstown's Baseball Hall of Fame. Regardless of the historical accuracy about the origin of the game, this small village in the countryside of New York State with the population of approximately 2,000 has become the home of baseball and its past. No entity possesses such a great ability to shape and manage MLB's history, legacy, and ultimately its very soul. In fact, in many cases, individual teams are able to construct their local histories thanks to the Hall itself. Often, images and memorabilia are obtained from the Hall of Fame to adorn the stadium-scape of MLB teams. It is also the Hall of Fame that brings the experiences of both historical events and canonized artifacts of the game today into the eye of the public. Wandering the Hall, one can see Babe Ruth's bat along with Trevor Hoffman's hat worn during his 600th career save. From the tens of thousands of artifacts, hundreds of thousands of photos, and countless documents meticulously stored and preserved in the Hall's holdings, a narrative history of baseball is created, tracking the game from its humble origins to its contemporary life. It is also here that the greatest of the game are enshrined in a sacred space, a site of pilgrimage for the converted.

As it wields so much power in creating the history and soul of baseball, this chapter focuses on an interview the authors conducted in 2011 with Senior Director, Communications and Education, Brad Horn, of the Baseball Hall of Fame, to better understand how the Hall operates, and, most importantly for this book, what part MLB plays in shaping this narrative in American life and abroad. MLB has a vested interest in the Hall. As of December 2011, four of its Board members are associated with MLB, including its Commissioner Allan H. "Bud" Selig. While the Hall is an independent not-for-profit organization, MLB is a massive profit-generating powerhouse. Since the Hall preserves much of MLB history, it is only natural for any visitor to question what the relationship between the two entities might be.

The Hall also benefits from funding and donations of artifacts from MLB. Teams offer their congratulations to inductees and honor deceased Hall members in Hall of Fame publications. Browsing through the Hall, one can see that individual players and teams are responsible for many artifacts contained within. Horn's name was actually first seen in our research in an article discussing the working relationship of the Hall to MLB in regard to the World Series each year. As Horn has stated, "We're unique, I'm unique, in the sense that in this environment I have the ability to talk with players and teams as it happens, as it unfolds. We work very closely with MLB, with the two teams playing, so that when the series concludes, we're able to take back to Cooperstown eight to 10 historic moments that we can preserve for future generations" (Hayes).

The Hall of Fame is definitely upheld as a determinate force in shaping the legacy/historical narrative of baseball. For instance, consider a discussion with Marvin Miller, a former executive director of the Major League Baseball Players Association, in the *New York Times*. Miller, disappointed in falling short of getting the votes needed to get into the Hall stated, "You can leave the individuals out" continuing, "but you can't leave out the impact the union has had. You can't be anything but fraudulent if you pretend that you are the archivist and recorder of the history of an institution like Major League Baseball but leave the union out it." Horn responded by citing that the Hall had featured a "year-long exhibit on labor that featured Miller" in 1998 (Sandomir "Miller"). Regardless of the politics of this specific situation, one can see in this discussion the negotiation that occurs in determining the legacy and definitive story of MLB as not only an economic product, but also a product of culture.

As the Horn interview will indicate, though, the Hall is far from an absolute appendage of Major League Baseball. The Baseball Hall of Fame, a non-profit entity, exists as a place where the story of baseball as whole comes into play, around the globe: Little League, Negro League, Women's Professional League, and even through exploring relationships of the game to other sports such as cricket. The Hall is also focused as being a site of historic preservation of the game itself, funded through memberships and other funding sources above and beyond MLB.

Still, one must acknowledge the fact that this non-profit organization can mean a lot to the practice of MLB today as a cultural and economic product. We sat down with Horn to discuss these realities and the way that the Hall constructs, maintains, and displays not only the history of the game, but also very much contributes to its present and future as a sport in the eyes of American and international fans/practioners of the game. MLB, teams, players, Hall electors, and the Hall itself have a vested interest in telling/creating the story of baseball and all possess a certain influence. The life of the Hall reflects these relationships of power and control in its ability to both work with and independently of Major League Baseball. Hence, a look into the Hall provides an important look into the power relations that construct this hallowed space of a culturally and economically driven product. As stated by Hal Bodley, a senior correspondent for MLB.com, in the Hall's 2011 Yearbook, there is a necessary symbiotic relationship:

> From a small Museum on Main Street in the tiny Central New York village of Cooperstown, the Hall of Fame — over the course of 75 years — has grown into the stately institution that serves as the protector of our National Pastimes' legacy. Nothing, except for the players themselves, has helped make base-

ball what it is today more than the Hall of Fame. By the same token, baseball, with its enormous popularity, has been a force that has lifted the Hall of Fame to a height that other sports museums cannot approach [7].

As MLB continues to be the driving force of baseball economically and as a popular culture force in the United States and arguably abroad, it is a main force in establishing and maintaining the life of the Hall. As Horn's interview suggests, the Hall readily acknowledges the role of MLB in its life, but also points out the important independence that the Hall as a historical and cultural institution itself possesses. As there is some influence/representation from MLB, it is important to understand the relationship further, and to consider, regardless of the level of involvement, how the Hall continues to contribute to the life of MLB as a cultural and economic institution.

Interview with Brad Horn

YUYA KIUCHI: Thank you very much for allowing me to interview you this morning. I would like to start by giving you some information about how the project started before delving into questions. This project started when Mat and I were both graduate students at Michigan State. We were pursuing our Ph.D. at the time. I had a friend, a high school friend, who worked for the Red Sox as a trainer, and then I also had a friend who worked for the MLB Japan office. So through those people I got a phone call from the Red Sox seeing if I was interested in being their translator for their new Japanese player. I think that was going to be Daisuke Matsuzaka and at the time I was still going for my degree so I had to say no.

BRAD HORN: Oh, okay.

KIUCHI: That was a very, very unfortunate thing. That didn't work out but Mat was in the same office with me and that's when we started talking about "you know it's quite interesting to see how some random things happen with the globalization of Major League Baseball." It seemed to touch upon issues that we rarely thought about and then from there we started writing about the globalization of Major League Baseball; how the relationship between the Japanese league and the American leagues worked together; and so on. Then eventually we said, "okay, let's write an academic book on this," so that we could talk about things that many people, typical baseball fans, were not really talking about. They talk about teams. They talk about players and their legacy. But they don't really talk about globalization, or Americanization. Probably they don't talk much about the management side of the League or baseball in general.

HORN: Right.

KIUCHI: Then a part of the discussion comes up when we ask, so what does the Hall of Fame do especially in relation to baseball in general, or to globalize the sport and also MLB.

HORN: Right.

KIUCHI: And then since the book is about MLB, our interest was the relationship between the MLB and the Hall of Fame because this is the Hall of Fame for Baseball, not MLB.

HORN: Correct.

KIUCHI: And I think it is a very difficult balance to obtain. So, the first question is, before we talk about the Hall of Fame and MLB, I was wondering if you could elaborate on your relationship to the Hall of Fame and what you do. Of course there is so much information out there about you already. But if you could elaborate on it, that will be great.

HORN: Sure, me personally?

KIUCHI: Yes.

HORN: Yeah, sure. I joined the Hall of Fame in February of 2002 as the Director of Public Relations. So during my first six years here, I was overseeing daily efforts, our publications, such as the yearbook, our website content and the overall messaging for public audiences for the National Baseball Hall of Fame. In 2008, I became Senior Director for Communications and Education. And broadly defined, my role is being responsible for all the outreach, all the external affairs that transpire for the Hall of Fame. Now, it covers many different individual skill sets. It's the primary contact for the media relations. It is the primary contact in club relations, dealing with teams on issues, dealing with artifacts that are acquired to come to the Baseball Hall of Fame. All of the overall advertising, marketing, branding that the institution does in a public sense, as well as oversight of our educational mission, which is our programs that we do on site for school children.... The video conferences we do, where we take our sixteen lessons that are designed around core curriculum subjects such as math, science, geography, cultural diversity that are all taught through the lens of baseball, delivering those video conferences point to point and all of the programs we do in the museum to enhance the public experience. So whether that be programming tied into an exhibit opening or a special event that we're doing here at the Hall of Fame to provide exposure to Hall of Fame members, those are the primary roles I oversee. And then as one of the six-member senior team ... our president, this is who oversees the entire operation, our senior vice president, who oversees administration and finance for the institution, a chief who oversees the museum experience, the exhibits, the collections, what the museum looks like and the items that we have in our possession. There is a chief who oversees the development of the fundraising, and the relationship of what we call museum members, those who give money to support the Hall of Fame mission. And then a chief who oversees retail licensing and revenue streams. So that six-member team, of which I'm a part, guides the institution on a daily basis. We are the senior management for the organization.

KIUCHI: Okay, and then for the Hall of Fame I would assume that the term "baseball" is self-referenced not only to Major League Baseball or not only to American baseball, but rather anything under the huge umbrella of baseball?

HORN: It does. We, our foundations, are in the name of the institution, the National Baseball Hall of Fame and Museum. But certainly over the years we have become more globally diverse. Our job at the end of the day is to reflect baseball, preserve its history, to honor its excellence and to connect generations. And over the last thirty years, individuals from other nations aside from America have earned election to the Hall of Fame and it's only become more and more prevalent. The game has become entirely global. Major League Baseball is now very global and as such, the Hall of Fame is becoming very global. In fact, two of the three Hall of Fame electees this year were born outside of the U.S. Bert Blyleven was born in Holland, and Roberto Alomar was born in Puerto Rico.

KIUCHI: As the globalization of baseball takes place, would you find it difficult to define American baseball? Like baseball played by Americans, baseball located in the United States or ...

HORN: Not so much, because we believe that baseball remains the national pastime.

KIUCHI: I see.

HORN: And our focus is in sharing distinctly American experiences. Take a couple of quick examples. One of our common themes is character encouragement, and we show the impact of Jackie Robinson, Lou Gehrig, and Roberto Clemente. Three individuals, Clemente was born in Puerto Rico, but three individuals whose achievements in American baseball went beyond the game. And so we talk about Jackie Robinson breaking the color barrier in baseball in 1947, happening a full fifteen years before Dr. Martin Luther King gave his "I Have a Dream" speech. Jackie Robinson being fifteen years ahead of the color barrier, Roberto Clemente being on a humanitarian mission when his plane went down, and Lou Gehrig having the courage to face a life threatening disease and really, be dying, as he was trying to continue playing the game of baseball. All from the guy who had been known as the "Iron Horse" for achieving so much on the field. So the content is rich in its American history. We are exploring connections with the global history. So we have influences from the Japanese League, Kinugasa, the Japanese Iron Man. We have artifacts from history. We have many, many stories from the Negro Leagues, which ran concurrently to Major League Baseball in the '20s, '30s, '40s, '50s, but because of the biases and discrimination that took place in the U.S. at that time, these individuals were not allowed to play in Major League Baseball. That's a very important story for us to tell. We talk about the role that women played and when baseball took a backseat to World War II, how men left to fight in the war but women took their place on the field, and very popular, played baseball at a very high level. And then how women are pioneers in the front office and playing today. So there are many spokes to the wheel of baseball but the American story remains at the heart. We are not changing our mission to detail the history of baseball in Latin America, but we have incorporated an exhibit in Spanish and English that talks about the game's culture in Cuba, or Puerto Rico, or Dominican Republic, which has become such a huge exporter of baseball talent to the U.S. So our heart remains focused on American baseball but the windows are opening to the world and we continue to look. You know, if we were to look thirty years into the future, that will continue as we look to document the game.

KIUCHI: So baseball as an American story, as an American pastime.

HORN: Absolutely, baseball as the fabric of America. That's an enduring theme that has been central to our mission and continues to be so. And I don't think we will stray from that because it is so distinctly American at its roots.

KIUCHI: That is true.

HORN: Even though it's debated. People will say that it may not be truly an American game, but its history is intertwined with America at every step of the way.

KIUCHI: So with that context, MLB, of course, is one of the biggest, if not the biggest, component in today's baseball at least for fans, media and almost everyone that is involved. So what really is the relationship between the Hall and MLB?

HORN: Absolutely, it is a relationship that requires mutual understanding and respect for each institution. At the heart of it we are entirely independent. So the charter mission of the National Baseball Hall of Fame, as a not-for-profit educational institution, is to preserve the history of our game, including Major League Baseball's game. To preserve the history of baseball by collecting and documenting artifacts from its history, by participating in activities that foster an appreciation for the sport, and by helping fans understand the role that baseball, in its largest form, plays in American society and culture. So we are entirely independent. Major League Baseball is a for-profit entity. What their entity is, is entirely different from ours. They exist to ... they have thirty major league teams; they provide baseball at the highest level. But ours is distinct in incorporating the history of the game. Now, we work very closely together. We are governed by a sixteen-member board, which I see you have a copy of our yearbook there, if I may open it to the page here for reference for you. This is our board of directors, which governs the institution. As I mentioned the senior staff earlier, that's the six of us here. But the board, of which Jane Forbes Clark serves as chairman, there are three teams represented, William DeWitt is owner of the St. Louis Cardinals, David Glass the owner of the Kansas City Royals, Paul Beeston the chief executive of the Toronto Blue Jays and Commissioner Selig. So you see of the four, of the sixteen members, twenty-five percent represent team ownership of Major League Baseball. So they're a very important part of the process of shaping the management of the Baseball Hall of Fame, but the day-to-day management takes place at the senior staff level of the organization and we work with Major League Baseball on many projects. Let me give you an example. For us to be able to acquire artifacts from, I don't know if you saw the third floor exhibit on the San Francisco Giants, and the World Series.... In order for us to preserve those moments as they happen we need the access from Major League Baseball to say yes it is okay for you to be here to acquire these artifacts so that when the last out is recorded I'm on the field asking players for their artifacts.

KIUCHI: There was a newspaper article about you collecting items.

HORN: Exactly. So that is a unique story because people wonder how these items get to where they are at. So that is a part of one example of access they provide for the Hall of Fame. Also we are launching a project just this week called "One for the Books." There are teams that have been generous: the Arizona Diamondbacks, New York Yankees, Chicago White Sox, Boston Red Sox. They provide for projects. There are a total of eight teams that are supporting this exhibit on their own. And that is independent of Major League Baseball and is their right because they are making individual gifts as teams to this exhibit. So there, it is an independent relationship, and it does not have ties or bonds that make us beholden to their desires.

KIUCHI: So there is no financial input from MLB at all?

HORN: MLB and its teams have been very gracious with the Hall of Fame over recent years. In addition to the teams I listed, another half-dozen have contributed to special projects for the Hall of Fame. Though there is no direct funding stream from the MLB to the Hall of Fame, they have been extremely supportive and generous in helping to support, and often times, fund, our projects and initiatives.

KIUCHI: So as far as day-to-day operations are concerned, MLB has no influence or no financial....

HORN: Right, correct. And the commissioner sits on our board; he, as any other board member would, can say I recommend you guys do that or I recommend you do that or shouldn't the Hall of Fame be doing that.

KIUCHI: Just as any board of directors member.

HORN: As any director would, right. So it's not a mandate; we are unique from other sports halls of fame in that regard. You know if you look at the Basketball Hall of Fame, or Hockey Hall of Fame, or Football Hall of Fame, those major sports are governed under the control of their respective leagues. So the independence works importantly for us in a number of ways. First of all, it allows us to impartially tell the story of baseball history. If there ever were a moment in baseball that was so important from a historical standpoint that Major League Baseball felt embarrassed by, or would not want to promote in that way, this museum is not a center for promotion, it's not a place to promote entities. It is a place to document the history in a serious manner, to tell the story of American history. So that's the really critical crux of what we do and we feel that independence allows for that to happen unabated so no one can question whether we are, you know ... if we feel it's an important story, we feel that it is an important story as an institution not because MLB or someone else said that is was.

KIUCHI: Well, one of the things I have noticed as I was touring the museum yesterday, thinking about the relationship between the Hall and MLB, was that I saw obviously a lot of things from teams, from MLB players and so on, but I didn't really see a logo of MLB.

HORN: Interesting, okay.

KIUCHI: And that was, I almost felt that was intentional distancing from the League or ...

HORN: It's a good point. You know I have been here ten years and never has that come up that we don't feature their logo. You know, at Today's Game Exhibit, we have a bulletin board as designed to be a clubhouse, and there's Major League Baseball documents on that, but that might be the only place you will find it. And it's an interesting observation. I don't think there's any intentional un-inclusion, to put it that way: it just doesn't fit maybe in the context of what we are trying to document, as we talk about stadiums, ballpark experience. If we were to have a business model or business exhibit, I would think probably a logo would be an important piece.

KIUCHI: Because there was a section where it clearly stated baseball has become not just a pastime but it has become, I think the word they used was an "enterprise" or something like that.

HORN: Yes, enterprise, exactly.

KIUCHI: And then there I thought well this really is, you know, connected to MLB but then again as I said earlier I didn't really see the logo, I mean not that the logo is the important part but as much of a reference it is to the league itself, so ...

HORN: Absolutely. That is a very good point, I think that, that part of, and again I am not sure if it's intentional but I don't believe it is, but it's a part of the celebration of the entire industry of baseball.

KIUCHI: Ah, okay.

HORN: Little League Baseball is a vibrant industry in this country.

KIUCHI: True.

HORN: Now do we document its achievements? Not so much, but you know there was a female pitcher who struck out every batter she faced, out of up-state New York about five years ago, we took her jersey in. There was a female pitcher in Florida who threw back-to-back no-hitters at the Little League level; we took her jersey. So we're not just limiting our story to Major League Baseball. The reason we probably don't feature the Major League Baseball logo is why we don't feature the Japanese Professional Baseball Leagues and we take artifacts from them. We don't feature the Little League Baseball logo. There are many entities that comprise baseball within it. We say that baseball is a capital B and Major League Baseball would say that's different because I'm sure that they refer to themselves as baseball with a capital B. But we never make that direct correlation. For us, it is more global. MLB is a part of the story we tell. And now most of the artifacts you'll see in the museum are from MLB achievements because that's the highest level but we couldn't without that spirit of cooperation.... We could not properly document the game's history if Major League Baseball were to say ... if they didn't have ... if there wasn't a good balance, a good relationship, because of those assets their granting us the use to display.

KIUCHI: So you would really characterize the relationship between the Hall of Fame and the League as very positive, independent but very positive.

HORN: Absolutely. Independent but very positive. And we work hand in hand because the history of baseball is so unique with this sport. In no other sport is the history really celebrated, but it is in baseball. And it's important to today's game to know who Hank Aaron was, who Willie Mays was, who Babe Ruth was and this is the place where the history lives. Now Major League Baseball is more focused on the season, and they're focused on that night's game or that championship year, or the pursuit of a World Series, or maybe doing good works in their community as a give back, or their television contracts, ratings, but when that moment ends, it's the history that is preserved. And so we work very closely, you know, the Hall of Fame carries a reverence with teams, it carries a cachet that Cooperstown is very vital. You know I had to pop out of [this] meeting to speak with someone at one of the teams for a joint project; we are making an announcement this morning. So we are working together on a joint press release for something. So that shows, this is more involving an individual, but it shows how we work together in that regard. So I had to talk to him. So not a day goes by that we as an institution don't communicate with someone at Major League Baseball or at a club level but it's not from a management perspective of what you are doing, it's relationship building. It's us working together. We have a relationship on a PR side with teams in which we send them public service announcements that promote the Hall of Fame. We ask them to run them in their ballparks in between innings, prior to games, we have a program ad that we ask them to run in their publications that's a trivia quiz that promotes the Hall of Fame. And all of the thirty teams, Major League level, cooperate and about one hundred twenty minor league teams do. So we are giving them content that they can plug into their offerings that promote that Hall of Fame, that are pre-produced. And that's a big part of what we do. We get calls from teams that say, both at the major and minor league level, "Hey we'd like to honor Jackie Robinson, how can we work with the Hall of Fame to do that?" We say "Well we have plaque postcards; we can sell those to you and you can then be supporting our non-profit mission. We can send you video free of charge that we have produced that's a tribute to this player." So we try to reach into those communities and work with those teams because that's where baseball fans are. So the seventy million fans that went to a Major League game last year, the forty million that went to a minor league game, those are the most likely people who are going to make the commitment to travel to Cooperstown. So if we can expand our message and our brand with those audiences, teams allow us to do that at no charge. We in turn help support their celebration of history.

KIUCHI: What do you think the teams expect from the Hall of Fame because I would say, well my sense is that Major League Baseball is extremely popular and it's in everyone's mind day-to-day, where the Hall of Fame is something that comes up to their mind when there is an induction ceremony that takes place or when something else happens. But not necessarily a day-to-day thing.

HORN: I think that whether it's the league or team, and there's really not a difference because it might deal with the PR department of the league or another executive of the league, I think they look at the Hall of Fame as being the stewards of the game. They know that if history happens in their ballpark, the Hall of Fame is going to document it. And they don't have to call us to say "Do you want something from this game?" because the second a no-hitter is thrown, I'm on the phone, "We'd like the cap, get us the ball." So they look at the Hall of Fame as the active place where it's going to be celebrated. Major League Baseball knows that they have, that baseball has an institution that is going to commemorate its history. And I think that is very unique because in many businesses, many sports organizations, the history is always secondary. But every day there is an institution of eighty-five people working to commemorate what they do on a daily basis. And they don't have to come to us and say "Will you be doing this?" because this is part of our daily business. For seventy-two years now the Hall of Fame has been in business and every day that's what we do. In our library we preserve stories from things that happen yesterday in baseball, today in baseball. They look at us for input, for consultancy. Some unique examples: A team executive might call and say "We're thinking about honoring a World Series team of ours from fifty years ago. Aside from bringing in Hall of Famers" which they do on their own, "what are some of the other ways we can tie back to our team's history? Our team history may not be very good but what do you guys have from the 1948 team?" And then our staff will look and we'll say "Oh, we have these photos, we have these images from our material, we have video and you know we will provide that to you" because that's how we work with them.

KIUCHI: Okay, so with the close communication between the Hall of Fame and the League, have you encountered any difficulty because of the different approach to baseball? One being non-profit, the other being for-profit.

HORN: Sure and that's something that's vitally important to us.... It is that at the end of the day we maintain our non-profit mission. And sometimes Major League Baseball might want to come and do things that we have to seek remuneration for or that we have to protect our own entities. So sure, with every relationship there are moments where you have to say no. And it's a very open and good dialogue and there are certain instances where the Hall of Fame works with an entity that is not Major League Baseball, that is best for the organization. So we manage the best of what is going to be good for the Hall of Fame, not what is always going to be best for Major League Baseball. And vice-versa, Major League Baseball would probably tell you they make decisions not involving the Hall of Fame that they have to do to protect what they do. So it's, it can be complex but it is built on mutual respect for each other's institution.

KIUCHI: I think that's the very important key part of the relationship, I suppose, independent and respectful.

HORN: Independent and mutual respect, absolutely. I think other sports would be envious; you know we always are looked at as the bar by which others are measured, you know the standard if you will. And I think other sports would be envious of what our institution does every day to document the history in the way that we do.... From a very professional curatorial staff to researchers, to people who care about the history of the game to make sure that it's being preserved. And that's kind of what motivates all of us. We work in a not-for-profit environment, where we know that all we're doing every day as a staff is preserving the moments for fans.

KIUCHI: That's true.

HORN: It has nothing to do with us. We're merely caretakers. So if we are doing a program, like we had the Giants' World Series trophy here a couple of weekends ago, our role in working with the Giants, we were the proactive ones. We worked with the Giants on getting the trophy. All of those efforts are so that someone can come here and have a very emotional memory. There were fans that traveled from San Francisco that said the reason they came to Cooperstown was because the trophy was going to be here. And it allowed them to celebrate their team, their moment, their World Series the only one they ever had, at the home of baseball. So again that's not written that the World Series trophy must come to Cooperstown, but those are the types of events that we do that provide a connection for a fan. And so that's how the relationship between the MLB and the Hall of Fame benefits everyone.

KIUCHI: I see.

HORN: Because it's not one order-taker at the MLB processing everything, it's people at both organizations working together. So the Giants might call us tomorrow and say, actually they did ... this is a really good example because when the Giants were presented their World Series ring they asked if we could be at their ballpark. And Jeff Idelson, our president, traveled with several of the New York Giant World Series rings. He brought them with him out of our collection and flew to San Francisco and it added value for their players, and their executives and their fans because they did a segment that these items were directly from Cooperstown in celebration of the Giants. So that's a perfect example of a Major League Baseball club and the Hall of Fame working together on our levels to provide more for fans. And that's what the Hall of Fame serves. That's why we operate.

KIUCHI: So the teams don't really expect any financial remuneration for you to have a ball or for you to have a historic icon?

HORN: Yeah, and they know that for us, our resources are limited. We never pay for any artifacts, every artifact is donated whether that comes from you as a fan, or from the San Francisco Giants' best player, or the team has said well, we own the jersey, now we're going to give you the jersey. It's all out of the generosity because they realize the preservation of the Hall of Fame.

KIUCHI: How does the Players Association react to that? I know that players personally feel that it's a great honor to be here but….

HORN: Yeah, again there's no formalized relationship with the Players Association. We have worked with them on certain events in the past and I think that they view the player's generosity as the important way that we are preserving their history. You know if you were a player and you have the moments, you might not be a Hall of Fame player but you have had a great day at the ballpark; you've thrown a no-hitter or hit four home runs and the Hall of Fame calls, that's your connection to history. And a player makes that decision to donate their glove or their spikes. In a free-market environment those are items that could get, you know memorabilia is a different word we don't use — memorabilia as a word — we use artifacts, but it could get money on the memorabilia market. So I think a player sees that gift to the Hall of Fame as their contribution to preserve baseball history. We've had active and former players visit regularly. Ichiro Suzuki has visited four times. He loves Cooperstown. And players have a strong attachment to … you know one of the roles I serve is being on site to talk to individuals. You see the excitement of Cooperstown, "Wow my bat's going to end up in Cooperstown, great." So it's not a formal business relationship with the Association, that's probably how their membership views that and they might come to us tomorrow, if we would work with something with players and we would. We are the entity that basically is neutral to the labor and business side of baseball.

KIUCHI: I have a question about something I have always wondered ever since I came here for the first time, maybe in 2003, just as a visitor. I know that there is a historic connection to Cooperstown, but baseball being such a huge game not only in the United States but globally, and how so many people would want to visit the Hall of Fame but it's in upstate New York.

HORN: Absolutely.

KIUCHI: Is there any thought that you know you might have at least a branch office somewhere, you might move somewhere?

HORN: We feel that Cooperstown is the home of baseball. Now in a literal sense the home of baseball does not mean it was born here. We know that. We used to promote that is was, but we now know that baseball was started elsewhere. But Cooperstown remains the spiritual home of baseball and that is very important to the organization, to the board that Cooperstown is this shared relationship with the Hall of Fame. We average about three hundred to three hundred twenty-five thousand visitors a year. It's been very consistent. If we were to move to a bigger city, would the potential be there? Yes. There are many parallels with coming to Cooperstown as what it is to get to a Hall of Fame career. When you get to Cooperstown, it's very beautiful, it's very elegant, it's very timeless. You step out on Main Street today, not a whole lot different than maybe 1950s Main Street. Cars are different, but the appearance is very much the same. That's an important comparison because a Hall of Fame career is out of reach, one percent ever gets to the Hall of Fame. Now accessibility to fans, that's a different story because everyone should have the ability to enjoy the Hall of Fame. Now that we have technology as a focus, you know, technology is now the way, it's taken care of. Everybody can connect through an iPad, through mobile devices. So our challenge now is to take some of the history through that. But I think we always feel that Cooperstown will be the home of baseball and it's not to say never say never but it's not the same if someone experiences this in New York City, or Los Angeles, or anywhere in between.

KIUCHI: Do you feel that with baseball being an American pastime that this whole experience of being here is not just being inside of a building but participating in the pastoral idealism of the United States?

HORN: Absolutely. It's Americana at its finest. And we did a traveling exhibit from 2002 to 2006, you might have read about this called "Baseball as America." And we went to fifteen major museums in cities across the country: Minneapolis, Dallas, St. Louis, Oakland, Philadelphia, New York, Boston, L. A., major metropolitan areas where we could go into an existing museum environment. We took five hundred pieces and they were all themed in a very professional way about the relationship between baseball and America. And we put those in museums and it was a great success. And that philosophy will probably lead to future efforts to do that same matter. But just like any baseball team that returns home after a road trip, that's how we view Cooperstown. Cooperstown is one and the same with the Baseball Hall of Fame and it's part of the myth that is that we're almost larger than life. When you think about that twelve-year-old baseball player in this country, who have played since they were six, seven, eight, nine, by the time they are twelve, their father, their grandfather or the TV they are watching has said the word "Cooperstown." And they know there is this place where if you are good enough to play for a long time and you are one of the very best you may end up in Cooperstown. And if that say became Manhattan, it's not quite the same, similar ring. So very different in its approach and it's proven, it's withstood the test of time. You know the museum opened its doors for the first time in 1939. Seventy-two years later we're still, we are at our best place we have ever been. More artifacts, more exhibits, more people connected. We have thirty-thousand museum members who support us. They get our magazine and yearbook. Almost fifty percent of those thirty-thousand have never even been here. Because they now understand that we are dependent upon individuals to make this place what it is. And this does go back to your relationship question. At the end of the day, it's not Major League Baseball that is insuring our financial security, it's baseball fans. Because they are making contributions whether its forty dollars a year to be a member, or one-million dollars as an endowment donor, or they're sponsoring an exhibit. And fans can take many forms. The commissioner of baseball made a donation to this exhibit, fifty-thousand dollars, "The One for the Books." So we are truly the fan, the fans direct connection to its past. A fan can spend thirty dollars on a ticket to go to an Astros game in Houston, but that experience ends when the game ends. And something might have happened to them there and that's where they can come here and maybe relive it. They saw a player, the first game, first date; you know, we had someone here just come through the front doors last month and they walked through the front door and he stopped and he proposed to his girlfriend. So you know, this was the place of their first date, they were from downstate, a town called Beacon, New York, down near the Poughkeepsie area. Their first date two years ago was at the Hall of Fame, so he wanted to propose to her at the Hall of Fame. So that's how real life happens I guess. And it's the place where people come to seek an emotional connection, and that's why that is always at the very top for us. We know that if we have that emotional connection things like financing will come, things like programs are a natural outflow. If we stay true to our mission, and that's where the independence is so critical, it's something the Hall of Fame feels very strongly about where it stands in the landscape of baseball.

KIUCHI: For future development, do you have anybody designated to work on the online educational section?

HORN: We are working at it, yeah. We've changed some of our staffing to become more online focused. We spend, now where we used to spend five to ten percent of our time, we spend more like thirty percent. So it's in our future plans to become more technological and to take many of the assets here that are a bat, a baseball, online. To take a baseball, we will photograph it and give a three-hundred-sixty-degree presentation in the studio context so the user could, this might be a home run baseball from Mickey Mantle's five hundredth home run, to take it so they can see it on their mobile device, on their laptop, iPad. So that is a very big focus of ours. We hope to in the next three to five years have much of the collection in that regards.

KIUCHI: And if more people can watch it and then come here that would be a good thing.

HORN: Exactly, exactly. We know there are challenges of where our location is, we anticipate that if Ichiro would ever get inducted a number of visitors from the Far East would come and, how do we make that more accessible? How do we become more relevant to other languages, I'm speaking audiences, Spanish-speaking audiences, Japanese. I mean taking Hall of Fame plaques and making them relevant to individual cultures. That's a huge growth point for us and with funding opportunities in future years hopefully we will get there.

KIUCHI: Thank you, Brad, for your time.

Baseball as Part of American Culture

As Horn clearly states, visiting the Baseball Hall of Fame is witnessing "Americana at its finest." Furthermore, the visit is also a journey and an experience. Just as any Hall of Famer spends decades involved in baseball until their plaque appears in the Hall, fans experience the journey by driving through pastoral up-state New York state, walking in a small but welcoming and cordial town of Cooperstown, and approaching the brick building that houses the history of America's pastime. Surrounded by nature, the city offers a sense of timelessness. George Castle states that "baseball is the eternal game, melding past, present, and future" (vii). Cooperstown is a suitable place to house the history of baseball. As the interview showed, we had a lingering question of why one of the most famous and iconic architectures of such a popular sport must be located in a distant place and not in more accessible metropolis. Horn explained throughout the interview that while baseball is a sport and an enterprise, it is first and foremost an American pastime. This is to say that to enjoy baseball is to appreciate friends you see at games every week, the sound of the game, childhood excitement about hot dogs and Cracker Jacks, and everything associated with that day or evening excursion. In Cooperstown, visitors are invited to live baseball as the American pastime. The Hall of Fame authenticates this experience.

The Hall of Fame, however, also is a place where conflicts seem to happen. On the one hand, as explained, baseball continues to be an American pastime. A simple trip to a local minor league team game will reveal that this sport continues to maintain its original status. Additionally, it is deeply rooted in American culture. From day to day expressions and phrases such as "struck out" and "right off the bat," to popular references of baseball in movies including *The Sandlot* and *Field of Dreams*, baseball has symbolic value reflecting American idealism and a way of life. A trip to Cooperstown is a part of this experience. On the other hand, however, there is no question baseball has become a large capitalistic enterprise. It is a business with sales, profits, endorsements, and contracts. This is not an easy balance to maintain. The Hall balances this difficult responsibility by preserving baseball's history and simultaneously reflecting what it has become now.

Another conflict is an apparent one: the Hall of Fame's status as the National Baseball Hall of Fame and an epicenter of MLB's dominance. As Horn clarified, the Hall is an entirely independent entity from MLB. It aspires to include Little League, Women's League, and other non–MLB baseball legacies when appropriate. The Hall exists to promote baseball. Therefore it works closely together with MLB. For many fans and for researchers, stories and myths of MLB are what drive their interests. Horn's comment on mutual respect while maintaining independence is the key to sustain the Hall's original raison d'etre amidst the global expansion of MLB capitalism. George Vecsey makes an interesting observation about the conflicts that the Hall is experiencing and what the Hall continues to represent:

> The Hall keeps growing into a sophisticated, multimedia, online, year-round haven of souvenirs and records, available to serious researchers or casual tourists mainly interested in souvenir T-shirts of their favorite member of the Hall. Yet the Hall is saved from being totally Disneyfied by its location in sleepy upstate New York. The sport also got lucky because the annual induction takes place at the end of July, when little else is happening. No other sport is blessed with the living Norman Rockwell tableau of the induction ceremony: fans pile into rooming houses and bed-and-breakfasts around Cooperstown and chase down autographs from the stars; agile boys hang from tree branches and gape as the old players weep while being inducted into the hall [*Baseball* 47–48].

The Hall of Fame will continue to be modernized through its digital projects and inclusion of global baseball as it relates to American baseball. It will, however, keep its fundamental mission of preserving a significant part of American culture in a very American way.

7

Commodore Selig

*The Importance of Japanese
Baseball Players in
Major League Baseball*

From the 1970s well into the 1990s, the influx of Japanese economic interest into the American business sector drew casual criticism to outright expressions of nativism and fear on American streets. Such reactions, however, seemed a distant memory on April 5, 2007. The eyes of the United States and Japan focused on a young pitcher recently signed to the Boston Red Sox, Daisuke Matsuzaka. Having attracted the attention of both American and Japanese baseball fans since the end of the previous season, Matsuzaka reflected an increasing presence of and fascination with Japanese baseball players in the Major Leagues on both sides of the Pacific, which began fifteen-plus years ago with the arrival of pitcher Hideo Nomo. Since then, names like Ichiro and Hideki "Godzilla" Matsui have opened the floodgates of media exposure, endorsement deals, and focus on Japanese baseball players.

What then happened in this short period of time? Are the presence and proven talent of these players creating an effective program of cultural diplomacy? What is the significance of baseball diplomacy in what Mike Mansfield, the longest serving American ambassador in Tokyo, repeatedly referred to as the "most important bilateral relationship in the world" between Japan and the U.S.? Have Japan's financial woes in the forms of economic recessions during the decade of the 1990s neutralized the threat felt by some Americans, thus opening a door of acceptance for these players? All of these questions demand discussion, but it is one factor that overwhelmingly has assured the current state of acceptance and reception of Japanese players in Major League Baseball: the progressive march of transnational capitalism.

The attention paid to these questions extends far beyond a player's athletic abilities. Not to detract from their performance in the Major Leagues, but these players are representative of much larger economic powers looking to extend financial interest and gain across the Pacific. Additionally, it also reflects American interests in capitalizing globally, on available human and cultural resources for its own benefit. Current Japanese players in baseball are not only potentially individual cultural diplomats breaking down racism and bigotry, but are also foot-soldiers for corporate expansion and the extension of brand identities internationally including that of Major League Baseball, individual teams, and the corporations involved in the process. Furthermore, as much as American baseball teams aim to capitalize on the economic values of these players, the Japanese economy strives to generate profits by taking advantage of their individual symbolic value. There is also a sense in Japan that their resources have been taken advantage of, if not stolen, by American power. It is in these larger structures of transnational capitalism and consumer cultures that the real "acceptance" of one of Japan's most focused-upon imports has come. As the globalization of sports progresses, the significance of a nation as an idea and as an interest group increases (Miller, et al., 16). The international exchange of baseball culture over the past fifteen years highlights the multi-layered structure of an intricate system that globalized capitalism possesses.

Due to this complex flow of trans–Pacific capital, an examination of obvious and eye-catching signs of global capitalism does not suffice to understand the nature of this new type of cultural diplomacy. For example, the fact that the Red Sox spent over $103 million signing Matsuzaka drew in a curious public's general attention. What is more important, however, is the team's decision to spend as much; it was aware that if Matsuzaka successfully brought six extra wins to the team and helped win the pennant, his presence would enhance the annual profit in advertisement of the New England Sports Network by approximately $12.5 million. Consequently, the broadcasting station's value increases by the same amount. Since the Red Sox under the name of Fenway Sports Group own 80 percent of its stock, the team can make an extra $10 million only with advertisements at a local broadcasting station. Once other profits from broadcasting, merchandising, player placements in media, and others are calculated, there was more to win for the Red Sox than to lose. This is nothing but just one example of the vastness and dynamics of how the cultural exchange has become consequential in international business (Adams 57).

Although one chapter does not suffice to replicate the width and depth of this role of baseball diplomacy in global capitalism, an exploration into Major League marketing — both in a traditional "business" sense and a more contemporary "cultural" sense — will show that baseball is a cultural exchange between Japan and the U.S. and that this global economy functions around the players. From the American perspective, Japanese baseball players in the Majors show how an influx of non–American resources no longer signifies a disadvantage for the American economy and culture. This is a different situation than earlier economic concerns like automobile trends between the two countries when the number of Japanese cars imported to the U.S. increased, the American automobile industry suffered. The type of antagonism against the Japanese automotive industry felt in Detroit and other parts of the U.S. (which some critics speculated to have turned the Toyota recall case in 2009 and 2010 into that of "Japan bashing" and an attempt to "undermine Japan Inc.") does not seem to exist in the baseball business. In this type of culture-based exchange, an increase in the number of Japanese players does not bring a decline of the American baseball industry. In reality, it boosts the economy of the Major Leagues via merchandising and broadcasting rights. (Yamaguchi; Hayashi).

It is also important not to romanticize this cultural exchange. From the Japanese perspective, export no longer guarantees profits. While the outflow of baseball talents to the U.S. is beneficial for some industries such as broadcasting, advertising, and traveling, Chapter 10 shows it is concurrently damaging to the Japanese baseball industry. Fewer Japanese professional games are broadcast on television. The fan base weakens. As described later, many Japanese fans perceive the outflow of talented Japanese players as the threat to Japanese *yakyuu* [baseball]. Examining some of the recent developments in this baseball-driven trans–Pacific flow of capital allows us to observe some of the more recent characteristics of what Walter LaFeber calls the "new global capitalism" both of economy and culture.

Looking to Japan from the United States

In 1989, now executive vice president of the Cato Institute David Boaz wrote a piece in the *Wall Street Journal* entitled, "Yellow Peril Reinfects America: U.S. Hostility Turns to Japan." The article reviewed the economically and racially motivated anti–Japanese rhetoric present in the United States that had resulted from an influx of Japanese business interest in the United States, and the increasing competition coming from Japanese auto and technology companies. Boaz shares that the anger took many forms including "presidential candidate John Connally warning the Japanese they had 'better be prepared to sit on the docks of Yokohama in your little Datsuns and your little Toyotas while you stare at your own little television sets and eat your mandarin oranges, because we've had all we're going to take!'" (Boaz). Eighteen years after the article was written, an Associated Press piece lauded the fact that although Mike Lowell was the World Series MVP, "Boston had plenty of candidates. Especially in a year in which Japanese stars Daisuke Matsuzaka and Hideki Okajima helped put the world in World Series" (Walker). Obviously the discussion of American "Japan-bashing" and Matsuzaka's rise to fame are both subjects that are complex and are equally worthy areas of study in themselves, but it is fascinating to see how a nation that has exhibited both fear and fascination with Japan has so successfully adopted Japanese baseball players into its most historically regarded game, especially in the twenty-first century.

The presence and acceptance of these players is much more than a tale of an increasingly welcoming and less racially focused world. The reality of the situation has much more to do with a significantly larger system of global capital and the vested corporate interest in the marketing and promotion of a global sports entity. Much of the internationalization of baseball, especially in regards to the rise and presence of Japanese talent in Major League Baseball, is a story of what Walter LaFeber calls the "New Global Capitalism." Like his examination of Michael Jordan and the internationalization of the NBA, similar corporate power structures are at play in the utilization of names like Daisuke Matsuzaka, Ichiro, and many others to break down international boundaries of consumption. LaFeber describes the immediacy and reality of a rapidly interconnected world through media and technological innovation:

> As revolutionary technology thus integrated Americans into the rest of the world, many of them feared the strangeness and

challenges that they encountered. Americans had feared the strangeness and challenges of other peoples since the seventeenth century, but never before had such dangers been so instantaneous, so immediate, as they were in the new, tightly wired world [21].

LaFeber measures these new challenges to American identity and assures us that the march to global capitalism will eventually, even if at the expense of individual cultural identities, overcome these strange feelings: "In this developing battle of capital versus culture, capital will ultimately win" (21). This process seems to be at work surrounding this latest round of interest in the rise of Japanese baseball players into the Major League Baseball culture; capital is providing a new vision of Japan and its role in the global economy.

Part of this new vision involves a marketed sense of "cool." In an article for *Foreign Policy*, Douglas McGray discusses the rise of Japan's "Gross National Cool" and its connection to the world economy. McGray stipulates that Japan's decade-long recession essentially cut out notions of the country being an immediate economic threat. The opening created by this economic downturn has created a greater sense of openness and in some cases, fascination, with the country by Americans. Japan, McGray, says "succeeded not only in balancing a flexible, absorptive, crowd-pleasing, shared culture with a more private, domestic one but also in taking advantage of that balance to build an increasingly powerful global commercial force. In other words, Japan's growing cultural presence has brought a mighty engine of national cool" (53).

Taking into account LaFeber's model of international capital, we can consider McGray's article as a bridge linking capital and culture in a succinct fashion. The leveling of international boundaries in favor of the spread of global capitalism allowed Japan to effectively sell a less economically threatening vision of itself internationally. This is especially true for consumers in the United States, a country that only years before had, at times, been embarrassingly outspoken about its views towards the Japanese.

In regards to Major League Baseball, these contingencies of international capital and the selling of Japanese culture and identity need to be taken into account when dealing with the reception of, and media attention to, key Japanese players like Ichiro and Matsuzaka in the United States. One can see that *especially* in terms of media coverage that race and national ascriptions of character seem to have much less of a harsh focus when compared to the reception of Hideo Nomo and Hideki Irabu in the 1990s. Instead, what can be witnessed is an extremely lucrative and widespread campaign to mold "America's Pastime" into an international entity. Baseball is to be a game that exists beyond national boundaries and speaks the international language of capital.

The very systems of international capital that are being used to describe the outwardly well-seamed baseball of the twenty-first century were cited by many critics as forces that were creating discord for baseball in the 1990s. Reception to the expansion and use of players in Major League Baseball from Asian countries in the 1990s was seen by David Tokiharu Mayeda as much more racially focused. Mayeda cited players like Nomo as being in a racial limelight in the media and within the American populace: "Hard working and self-sacrificing, and quiet as (he was rarely quoted in newspapers), Nomo reaffirmed to readers that Asian nationals and Asian Americans were model minorities. It should be noted here that although Hideo Nomo is a Japanese national and not Asian-American, he and Hideki Irabu can still affect the way mainstream America views Asian Americans" (211). Along with the "model-minority" concern, Mayeda looks at the previously discussed focus on the Japanese as an economic threat. This threat is the one that according to McGray's article on "Japan's Gross National Cool" has changed so drastically in the last few years. Mayeda saw press coverage of Nomo and Irabu as indicative of this economic fear: "What readers can potentially digest, however, is another Japanese entity that is financially threatening an American institution. Irabu's Japanese heritage and national status were displayed prominently by the *New York Times* ... therefore a cultural sensitivity should have accompanied any articles, positive or negative, on Irabu." He continues later that in regards to the *Times*, "both Japan and Irabu were depicted as economic dangers" (213).

Obviously, Matsuzaka's contract with the Boston Red Sox created a similar focus. Yet, compared to the cultural insensitivity that Mayeda had seen with players in the 1990s, something had fundamentally changed in regards to the theme of economic threats. This discrepancy, as was alluded to, became one of the main protagonists for these studies when comparing media coverage of Japanese players in MLB in the 1990s versus the 2000s. As Robert Whiting in his book *The Meaning of Ichiro* describes, Japanese baseball players at the turn of the century had seemingly shed stereotypes of economic imperialists. He describes, "Americans liked them because of their belief, generally speaking, in the team ethos and their commitment to the idea that playing baseball was first and foremost its own reward—monetary considerations coming later. They were welcome additions to a game that seemed increasingly consumed by greed and ego" (205). Although a wonderful sentiment, this welcoming seems to be more dependent on two important themes Whiting unmasks: first, domestic economic gain, and second, marketing.

Whiting shares several estimates that prove the economic worth of the further internationalization of baseball as a product, including insight into the economic weight that Ichiro brought with him to Major League Baseball and Seattle specifically. Whiting cites ticket sales, hotel and airline reservations, souvenirs, and advertising as bringing in "over $100 million into Seattle's economy over a five-year span" (*The Meaning* 30). A good deal of this money is coming in from Japanese tourists and was the case with other teams across the nation as well.

Whiting proposes that Hideki Matsui's "most important contribution may have been financial, as he single-handedly created new ways for tourists to blow their money in New York. Sales of Yankees tickets to Japanese tour groups went through the roof, as did sales of Matsui goods." Whiting continues, "according to one estimate, the intense Japanese interest in Matsui brought in roughly 500 million much-needed dollars for the city's economy" (*The Meaning* 251). Similar stories have abounded around Matsuzaka's rookie year in MLB for fans here and abroad. From advertising in Fenway Park, to local hotels, to the sales of Matsuzaka products available in MLB retailers nationally, the economic impact on baseball has been massive.

The marketing responsible for this product recognition of MLB as an international product has astutely been able to keep up with, and in many ways, shape this reception. One only needs to look at the *Major League Baseball: International Business Review* to see how consumption has created and directed programs of international acceptance for American fans just as well as in Pacific Rim and in Latin American countries. Major League Baseball now broadcasts in 229 countries and territories bringing numerous broadcast deals, event sponsors, licensing agreements, player development centers, marketing promotions, local advertisers, and international events like the Japan All-Star Series along with it. With rapid growth in the Asian and European markets, MLB is experiencing robust growth as an international entity (Major League Baseball 5, 16, 24–26, 38–41).

Hence, the ideas of national boundaries are not something that

MLB would consider a restraint. Attention paid to Japanese baseball players in the recent years is a larger reflection of widening markets for sports entertainment. These individuals that, as LaFeber states, could transcend race, are also "less a person than 'something of a 24-commodity'" (16, 85). The reception and career of these individual players are receiving so much media focus, not because of cultural progress, but because of immense commercial progress. Keith Reed sees the exorbitant fees paid for Matsuzaka's contract as an investment in a new market versus solely an individual player: "Sox executives believe there is a big market in Japan and locally for endorsements involving the team and Matsuzaka, and that their new pitcher will boost the team's popularity in Japan past that of a certain pinstripe-wearing rival with a Japanese player of its own." Reed continues by quoting Red Sox senior vice president of sales and marketing Sam Kennedy, "We want to be the team of Japan. The Yankees are very popular over there because of [Hideki] Matsui, but now we think we can get in over there as well" ("Dice-K"). To keep up with this hope, the marketing machine of MLB, numerous corporations, and teams have reacted swiftly. Ads for Japanese companies have sprouted up in stadiums across the nation: some with Japanese language signage. Numerous American companies have translated their signs into Japanese as well, including Dunkin' Donuts and Lumber Liquidators (Reed "Sox").

Whiting chronicles that such investment has been a standard with several of the current Japanese players, including Matsui who had numerous "endorsement contracts for Upper Deck sports cards, Lotte ice cream, a Mizuno sports drink and Japan Airlines" (*The Meaning* 251). Ichiro inspired a "30 percent jump in ticket sales" when a bobblehead doll with his likeness was given away at Safeco Field as a promotional giveaway (Whiting *The Meaning* 29). This was complemented by the creation of sushi stands at Safeco Field selling "Ichirolls" and the sales of headbands with Japanese lettering (Whiting *The Meaning* 30). Japanese players, far beyond their athletic capabilities, are becoming symbols of the possibilities of internationally focused marketing for a supposed "American" product in MLB.

The economic realities of Japanese players in the majors were further showcased in Matsui's trade from the Yankees to the Angels for the 2010 season. Anthony McCarraon in the *New York Daily News*, as far back as November of 2009, considered the impact of losing Matsui: "He helped build Yankee — and Major League Baseball — business in Japan and the Bronx, whether by prompting Japanese companies to buy advertising signs at Yankee Stadium or drawing Japanese tourists to the stands." McCarron later quotes a Japanese news outlet who estimates that "the Yankees stood to lose as much as $15 million if Matsui did not return. Other estimates have been as high as $20 million per year." Such numbers were in dispute in the report, but one could see the economic wake left by Matsui continued as a main theme of discussion as he made his way to the Angels.

Much like the Yankees, Matusi seemingly fundamentally changed the Angels' baseball culture. NBC Sports reported during spring training that his "mere presence in Angels camp has increased the contingent of notebooks and cameras by about 15-fold" (DeMarco). Other reports nationally and locally attempted to decipher the Matsui-effect on the organization. Amidst discussions of his baseball talents, articles such as Michael Becker's piece in The *Press-Enterprise* also discussed the economic and cultural significance of Matsui's presence in Southern California. Becker quotes Angels chairman Dennis Kuhl, describing his presence in the following way: "As soon as we signed him, we had many inquiries from Japanese sponsors who wanted to be a part of the Angels organization because of him. During the year, I expect that we'll attract a larger Japanese audience than ever before.... He's brought a new wrinkle to the organization, but it's been a great wrinkle." Other reports showcased the immense amount of interest and attendance by members of the Japanese media, potential signage, and extending the brand name of Angels baseball and Major League Baseball through Matsui.

A looming question remains. Even though in terms of market forces and the largely positive press that has surrounded more recent Japanese players like Ichiro, Matsui, and Matsuzaka, has anything really changed in regards to American views of the Japanese culturally and within the Major Leagues? The massive amount of merchandise that has been sold points to some kind of, at least, consumable acceptance of Japanese players in MLB by Americans. This is the case even though these players only represent a small fraction of total players (even when compared against other international representatives in MLB like from the Dominican Republic). As we have seen, a great deal of investment in branding and creating internationally marketable images of baseball has created an "It's a Small World After All" aesthetic where harmonious page after page of the MLB sponsored *International Business Review* points to a rainbow of players, each respected and part of an international community.

Hence, do these economic realities reflect a real cultural shift? If this is the case, issues central to Mayeda's study of Nomo and Irabu have been pushed into the shadows by the media in favor of the financial discussions that these players have generated. Simply put, though, the march of international capital has not killed American xenophobia. To get to the heart of the matter, MLB's business office was criticized by a former MLB employee for "fostering an environment in which anti–Asian hostility thrived." The Associated Press reported on October 16, 2003, that the employee stated that she was "repeatedly subjected until her May termination to an 'unreasonable, offensive and demeaning anti–Japanese and anti–Asian hostility that pervaded the entire International Department'" ("Woman Says"). Major League Baseball is far from immune from such issues; discussions concerning race are ever-present and have followed the League whether in regards to discussions of minorities in coaching positions or numerous other concerns.

One could perhaps even issue the word economic "fad" in terms of influence, when one looks at articles like the *Sporting News*' "Setting Sun?" in their "Baseball 2010" issue. The article, along with admitting to Ichiro and Matsui's lasting influences on the game, also discusses "the once-ballyhooed talent pool for Asian stars appears to suddenly be drying up" (Gregor 16). The "list of failures, however, is overtaking the success stories," specifically citing how Dice-K's "stock was in freefall" (17–18). One has to wonder, with such neat bows ready to be tied on the influence of Japanese players in the United States, how much are people willing to think of the presence of Japanese players as a permanent change in the narrative of Major League Baseball? Of course, such thoughts could be countered with publications as far removed as *the Irish Times* discussing the wooing of "Japanese schoolboy Yusei Kikuchi" into the majors just a few months before *the Sporting News* piece was printed ("Sports Digest" 8).

Such occurrences that have come and that will be sure to arise as Major League Baseball continues to reach and compose itself of an international community are important to keep in mind as the juggernaut of transnational capitalism continues to roll in the twenty-first century. Yet, one must marvel at the immense power and sense of peace created in the media that has come through the marketing of these players as international capital-generating machines. That sense of peace and fascination exists because so much is financially dependent on sports diplomacy to continue to generate the capital that Major League Baseball has become accustomed to. In the meantime, we can see how larger economic relations shape the reception and use of cultural events like the latest media focus on Japanese players in baseball. Japan's economic life (whether at its pinnacle or in the recovery from recession), the domestic benefit of Japanese players in a competitive sports-entertainment industry, and the marketing done to ensure economic benefits to all involved, shape reception.

Looking to the United States from Japan

Watching Japanese baseball players play a vital role in their teams' victory in the MLB is a pleasure for many baseball fans and non-fans in Japan. It may even nurture a sense of nationalistic pride when Matsuzaka strikes out an American slugger or Matsui hits more than thirty home runs per season against American pitchers. Jim Street, a writer for MLB.com, reports that Ichiro already has his "foot in the door" as a Hall of Famer, after being selected to play in almost ten All-Star Games and receiving the Gold Glove Award nine times (Street). Thanks to these achievements by Japanese players in MLB, some industries see the Japanese fascination about American professional baseball as a great business opportunity. This trans–Pacific capital flow enabled this appealing market to generate large profits from MLB-related clothing sales to broadcasting rights. Baseball diplomacy, however, does not always bring entertainment to those sitting in front of a television set or business opportunities like it does to Japanese travel agencies organizing a weekend trip to Boston or Seattle just to watch a ballgame.

On the other side of this excitement about Ichiro, Matsui, Matsuzaka, and many other Japanese baseball players in the Majors, there is a strong sense of fear and concern about the gravitational force that Major League Baseball possesses. Many fans have expressed their ambivalence about a cultural crash between Japanese collectivism and American individualism, and how that might affect those Japanese players in the Majors, those still playing domestically, and ultimately the youth that aspire to one day become professional baseball players. A continuing outflow of talented players to American teams over the last decade and a half has become a cultural and economic threat both for fans and the related industry. While cultural imperialism would take place when a dominant culture exercised its centrifugal force over a less powerful one in the past, American centripetal force has caused ripple effects under the new global capitalist framework.

Tomonori Iijima reports the sense of threat that surfaced at the professional baseball owners' meeting on July 18, 2007. Keizi Oyashiro, the owner of the Nippon Ham Fighters and the chair of the meeting, admitted at the succeeding press conference that team owners had agreed that Nippon Housou Kyoukai (NHK), Japan's government-run television station, had broadcasted too much about MLB. Earlier in the year, Masayoshi Son, the owner of the Fukuoka Softbank Hawks, problematized NHK's televising policy by claiming that the broadcasting station "disproportionately" emphasized MLB in its program content. NHK audiences, indeed, had more opportunities to watch an MLB game than a Japanese domestic league game in 2007. While NHK broadcasted 127 Japanese games, it also broadcasted 260 MLB regular-season games and 30 postseason games, compared to the previous year, the number of games broadcast for Japan's league was increased by one game, whereas broadcast games for MLB increased by fifty-five (Iijima). The meaning of these numbers was particularly significant since NHK is the only government-owned television station in Japan, which is supposed to reflect the general interests of the Japanese population. It was not simply a matter of NHK's indifference in the domestic game but that of national indifference.

What happened with NHK in 2007 was not an isolated case. Although the total number of domestic professional baseball games aired on "television" (as widely defined to include cable, satellite, the Internet, and other forms of telecasting) has increased over the years, the popularity of baseball as television content has been on a steady decline. Nippon Television Network Corporation, the broadcasting station owned by Yomiuri Shimbun, or the parent company of the largest and most popular Japanese baseball team, the Yomiuri Giants, curtailed the number of broadcast Giants games by approximately 40 percent in 2007. Additionally, unlike in the past when television stations continued to broadcast the game until the end, even after the scheduled broadcasting time was over by delaying the start of the following shows or canceling them, most channels adhered to the original broadcasting schedules and left some avid baseball fans unsatisfied. The Nikkan Sports News, one of the leading newspaper companies in sports, is unsympathetic to the team owners' claims. They summarize these unsatisfied owners' comments by claiming they are simply looking for scapegoats. Iijima claims that it is not the broadcasting stations that are contributing the weakening fan base. It is the attractive value that the Japanese professional baseball has failed to maintain that turned the game into an ailing business. Regardless of the cause, team owners unanimously show their concerns that the Japanese leagues will eventually lose most of the talented players and dedicated fans to MLB (Iijima).

MLB, on the other hand, has been successful in expanding its broadcasting fan base in Japan. After Dentsu signed its six-year contract worth $275 million with the MLB in 2004 to broadcast the major games, Japanese fans have had more exposure to American baseball. Five years later, Major League Baseball International renewed its broadcasting agreement with Dentsu, a Japanese right-holder, through 2015. It was a part of the contract renewal between MLB and global partners including Meridiano Television, DirecTV Latin America, and Rogers Sportsnet. Through Dentsu, Japan Broadcasting Corporation, Tokyo Broadcasting System Television, Fuji Television Network, TV Asahi Corporation, TV Tokyo Corporation, and J Sports Broadcasting Corporation are able to telecast MLB games (Major League Baseball International Renews). This was a major contract both for the MLB and Dentsu. Although MLB has attracted many fans in Japan, Japan continued to suffer from the economic downturn that started in the 1990s. As much as Americans felt the consequence of the failing U.S. economy, the Japanese also experienced its impact in layoffs, bonus and salary cuts, and other tangible ways.

MLB did not expect to expand and secure its fan base in Japan only by showing its games on television. They exposed Japanese fans to the history and culture of "MLB.SPORT," a nightly sports news program on the Fuji Television Network that features a short weekly feature called "West Side Story." In this sub-program, audiences learn about the history of MLB, the history of ballparks, the rivalry between the New York Yankees and the Boston Red Sox, and many other fundamentals about American baseball culture (Kato). A similar effort took place in newspapers and on websites. Before the 2007 season started, MLB Japan conducted an online popularity poll for all MLB teams. It was one of the promotional efforts to nurture a sense of fandom for a particular team, and possibly replicate a geographical rivalry between the two cities on the other side of the Pacific (Major League Baseball Japan).

MLB did not attain this level of success in Japan easily. The contract renewal in 2009, for example, rang a cautious bell to the ears of MLB representatives. Although four broadcasting stations agreed to purchase broadcasting rights through Dentsu, Nippon Television Network Corporation, the aforementioned parent company of the Yomiuri Giants, decided not to air any MLB games starting in 2009. This was a seismic decision, particularly because Matsui, who at the time played for the Yankees, or Koji Uehara, a pitcher for the Baltimore Orioles, were once star players for the Giants. An anonymous representative from Nippon Television Network explains that despite fan interests in the Majors, the cost was too immense to bear. The contract among the conglomerate of TV stations, Dentsu, and MLB stated that each station was able to use game video clips for news and other programs with the maximum length of three minutes a day by paying the MLB over seven million dollars a year. This decision was not necessarily a surprise since Nippon Television Network went into the red in September 2008 for the first time in thirty-seven years. A savings of over seven million dollars was consequential ("Nittere").

To secure the process of business expansion through cultural diplomacy, MLB seeks more than just media appearance as its marketing tactics. One of its objectives in Japan is to make a shift from player-driven hype to a more general fan base that appreciates the game as a whole. In other words, despite the current popularity of MLB in Japan, most fans only watch games in which Japanese players play. They turn their television on to see Matsui or because of Matsuzaka. If Matsuzaka and Okajima were to leave the Red Sox, the team would be very likely to lose popularity increasingly amongst Japanese fans. One of the ways in which MLB's Japan office is attempting to pull fans into the sport itself is to place its players in magazines. Ryan Howard appeared in *G. Q. Japan*, David Wright in *Men's Non-no*, and Joseph Mauer in *Goethe*. Bronson Arroyo appeared on MTV's "World Chart Express" which was also broadcast in Japan (Major League Baseball Japan). Through these media exposure activities, MLB aims to attract Japanese fans not only to Japanese players but also to non–Japanese players. Additionally, the league aims to educate its Japanese fans about the culture of baseball so that the league would have a more secured and stable fan base through which it can generate profit.

MLB has also been successful in attracting a new demographic group to baseball, which is currently targeted at females. In the past, Japanese baseball attracted adult males. With the arrival of MLB to Japanese living rooms, middle-aged housewives began to cheer for Japanese players in the U.S. This new phenomenon is partially due to the time difference. The games are on television in the late morning in Japan when housewives traditionally spend time cleaning the house and doing the laundry with their television on (Kato).

To capitalize on this expanding demographic of fans, MLB particularly focuses on females between the ages of twenty-eight and thirty-five. While they tend to have a relatively large disposable income, they have traditionally not been baseball fans. The strategy is to market MLB apparel to this demographic. Since cultural difference between the U.S. and Japan makes it difficult to sell baseball jerseys, t-shirts and caps to females in Japan, MLB came up with a new product portfolio which is more acceptable in the mind of young Japanese females. Located in Harajuku where young people gather on weekends, "LB-03," one of the most popular apparel shops in Tokyo, agreed to sell such items (Kato). The store's official blog features the latest Major League Baseball apparel for women. Using black and pink as the base colors, the website is not anything commonly expected for an online baseball merchandise store to look like.

Similarly, Akira Machida, the store manager of the MLB Club House Store, explains that now that Major League Baseball is one of the most popular sports in Japan, consumers are willing to spend more money on baseball-related apparel. In the past, a majority of the store's sales came from Matsuzaka- and Matsui-related items that cost around $25 to $30. Machida now predicts that customers are more likely to purchase more expensive items. As an attempt to take advantage of this commercial opportunity, the store now sells replica jerseys for women, even though the line only included ones for men and children in the past. (Machida)

These capital-driven marketing efforts in Japan have so far been successful. As President George W. Bush mentioned at the Japan–U.S. summit meeting on November 18, 2006, the trans–Pacific flow of talent may be beneficial to the Japanese economy in some cases. Even so, if LaFeber's aforementioned prediction that capital wins at the expense of culture is true, what are the possible cultural consequences of baseball diplomacy? Is it possible that ultimately, the baseball culture will become *nothing but* a vehicle of capitalism?

Albeit harshly criticized by fans and players, Japan's National Professional Baseball League (NPB) maintains a strict policy regarding the Japanese players' ability to play abroad. For example, a player who belongs to an NPB team has to spend at least nine seasons until they can obtain the right to negotiate with an MLB team. Although some players who had taken this option have played well in the U.S., many players fear that they will have passed the prime of their career after nine years in Japan. Additionally, the NPB team to which the player belongs will not receive any transfer fees unlike the transfer case to another team in Japan. Or, a player is eligible to play in the MLB only if his team releases him. Unless the team is understanding about the player's wants, it is unlikely to let go of a key player who has a potential to be successful in MLB but who can probably help the team win the NPB season. Although there are several other ways for players to play MLB, both fans and players perceive the NPB's policy as an attempt to exclude the MLB from the Japanese baseball society. To judge if this policy is a fair one or not is not within the scope of this chapter. It is, however, true that this exclusive policy of the NPB has so far been successful in keeping Japanese players within Japan's domestic leagues as much as possible and to enrich the domestic baseball culture, even at the expense of many talented players' careers.

Despite the isolationist attitude of the NPB, it is evident that it has impacted globalized baseball. One of the major consequences is the clash of two different value systems. As the capital-based American baseball culture interacts with Japanese culture, an inherent and traditional difference between Japanese and American culture is particularly highlighted. Although essentialism never does justice to the complexity and diversity within culture, as past sociologists and anthropologists including Edward T. Hall and Ruth Benedict have analyzed, Japanese society has prioritized collective good over individual benefit. On the other hand, American society has been characterized as individualistic by various Japanese cultural scholars. This fundamental difference between group-oriented Japanese culture and individual-oriented American culture seems to explain how differently Japanese baseball fans and media consider the success of Ichiro and Matsui. Many fans have expressed ambivalence about Ichiro's pursuit of individual achievement while showing a sense of empathy to Matsui's collective idealism.

Although "Americanized personality" is too strong an expression to describe Ichiro's professional attitude, Ichiro has emphasized his personal achievement more than his team's success. Some of his comments reflecting this philosophy include: "I am happier when I hit four hits in a game and my team loses than when my team wins and I hit none," and "When I meet players who are playing just to win, that angers me." Although these quotes do not mean Ichiro cares less about winning, individual achievement is a major benchmark for his career. Shigenori Matsushita concludes that it was partially because of this idea that Ichiro decided to play for the Mariners when he could have obtained free agency to transfer to the Yankees or the Red Sox where he might play in the World Series. He argues that there was something more important for Ichiro than winning the World Series. Matsushita claims that that something was the five-year contract that included $90 million, as well $32,000 annual residence fees, an SUV, four first-class round trip tickets for him and his family between Japan and the U.S. annually, and a guaranteed personal trainer and interpreter (Matsushita).

Matsui, on the other hand, is a collectivism-oriented player. He says, "Baseball is a team sport. What is the point of competing on an individual basis within the team?" While Ichiro sets his target as 200 hits per season, winning the World Series is Matsui's target. Many Japanese fans and baseball analysts recognize the proximity to traditional Japanese value systems of Matsui's baseball philosophy. To express his admiration, Matsushita quotes Matsui: "I am fine even if I could achieve nothing as long as my team achieves something."

Such ambivalence about the capital and individualism driven culture in MLB also appears in Japanese media reports on seasoned players' attempt to join MLB from Japan. Takashi Saito was once thought to be at the end of his career in Japan. But he later became successful as a closer in Los Angeles. Masumi Kuwata signed a contract with the Pirates as a Minor League player. Hideo Nomo and Shingo Takatsu attended spring training in 2008. Several Japanese players around the age of forty have crossed the Pacific to make it to the Major Leagues. Media reports about these players portray them as the embodiment of non–capital-driven dream seekers. As the *ZAKZAK* article entitled "There Is More to the American Dream Than Money" shows, "there is nothing new about young players signing expensive contracts." This new and older demography of Japanese baseball players coming to the U.S. with a very small signing fee reflects how they began to test their individual talent in a new environment. Instead of focusing on "playing for the team," these seasoned Japanese players play to challenge their own individual limits.

A Complex Cultural and Economic Exchange

Baseball diplomacy that operates within the framework that LaFeber terms as "new global capitalism" has different consequences, both positive and negative, compared to the product- and material-based trans–Pacific exchange in the 1980s and before. A see-saw like understanding of globalization is no longer valid. In the past, when the Japanese auto industry did well, American industry suffered. In the new global capitalism, both parties may suffer or benefit. Some of the examples have shown how Japanese Major League players have allowed both American and Japanese corporations, baseball organizations, and other relevant entities to generate profits. Such economic-based arguments, however, do not suffice to understand the new trend. Although LaFeber suggests that capital gain is more emphasized over cultural consequence, this study has shown that the nature of cultural exchange is more complex than concepts such as "domination" or "loss of culture" can explain.

An increasing number of non–American players in MLB results in an outflow of baseball talents from non–American baseball leagues. While increasing economic interest in the game, this process still can potentially challenge, for some, the "American-ness" of MLB. These players, largely though, have seemingly found a much warmer reception than some other products of the Japanese industrial-entertainment complex.

In addition, unlike the material and product export business, the intricacy of talent-based capitalism is that the outflow of resources may result in loss of money in the exporting market. Although relevant industries in Japan, MLB's Japanese office, and the Japanese professional baseball league try to identify various ways to generate profit through Japanese baseball players in the U.S., they has not been successful erasing the common idea that the trans–Pacific baseball diplomacy resulted in the loss in Japanese culture and sport.

The preceding pages have not sought to successfully diagnose and understand every aspect of the complex cultural and economic exchange that is reflected in the rise of Japanese baseball players in the U.S. Major Leagues. The subject continues to evolve each season and with each acquisition or trade. The subject also continues to evolve as these players create seemingly permanent residencies in a sport that has found great economic success in the last several years. Just as it is an exciting/problematic time for those financially invested in the baseball world around the globe, so it is the same for fans as well as cultural critics that look to the future of the sport in national and international consciousnesses. Keeping an eye on these relationships of culture and capital can only help us understand the competitions both on and off the field in the life of baseball as an international presence.

8

It's All About the Capital

Major League Baseball and Its Capital-Driven International Strategies in the World Baseball Classic and the Olympics

In 2005, concurrently a hopeful yet troubling year for global baseball, MLB witnessed one of the most obvious international strategies in recent years to market its cultural product for capital, rather than solely for pure athleticism. In other words, in 2005, it became very clear that, in the existing and prospective international baseball markets, MLB was committed to promote its asset in order to promote its sport mainly to generate profit. The League's decisions reflect its view on the sport as an investment. Within the framework postulated by Arjun Appadurai, MLB's emphasis on the financescape is evident. This approach also meant that the League was willing to move away from those projects that could possibly be beneficial to the general growth and expansion of the sport in the international athletic sphere but lacked the promise to generate global capital. Examining MLB's involvement and lack thereof, respectively, in the World Baseball Classic (WBC) and the Olympics shows that MLB has become an international baseball business leader but not the international leader of the sport.

There were two major events in 2005: the inaugural press conference for the WBC and the International Olympic Committee's decision to exclude baseball from the 2012 Olympics. On the one hand, in July 2005, the International Baseball Federation (IBAF) had a joyful moment as it held a press conference in Detroit, Michigan, to announce the launching of the World Baseball Classic. Major League Baseball, along with the Major League Baseball Players' Association, helped this development along with non–American professional baseball leagues and federations, including a number from Asia. Present at the press conference were baseball commissioner Bud Selig and Donald Fehr, the executive director of the Players Association. MLB players from abroad adorned themselves in the jersey of their respective national team. This new tournament promised that fans would be able to enjoy the highest quality baseball that even the Olympics could not measure up to. On the other hand, in the same year, the International Olympic Committee (IOC) voted baseball out of the 2012 Summer Olympics in London. Baseball in 2005 was no doubt a major sport even outside of the U.S., but in the eyes of the IOC, it lacked the appeal.

An increasing number of exchanges of players between the MLB and other leagues and the rise in the number of MLB games played overseas attested to the fact that baseball was not just an American institution. However, the IOC deemed golf and rugby sevens to be more appropriate for the Olympic Games than baseball and softball. This was a vexing development for many Americans. Particularly after failing to win the gold medal at two consecutive WBC tournaments, some American baseball fans began to feel a sense of lost ownership of the sport. The MLB no longer seemed to be the global baseball powerhouse. The MLB undoubtedly generated great financial profit, but it seemed to have lost the centripetal force that ensured the steady growth of baseball. Baseball as a business was American. But baseball as a sport or culture no longer appeared to be purely American.

The implication of this ecological change around baseball in 2005 is two-fold. On one level, despite the MLB's major solid presence in American popular culture, baseball still lags behind many other sports globally. The IOC's decision is just one of the examples of America's most associated sport being not as popular in many other parts of the world. On another level, and more importantly, the global expansion of baseball is an unchallengeable fact. It is a marketable and profitable sport. Concurrently, Appadurai's idea of ethnoscape also explains the international flow of MLB expansion. More American baseball players play globally. More non–American players play in the MLB. The world has witnessed numerous games and events sponsored by and associated with MLB. Two successful WBC tournaments also reflect the growing international interest in baseball. This perplexing and shifting global ecology of baseball raises a question about MLB's role in international baseball. MLB arguably is where all, if not most of, the best players in the world aspire to come to play baseball. It is also one of the most successful professional sport leagues. To some extent that still is the case. To be scouted to play in MLB, for example, is a dream for many Japanese high school and young professional ballplayers. But the WBC revealed that the home country of "the World Series" did not have the "best" team in the world. The U.S. failed to qualify for the semifinals in 2006. In 2009, the U.S. lost the bronze medal game to Venezuela. The WBC all-star team included only one American player. All of these events seem to suggest that the U.S. and MLB have an increasingly limited impact on the global development of the sport, but this is not neccessarily the case entirely.

The debate over the role of MLB in global baseball was featured in the *Wall Street Journal* in April 2010 when John Miller published his commentary that claimed America's pastime was no longer American. He explained that on the one hand, the international popularity of baseball is increasing. Miller uses Dominican boys' aspiration to become successful MLB players and the popularity of Japanese high school baseball as examples of the rising fan base outside of the U.S. On the other hand, Miller argues that "the increasing American taste for sports that offer fast-paced and violent action" caused the decline of baseball in the American consciousness. While some agreed with Miller's assessment, the support was far from unanimous. A reader of the *Journal* expressed his frustration in his letter to the editor. Seymour Yusem wrote, "Would Mr. Miller say that Canadian hockey is fading as a national pastime because European and American teams can defeat Canadian teams?" Another letter by an anonymous writer claims that baseball had never been more popular, even "during baseball's so-called golden years of the 1950s" ("Major League Baseball Has").

There are numerous ways to interpret what these comments mean. However, there is no doubt that MLB exists in a very different social environment compared to the period when "international baseball" referred only to Latin American players in the League, Little League international games, or a limited exposure at the Olympics. What becomes evident was that examining MLB's involvement in the WBC and the Olympics showcased its interests in leveraging on its unique asset — in the forms of talented players, legends and myths that fans like to remember, and merchandise and other forms of legal rights— simply in order to maintain and grow its successful business.

Studying the relationship between MLB and the WBC shows that it made sense that MLB was much less upset with the fact that the U.S. national team did so poorly during the WBC. While fans and critics speculated numerous reasons why the team failed to win the championship two tournaments in a row, the League considered the tournament rather successful because it produced a very high return of investment. With the same logic, MLB was less inclined to be involved in the Olympics. Capitalism dictates how many fans and team owners hesitate to partake in the event for fear that teams' assets, or players, might be hurt. This analysis studies the way in which MLB's international business plan has focused disproportionately on its capital gains or cultivation of business markets rather than pure athleticism.

MLB and the WBC: The Betrayed Expectation of MLB

The relationship between the MLB and the WBC is not a simple one. To consider the WBC as a genuine attempt to promote global baseball culture is a naïve assumption. The tournament, in reality, came into existence to expand and promote MLB, not baseball in general, in the global market. The WBC is just one of the global expansion business strategies for Major League Baseball. Examining the early history of the tournament reveals the true raison d'être of the WBC as a means for MLB to further cultivate its international market. The IBAF, the international organizational body of baseball, does not play the role that FIFA, its counterpart in soccer, assumes with the World Cup. Although the IBAF is the sanctioning organization of the WBC, it had little to do with the launching of the WBC.

The IBAF has a clear view on its overall responsibility as the sanctioning body of the tournament. As an international body that organizes baseball, it oversees the WBC. On paper, professional baseball leagues and their player unions including Major League Baseball, the Nippon Professional Baseball (NPB), the Korea Baseball Organization (KBO), and the Major League Baseball Players Association, "supported" the IBAF. This construction too suggests that the IBAF was the organizer that was supported by these leagues. The reality, however, is more one-sided, and in favor of the MLB. The twelve-member organizing committee had four MLB-related officers, two from the MLB and two more from the MLBPA (Furuuchi 32). In many ways, the MLB was more influential than the IBAF that had two members on the committee. The MLB and the MLBPA undoubtedly played a more central role in the development of the WBC. The IBAF was outpowered and outnumbered. In reality, these two bodies initiated and established the base of the tournament and invited other leagues. The *World Baseball Classic* official tournament web site makes a clear statement on the origin of the tournament:

> Major League Baseball (MLB) and the Major League Baseball Players Association (MLBPA) have joined together to establish the World Baseball Classic. The tournament, sanctioned by the International Baseball Federation (IBAF), will be conducted jointly by MLB and the MLBPA in cooperation with Nippon Professional Baseball (NPB), the Korea Baseball Organization (KBO), their respective players associations and other professional leagues from around the world.... The World Baseball Classic is the first international baseball tournament to feature players currently playing in the major leagues. In addition to providing a competition between the top players in the world, the World Baseball Classic was created *in order to further promote the game and Major League Baseball around the globe* [authors' emphasis added].

What these excerpts show is that the IBAF was simply a sanctioning body to legitimize the tournament as an official baseball event, whereas the leadership role existed with MLB.

The MLB's larger clout over other associations was made ever more evident when the MLB and the MLBPA announced the outline of the tournament, even before the first pitch in 2006. It was not because of logistical reasons that no representative of the NPB appeared at the press conference in Detroit announcing the tournament. When the NPB received its invitation to the first WBC, it was clear that the organization would not make any profit from the first-round games. The first round of games in Asia financially belonged to Yomiuri Shimbun, the largest newspaper company in the world, which also is the owner of the Yomiuri Giants. It had purchased the rights to sponsor the preliminary tournament in Asia for approximately 200 million yen. Because of this contract, regardless of the number of tickets sold or the price of broadcasting contracts, profit belonged to Yomiuri, not to the NPB. This was the main reason why the NPB and the WBC were not in agreement even when the press gathered in Detroit (Furuuchi 27–28). These arrangements were coordinated by MLB. The NPB suggested that the IBAF should be in charge of the tournament. After negotiations, however, the MLB's leading role never changed. Mitsumasa Etoh, a researcher in sports business, explains that Japan's aforementioned agreement was only possible after MLB and NPB agreed to continue to examine a more proper way of organizing the tournament. When the NPB finally agreed to partake in the tournament, its agreement did not go to the sanctioning body, the IBAF, but to the MLB. This is another piece of evidence that shows there was no question about the MLB's preferential status over other associations and leagues (Furuuchi 31–32). The same power struggle happened with the Korean Baseball Organization. The MLB and KBO only reached an agreement after the MLB revised its profit distribution scheme (Etoh).

Fans also noticed the one-sidedness of the WBC once the tournament started. They reacted harshly when umpires made questionable calls favoring the American national team. From the beginning of the tournament, fans and critics challenged the selection process of umpires. Twenty-two of the thirty-two umpires were American. All of these twenty-two were Minor League umpires because the Major League umpires were fulfilling their spring training camp responsibilities. Other similar international tournaments such as the FIFA World Cup or the Olympics would not have had such a homogeneous group of officials to officiate matches between two national teams.

On March 12, 2006, an American home-plate umpire, Bob Davidson, overruled the second-base umpire's safe call after being challenged by the American national team manager, Buck Martinez. This call supposedly cost Japan at least one run, if not more, leading Japan to lose to the U.S., 3–4. On both sides of the Pacific, this controversial call made headlines (Etoh). Writing for the *New York Times*, Lee Jenkins wrote that American players "looked as if they had been awarded unexpected bonuses" of an undeserved victory (Jenkins; Fraley). A similar case cost Mexico a home run on March 16, 2006, during a game against the U.S. (Etoh). To speculate on the nature of these calls is not, of course, within the scope of this project. It is, however, significant to note that the tournament, despite the criticism, continued to be seen as a place to show an American sense of superiority to the rest of the world in baseball. A former manager of the Los Angeles Dodgers, Tommy Lasorda, summarized what many global fans considered as American arrogance and desperation. At the beginning of the second tournament, he was quoted in an article on ESPN.com: "We cannot allow those clubs to beat us. It's our game.... Baseball is America's game. It doesn't belong to the Italians or the Cubans or the Koreans or the Japanese.... It's our game, and we're not going to let them beat us" (Associated Press "Lasorda").

The fact that MLB was able to organize the tournament for their own interests without publicly admitting its true intention added to the frustrations among international fans. The WBC appeared to be a place to promote international baseball. In reality, such an idealistic view was nothing but naiveté. The tournament was planned for the promotion of American baseball as a means for capital gain. But once the tournament started, it was clear that the American national team's superior performance was not going to be the means for the MLB to market and represent itself. During the 2006 tournament, the U.S. had at best a subpar performance. After beating Mexico, 2–0, on March 7, it lost to Canada. While the U.S.'s third game was the highlight of the tournament for the team, beating South Africa, 17–0, to qualify for the second round, the U.S. lost to both South Korea and Mexico and only had the aforementioned contested victory over Japan. Securing the fourth position, the U.S. team did slightly better in the second tournament. The WBC did not turn out to be where American professional players overwhelmingly showcased superior skill or ability to the world.

The U.S.'s mediocre at best performance was partially due to the lack of star players. The MLB did not like its players to play before its main season started. Although more MLB players played in the WBC than in the Olympics, some leading players refused to play during the preseason period. The apparent irony was that MLB took the initiative to start the WBC. But its teams did not support the tournament unanimously. At the meeting of team owners during the planning phase, George Steinbrenner, the owner of the Yankees, voted against the tournament. He argued that his team practiced and played to win the World Series. He did not want his players, in whom he had invested so much, to be hurt and ruin the rest of the season. As a team, the Yankees sent a letter to its players requesting that they would not participate in the WBC. Additionally, there was a concern about more stringent anti-doping testing at the tournament than during the regular MLB season. As a result, it was far from the "Dream Team." Fans seemed to prefer to focus on preseason camp games. Unlike Japan that had a pre-tournament camp several weeks before the opening, the U.S. national team did not meet until just a few days before the tournament began (Furuuchi 29–30).

MLB and WBC: The Rise of Different Baseball Styles

If the MLB truly sought to popularize its own values and playing style across the world, it clearly lacked the understanding as to how globalization worked. Globalization of any form including culture, as with the case with MLB, does not bring homogenization. It rather "reveals the inadequacy of sameness as communities assert their uniqueness" (Nauright 1330). Through this cultural exchange, "the local dialectically absorbs, shapes, alters, and opposes wider tendencies while creating and promulgating its own" (Miller, et al., 19). The WBC was not an exception. Unlike what MLB originally intended, the WBC did not show the dominance of baseball played by Americans in the global baseball culture. Instead, it showed how diverse the sport had become, how MLB's way of playing baseball was no longer the norm in the international arena. Rather than promulgating the MLB style of baseball to the rest of the world, the WBC taught Americans and MLB that there is more than one way to play the game.

Nauright's observation about globalization was no surprise to American baseball players having been exposed to non–American baseball. Robert Whiting extensively shows in his book *You've Gotta Have Wa* that American players were confronted with a completely new way to approach the game when they started playing in Japan. It was the same game, but with a very different way of training, playing, and partaking in the team. The localism that is an essential part of globalization should not have been a surprise for American baseball fans. When Daisuke Matsuzaka joined the Red Sox, fans noted this Japanese player was perplexed by how little he was expected to pitch during training. He had been used to pitching far more than the American standard while he was in Japan.

Filip Bondy's article in the *New York Daily News* explains that the American way of baseball was not the only way of baseball, but also no longer sufficed to match up against the Asian baseball style. Derek Jeter was one of many players that were impressed with the Japanese team's fast-paced game and tactics. He commented, "I don't know how you emulate swinging and hitting while you're already halfway down to first" (Bondy). Another analyst called Japan's baseball style as "picture-perfect" (Zinser). There are abundant speculations on why such a difference developed. Bondy argues that American baseball players tend to take practice sessions less seriously than Japanese counterparts, resulting in a failure to improve their basic skills. He also suggests that the U.S. lacked strategy. He writes, " The U.S. team ... [was] still playing big ball against pitchers who were simply too good for such aspirations. Their heads remain stuck in the steroid era" (Bondy). Zinser's analysis resonates more with Thomas Blackwood's historical study on Japanese baseball that connects the sport to the Taoist idea of "Way" (Blackwood; Zinser). Regardless of the origin, Doug Glanville explains that the diverse styles in baseball are beneficial. Although somewhat idealistic, Glanville states that globalization of the sport opened up a new business market and has turned international players into an integral part of baseball, rather than just "fillers" (Glanville). The success of non–American players and teams clearly show that the MLB, its players, and its Americanness no longer served as the global standard. They were far from being sufficient to secure more than a few victories in the WBC both in 2006 and 2009.

MLB and the WBC: American Baseball Capitalism and Its Reach

Although the WBC showed to the world that the U.S. national team did not represent the international standard of baseball, it served as strong proof that the American way of baseball capitalism was effective, efficient, and strong. In other words, the role that MLB ultimately plays in international baseball is as the business leader.

The financial background of the WBC is MLB-centered as well. Most of the tournament profits come from official sponsor fees, ticket sales, and broadcasting rights. While twenty-six companies sponsored the first World Baseball Classic in 2006, the number more than doubled three years later to fifty-six. Of the profit 53 percent was distributed to national baseball associations and leagues whereas 47 percent was spent as prize fees. The MLB received 17.5 percent of the profit as profit sharing. The MLBPA received the same amount. This means that MLB-related organizations alone received 35 percent of the remaining 53 percent of the profit. The NPB received 7 percent, the KBC received 5 percent, and the IBAF received 5 percent. The overall award fees amounted to $14 million, almost doubling from the $7.8 million three years earlier. Although the WBC does not publicize how much exactly the MLB and the MLBPA made from WBC tournaments, Furuuchi is confident that these two organizations made the most profit and the structure of the tournament ensures that it remains profitable for both the MLB and the MLBPA (Furuuchi 34).

Just like any other international sporting event, the WBC relies heavily on global media coverage to maintain and cultivate its fan base. MLB made a large profit from broadcasting as well. When a game starts in California later in the evening, it is already lunch time in Japan and Korea. As discussed elsewhere in this book, MLB has used the time difference to its advantage by targeting a new customer base. So far, the tournament has been successful in securing record ratings, compared to the 2006 tournament, ESPN ratings increased by 8 percent in 2009. Approximately 1.6 million people, on average, watched a game on ESPN. The U.S.–Japan semi-final game had a 2.2 rating and was the most-watched WBC game in the U.S. If the U.S. had advanced to the final, it might have had a higher rating than the Japan-Korea final, which had a 1.4 rating (Lemke "A Different"). These numbers are not very high. But the tournament's success existed outside of the U.S. The rating for the final game in 2009 reached 36.4 percent in Japan, which is very uncommon for a program, let alone a sports program, aired during the day on a weekday. This figure means that 71.7 percent of TVs that were on during the game time in Japan tuned into the game (Furuuchi 9). Media, as Chapter 5 shows, are one of the most powerful drivers of MLB revenue.

This financial success, however, is not guaranteed to continue with the World Baseball Classic in 2013, especially as the divide between the MLB teams and the WBC appears to be deepening. While the divide between MLB's interests and those of other leagues is widening, the gap between the League and its own promotional tournament particularly reflects the capitalistic attitude of MLB. This disagreement primarily stems from the physical toll of the tournament on the players. The WBC organizers are in discussions to consider if the tournament should be shortened. Although the tournament itself was initially developed by the MLB and the MLBPA, after two WBC events, many players and coaches have voiced their concerns about the negative impact that the WBC might have on the overall performance of the team and players participating (Lemke "A Different"). Players may get hurt or feel fatigued toward the end of the regular season. Either way, teams' assets should be best leveraged during the regular-season games and postseason games and not preseason festivity games, at least according to the team managers.

In 2009, four U.S. players indeed went back to their respective teams injured after the WBC (Snyder; Passan "Team"). One of the injured players, Ryan Braun, stated that "everybody's concerned. We recognize the importance of being healthy for the start of the season and going back to our teams in good shape. There's probably a little more intensity, a little more adrenaline than we're used to having this time of year" (Passan "Team"). Len DeLuca, the senior vice president of ESPN, echoes these concerns well. He comments, "The general managers are paid to win in October, not March." Although it is often challenged if the WBC truly contributed to the injury of players, and the MLB's executive vice president of labor relations, Rob Manfield, argues that many injuries sustained by WBC players are minor in nature and similar to those experienced during spring training, whether or not they participated in the WBC, the negotiation between the MLB and the WBC continues ("DL Starting List"). In addition to injuries, a more subtle impact on the body from the fatigue caused by the trans–Pacific and trans–Atlantic travel continues to raise questions about how the tournament should be organized.

The language of cost and profit permeates within these controversies. Teams are concerned about their investment. Players are worried that possible injuries may affect their career, which directly affects their income. While MLB may benefit from the WBC, teams are more concerned about the regular-season games. From the tournament perspective, however, the tournament generated sufficient revenue without many MLB stars. In prize money alone, participating teams split $14 million. The MLB paid $15 million out of the WBC revenue to IBAF (Passan "Future"). As Passan argues, the WBC is too profitable to go away (Passan "Team"). But it is clear that it has developed in a direction that the MLB and the MLBPA were not originally intending. The tournament has proven that MLB is no longer the global leader of baseball culture, even though many young players all over the world aspire to play in the MLB. It has become an enterprise no other national professional baseball league has attained. This is partially why, Furuuchi speculates, MLB was not particularly disappointed when the U.S. lost the WBC title. In Japan and South Korea, and possibly in Italy and other parts of the Europe, there were small children watching WBC games, hoping to be a professional baseball player. Many of them may dream to play probably in the U.S. (10). They are possible customers and consumers of MLB. As a sport, MLB has lost its footing as representing the "ideal" mode of play in globalized society. As entertainment and a business, however, MLB continues to be the most successful endeavor in baseball.

MLB and the IOC: Striking Out of Baseball

Although MLB suggested the Olympics do not exist on its top priority list, the IOC's decision to exclude baseball from its Summer Games nonetheless became a major topic of debate. The distance that MLB tried to maintain from the IOC is almost perplexing when contrasted to the outcry to bring baseball back to the Games. The same logic that MLB utilized to justify WBC's success despite the U.S. national team's performance explains why MLB does not appear particularly concerned about the Olympics exclusion.

Baseball was a short-lived sport in the Olympics. Although the Olympics first included baseball in the 1904 St. Louis Olympics, it was not a medal competition, but a demonstration event. The more formal version of the baseball competition in the Olympics only started in 1984 in Los Angeles, without any medals awarded. It was only in 1992 in Barcelona when baseball was first recognized as a medal sport (Astleford). Since Barcelona, it has only appeared in four Olympics, including its final appearance at the 2008 Games in Beijing. There were great speculations about why baseball, along with softball, was cut from the list of games to be played in 2012. Writing for *The Guardian*, David Lengel suspects that anti–Americanism within the IOC affected the decision (Lengel). An American softball player, Dot Richardson, also agreed. She commented, "I've always seen in athletics an anti–American sentiment throughout the world. Most of it is through jealousy or envy" (Associated Press "Secret"). The European bias against American sports could have also been a reason. Or, Europeans are not as interested in baseball as Americans hope or believe. The U.S., on the other hand, is not as influential at the Olympics as Americans wish to believe. Seven out of eight modern IOC presidents have been from Europe, after all (Zuckerman "No"). Dan Steinberg remembers an earlier debate as the IOC was considering the inclusion of baseball. He explains that the IOC was against the idea of having baseball as an official sport because of its "unpredictable length" (Steinberg "USA"). There are endless possible reasons.

One of the most potent reasons was the doping scandal that swept MLB, a league that remained "radioactive" from its scandals (Vecsey "Olympics"). The IOC reportedly felt that the MLB did not punish players with a doping history harshly enough (Lengel). Jere Longman, contributing an article in the *New York Times*, also explains that "among the issues that would have to be worked out is drug testing, which is far more stringent on the Olympic level than on the major league level." Lengel argues that while the MLB's lack of interest and cooperation was a "competition" frustration for the IOC, the gap between the MLB's anti-doping policy and that of the IOC generated a "political" reason to exclude baseball. It is evident to Lengel and Longman that MLB had a lot to do with the IOC's decision.

While other possible reasons for the Olympics elimination also signal the IOC's biases and preferences, they also tell more about MLB's general disinterest in an event with a mediocre business opportunity for itself. This is to suggest that reasons why baseball will not appear in London in 2012 can partially be explained by MLB's disinterest in the Olympics as a marketing event. For example, MLB had refused to send its players to the Games despite the IOC and IBAF's continuous request. Basketball, for example, saw U.S. "Dream Teams" featuring NBA players. The NHL suspends its season for the Winter Olympics. Baseball fans, however, never saw the "dream" baseball team with MLB players. Even after the IOC approved of the participation of professional baseball players in 2000 for the Games in Sydney, MLB did not send any of its players to Australia. Although they won the gold medal with former Dodgers manager Tommy Lasorda, they were unsuccessful in even qualifying for the Olympics in Athens in 2008 ("They'rrre").

The lack of participation by MLB players was no doubt a reason for the IOC's decision to oust baseball. Jacques Rogge mentioned that if MLB agreed to send its players to the Games, it would be more likely for the sport to be readmitted to the Olympics (Fitzpatrick; "Baseball Teams"). He commented: "It would do good for baseball, like every sport, to have the stars.... We have LeBron James in basketball. We had Michael Jordan, Scottie Pippen and Magic Johnson on the Dream Team. That trend has continued in basketball. And we have all the stars of the NHL. So we would love to have as many stars of the major league as possible. I'd love to see [Alex] Rodriguez" (Fitzpatrick).

Although the previous two WBC tournaments suggest that the U.S. may not have the best team in the world, it is still unarguable that its national team could contain the biggest stars in the world. An IOC member from Britain, Craig Reedie, commented after the IOC's decision in 2005 that, "The lack of the MLB players — I think people [at the IOC] have looked and said, 'well, all right, if there's to be a change, that seems to be the logic of it.'" Carlos Rodriguez, the president of the Cuban Baseball Federation, concurs. He stated, "Those who bear most of the blame are the owners of the professional leagues who refuse to free up their ballplayers to compete" ("They'rrre"). Many of the players on the U.S. team are young players, of which only a few, in a few years, may make it to the MLB. There is a clear similarity in the team demographics between the WBC and the Olympics; they aren't "Dream Teams."

Jeff Blair of *The Globe and Mail* cites money as the reason for the separation between the IOC and MLB. From the IOC's standpoint, there is little financial value in baseball without its best players. The MLB, on the other hand, does not make enough financial profit by closing its season temporarily and risking injuries to its players. Although Bob Watson, a member of the MLB commissioner's office, was quoted as suggesting a possibility that club owners might be willing to suspend the season for the Games, Blair claims that "[Watson] knows that's not going to happen." Blair continues to write, "The fact is, the U.S.-based lords of the game view the IOC as a bunch of effete, sandal-wearing, Euro-centric foofs who have no appreciation for an anachronistic game played without a clock." Blair speculates that the WBC is more likely to get the support from the MLB.

The MLB considered the Olympics to be a distraction from its schedule and did not volunteer its top players to the national team. Unlike the WBC, the Olympics take place in summer, while the MLB season has been ongoing for a few months already at that time. If the WBC had enough difficulty convincing teams to release their players to play before the regular season starts, the Olympics would have a tougher time gathering players that can determine wins and losses for the teams. The executive director of the MLBPA, Donald Fehr, expressed, "you can't shut down Major League Baseball, you just can't do it and nobody can reasonably expect us to" ("They'rrre").

Not many American players seemed to disagree with Fehr. They are not invested in the Olympic Games as much as players from other countries are. Jose Contreras, a Chicago White Sox pitcher who had played for the Cuban national team in 2000, commented, "[The Olympics are] like the World Series for people here." It is not the case for many Americans. Ben Sheets, one of the pitchers on the 2000 national team for the U.S., who later played for the Milwaukee Brewers, explains, "There isn't any player growing up thinking they want to play in the Olympics.

[Winning the gold medal] was one of my greatest moments, but it has nothing to do with the big leagues." His lack of interest in symbolic achievement is clear. Fehr responded to the IOC's decision to eliminate baseball by saying that it "won't affect baseball very much one way or another.... Baseball will go on just fine. It's never depended in any way, shape or form even slightly on the Olympics" ("They'rrre").

This is not to suggest that MLB is the only reason why baseball has disappeared from the Olympics. There are other explanations, as well. For example from the logistical perspective, the decision to eliminate baseball had a positive outcome, at least for London. In reality, the financial impact of the elimination decision for London is something to consider. Although 2012 Olympics spokesperson Mike Lee explained that the local organizing committee was "delighted to be delivering the Olympic and Paralympic Games, whatever the side of the program," there was no question that baseball and softball were two sports that required the construction and remodeling of facilities. In financial terms, the BBC estimates that the decision saved London at least fifty million pounds ("Fewer").

MLB and the IOC: Trying to Bring the Game Back

Although fans speculated that the elimination would not affect baseball or the MLB, the outcry to bring baseball back to the Olympics continues to exist. This was a revealing experience for baseball internationally. On one level, baseball fans were well aware that the U.S. did not necessarily have the best Olympics baseball team. Cuba and South Korea had done well, often times better than the U.S. Observers of American baseball, however, also knew that the team did not contain any of the highest level American ballplayers. From this perspective, it was evident that the Olympics were not a very important event for the MLB, its players, and probably for MLB fans.

Additionally, it is not difficult to speculate that players, team managers, and fans believed to some extent that if the MLB decided to partake in the Olympics, the U.S. would be able to dominate the tournament. After all, the debate surrounding Olympic baseball took place before the first World Baseball Classic tournament, where the U.S. failed to win the title unexpectedly. On the other side of the same coin were the fans that expected baseball to remain in the Olympics. They might have thought that the MLB did not have to participate in it, but they wanted the sport to be a part of one of the largest sporting events in the world.

After the elimination decision for the 2012 Olympics, fans, players, and others in the baseball community voiced their hopes that the sport would be brought back for the 2016 Olympics whose venue at the time was undetermined. Jacques Rogge, IOC president, did not deny the possibility of baseball coming back in 2016. He mentioned, "needless to say, these sports are very, very disappointed, but it does not disqualify them forever as Olympic sports" ("Fewer"). Hector Pereyra, the president of the Dominican Baseball Federation, and Felipe Munoz, his Mexican counterpart, for example, were determined to work towards this goal. Pereyra mentioned that "this is the moment to start the race to return to the Olympic stage in 2016" ("They'rrre").

So 2008 became, at least temporarily, the last year of baseball in the Olympics. Around this period, the U.S.'s lobbying activity was at one of its highest levels to resurrect baseball for the 2016 Games. Both the International Baseball Federation and MLB lobbied for the return of the game. IBAF's Harvey Schiller and MLB's Jimmie Lee Solomon, executive vice president for operations, both negotiated with the IOC (Fitzpatrick). At a press conference, Bob Watson, the general manager of USA Baseball and vice president for on-field operations of MLB, commented, "I believe the Olympics are definitely going to want to have baseball back in the fold" (Longman). He continued to mention and indirectly respond to Rogge's complaint about the absence of MLB players by stating that some MLB teams were beginning to be "cooperative" as long as there was some insurance against injuries (Longman; Blair). Schiller mentioned that the scheduling of MLB games could happen so that teams would be more willing to send their players to the Olympics (Zuckerman "Making").

Players that experienced the 2008 Games also seemed to support the return of baseball. Although they were not MLB players at the time, they were considered to be prospective MLB players. After winning the bronze medal in Beijing, Jason Donald, a prospective player for the Phillies at the time, said, "I think [the elimination of baseball from the Olympics] is a real shame." He continued his comment by arguing that baseball was a global sport that deserved to remain in the Olympics. "For those who say it's not played enough around the world, that's a joke.... Look at the Far East. Look at North America. Look at South America. Everybody plays it with the exception of Europe and Africa. And I'm sure the game will grow there like it has everywhere else" (Fitzpatrick).

MLB and its players were aware of the aforementioned doping problem. As Lengel and Longman argued, MLB's less stringent policy was one of the speculated reasons why the IOC preferred not to have baseball at its Games. Cat Osteman, an Olympic softball player, commented that when baseball was eliminated from the Games, doping was a major problem with the MLB. But she argues that it was no longer the case in 2008 (Vecsey "Olympics"). IBAF's Schiller explains that the steroid use that caused a major scandal in MLB had never been "a real problem [among baseball players] at the world and global level, at the Olympics or any other international competition" (Zuckerman "Making"). Although he denied that doping was ever a reason why the IOC had to exclude baseball, he also pointed out the fact that the IBAF and the MLA had been working together "to ensure there was full World Anti-Doping Agency-compliant drug testing for [the 2008] World Baseball Classic and for future international events" (Vecsey "Olympics"; Zuckerman "Making").

Apart from the optimism and lobbying activities was the fact that the venue for the 2016 Games had yet to be announced at the time of these comments. The IOC met in Copenhagen in October 2009 to determine the 2016 venue. It was at this same meeting that the executive board was going to finalize the list of sports. Madrid, Tokyo, Rio de Janeiro, and Chicago were in the running to host the 2016 Games. This list gave hope to those who wished to have baseball back. Bob Watson was not an exception. He showed his confidence that baseball would be back in 2016 at a press conference in July 2008, especially if the hosting city was either Chicago or Tokyo, two cities where baseball is popular (Longman).

Many Americans felt the same way. The sense of hope was encouraged further with President Obama's backup. Having worked in Chicago, he was particularly interested in bringing the Olympics to that city. By summer 2008, Obama had become one of the most popular global icons (Kiuchi 197–198). His popularity, baseball fans hoped, would help Chicago win the bid. Jimmie Lee Solomon commented:

It's hard to tell what the impact of Barack Obama winning is going to be on our country, our world, baseball and the Olympics.... Right now, everything I've seen has been positive.... I would like to believe that our bid to get back in the Olympics would be enhanced by having Barack Obama in office. I'm not sure exactly how that would work, but we want to be back in the Olympics. We've made no bones about that [Bloom].

Don Fehr, the executive director of the MLBPA, concurred with Solomon. He said, "I think Sen. Obama's election is an event of profound significance to a lot of people around the world.... I would be surprised if it was not received that way in Olympics circles, also" (Bloom).

This hopeful sentiment empowered the representatives of baseball during the IOC program committee meeting in mid–November 2008. In Lausanne, Switzerland, Harvey Schillar and Curtis Granderson, who at the time was a center fielder for the Tigers, were going to make a thirty-minute long presentation in front of the committee, followed by a thirty-minute-long question-and-answer session. The same was true with proponents of other sports including softball, roller sports, rugby, gold, squash, and karate (Bloom). This committee meeting was a precursor to the IOC executive board meeting in August 2009 and the full Congress meeting in October later that year.

Despite MLB's alleged shift to being cooperative, having increased anti-doping awareness within MLB, and President Obama's presence, baseball failed to win popularity within the IOC in 2009. At the executive board meeting in August 2009, the board proposed to add golf and rugby sevens. This decision was going to be voted on at the IOC Assembly two months later. After baseball failed to be nominated to the Assembly, this marked the end of efforts to bring baseball back to the Olympics.

American media expectedly reported this decision with mixed sentiments. An article on *ESPN.com* and another in the *New York Times* kept their tones down by celebrating the possibilities for the two sports admitted to the Olympics while objectively stating the fact that baseball was not successfully incorporated. However Jeff Klein, also contributing to the *New York Times*, reflected a sense of disappointment by quoting Schiller as saying "On behalf of the millions of people who play the game at every stage, I'm personally disappointed that they won't have a chance to participate.... Baseball is the only sport not on the Olympic program that also is the national sport of so many countries."

Japanese media, including *The Daily Yomiuri*, however, reported the news without any sense of surprise. An article about this in Japan's leading newspaper stated, "Baseball is only popular in a few regions around the world, and this may be the main reason behind the executive board's action. Although baseball is popular in Japan and the United States, there is no denying that the game takes a backseat to soccer and other sports in Europe" ("IOC"). The article continued to speculate that doping issues, the future popularity of the WBC, and the absence of MLB players all contributed to the IOC's decision as well. There is no doubt that the MLB's lack of investment in the Olympics, scandals surrounding the league, and other MLB-related issues, at least partially, contributed to the continuing exclusion of the sport from the Olympics.

MLB's Emphasis on Capitalism over Culture

American baseball is a major business enterprise. Although the American economy is still ailing, the revenue for the 2010 season for the MLB is estimated to be $7 billion, a record-high in its history. Although the average per-game attendance went down by 0.6 percent compared to 2009 (the decline in 2009 from 2008 was 6.6 percent), Commissioner Selig commented, "There's no question, this is the golden era for the sport and given the [weak] economy this may be the most remarkable year we ever had.... Every economic option in our business is up this year. We're at numbers nobody ever thought possible" (Klayman). The MLB's business model continues to be successful.

The reach of the American baseball business model, just like that of other sport businesses and non-sport businesses, extends globally. As Furuuchi suggests, Japanese and many other international baseball leagues have been affected by this model. America's national pastime is no longer just a pastime. It is a business enterprise where investments are made in limited human talents and investors control how the bodies operate in order to generate greater profits.

However, on the other side of this, baseball's successful business story defines a less optimistic future of the sport. Baseball as a sport or a culture as conceived in the U.S. has not been as successful as the business in dominating the world. The lack of interests by MLB players, MLB owners' concerns about their expensive players, doping problems, and European resistance to American culture and preferences for other sports are just a few of the possible reasons.

But what we have seen in the past fifteen years or so suggests that Walter LaFeber's assessment that "in this developing battle of capital versus culture, capital will ultimately win" is true (21). The culture of America's national pastime, baseball, has been inundated by modern capitalism, ironically, another major driving force of American culture. Globally, baseball continues to spread throughout the world without any cultural leadership. Baseball business, on the other hand, remains in the hands of Americans, probably to the detriment of the traditional and pastoral idealism of the sport.

9

MLB in Japan and Around the Globe

An Interview with Jim Small of MLB

Major League Baseball is an international cultural and business product. In order to complete the circle a bit that started with the chapter examining Japanese players in MLB, it would be prudent to consider how MLB not only operates with global concerns in mind, but also how MLB operates in a specific foreign market. Though our focus on Japan dominates this section, it should not be considered the only market/culture that should be examined critically. Indeed, the examination of MLB as a global product has been a concern for many years. We have focused our attention on Japan as it is perhaps the newest and most powerful international market to arise in the first decade of the twenty-first century. MLB has had quite a past in many countries, however.

MLB's presence can be felt in the form of international licensing, merchandising, broadcast deals, and in various developmental programs and academies. Players, coaches, and MLB culture traverse the globe on continents such as Asia, Europe, and Africa, and in Latin America. The latter area is the focus of several academic works. The prevalence of MLB in Latin American countries and the prevalence of Latin American players in MLB have produced significant insight and criticism, including Guevara and Fidler's *Stealing Lives*, Alan M. Klein's *Growing the Game*, and Wendel's *The New Face of Baseball*. Such work is essential to understand the globalization of MLB. The positives and negatives can be witnessed currently in the game in comments like White Sox Manager Ozzie Guillen's lament, "I say, why do we have Japanese interpreters and we don't have a Spanish one. I always say that. Why do they have that privilege and we don't?" He continued, "Don't take this wrong, but they take advantage of us. We bring a Japanese player and they are very good and they bring all these privileges to them. We bring a Dominican kid ... go to the minor leagues, good luck. Good luck. And it's always going to be like that. It's never going to change. But that's the way it is" (Associated Press "Guillen").

Such sentiments reveal the reality of the true global nature of the game and possible issues of power and control that are at play. MLB in Asia and Japan more specifically as a focus came through the research, though, due to the speed of recent development in Asia the past decade. It is this recent development that guided us to the relatively newly established office of MLB in Japan. Comparatively, the history of Latin American influence in MLB has been a longer established one, dating back to the early twentieth century. As Latino presence increased during the 1950s and 1960s, the frustration that Roberto Clemente felt due to racial tensions with the Pirates in 1955 was not an exception. As Wendel discusses, it was "only in the last two decades have so many Latinos shared the same field with their U.S. counterparts;" until then, Jose Cardenal, Minnie Minoso, and others felt like Clemente did (xi, 29). But MLB as an international entity includes much more than just Latin America. Regional offices exist in Australia, the United Kingdom and China, but it is the Japanese office that has seen perhaps the most precipitous growth since the introduction of the American public to Ichiro.

MLB is now firmly entrenched in Asia, and Japan more specifically. MLB is present in numerous different forms. MLB games can be viewed on television and MLB entities are now part of Japanese popular culture. MLB has a history of exhibitions and all-star tours that date back decades, when figures like Babe Ruth and others traversed Japan spreading the gospel of baseball. Baseball in Japan is actually traced back to 1872 when Horace Wilson, an American teacher introduced the game (Baseball Hall of Fame). The Japanese Baseball Hall of Fame reflects this intertwining of the two countries with posters displayed from tours like Ruth's 1934 All-Star Tour to memorabilia from the latest Japanese success story in the MLB. It was this tour, in fact, that was credited by the Hall as doing much "to encourage the start of professional baseball in it." Hence, one can see baseball has been international for some time. It is within the decade of 2000–2010 that MLB has *really* grown its presence, for farming talent, as well as establishing the MLB brand in Japan and other parts of Asia.

In Japan specifically MLB has established itself as a media *and* consumer event. MLB's office in Japan has successfully negotiated countless promotions and merchandising opportunities. MLB publications can be picked up at newsstands, bookstores, and stadiums. These publications naturally highlight the careers of native Japanese players and the teams they are associated with in the United States. The focus has increasingly widened to include many star players that would be dealt with in American or Latin American publications. Stars like Albert Pujols, Tim Lincecum, and Ryan Braun along with Ichiro and Matsuzaka feature prominently on magazine and book covers. MLB's merchandising and promotions opportunities range from MLB-related imagery on breakfast cereals all the way to Sapporo beer. In addition, the culture of MLB has made its way into retail stores and even into the Nippon League (NPB) itself.

A stroll around the Tokyo Dome, for instance, features various restaurants, fan shops containing Yomiuri Giants merchandise and other assorted merchandise for other Nippon League teams. In addition, one can also find a healthy supply of MLB merchandise. The merchandise is featured in MLB-specific stores, as well as within general souvenir shops. Yankees and Red Sox trinkets are hung next to each other, as MLB-themed magazines await on the racks. Though a focus on Japanese-born players is still predominate, the aforementioned turn towards other MLB stars is increasingly growing.

As one can imagine, such infiltration of MLB cultural and economic influence can be considered a blessing to those taking part and consuming the culture of MLB, but it can also be seen as a possible point of contention. Like any globalizing power, the results and feelings are mixed. Though many fans may be generally supportive of MLB's influence and supportive of Japanese players playing in MLB, concerns of power and economy especially problematize the role of MLB in Japan. There is a potential threat seen by some that "MLB's superior financial muscle might eventually lead it to a takeover of NPB and the baseball market" (Whiting *You* 361).

The favorable effects for those seeing MLB as a welcome influence are present at both cultural and economic levels. Some fans welcome the culture of MLB, especially as more Japanese players have made names for themselves in the past decade in MLB (Whiting *You*). As Ichiro seems to be a safe bet for eventual inclusion into the National Baseball Hall of Fame, the presence of Japanese players in MLB appears to be primed to be a continued relationship. Much like Latin American players, Japanese (and Asian players generally) are entrenching roots in the life of baseball that fundamentally have changed the game into an international event.

MLB players are potentially lucrative spokesmen for Japanese businesses. The businesses can capitalize on League/team identities. They can also feature specific players that in some cases are handled by the Major League Baseball Players Association, who would deal with the following:

> Any company seeking to use the names or likenesses of more than two Major League Baseball players in connection with a commercial product, product line or promotion must sign a licensing agreement with the MLBPA. The license grants the use of the players' names and/or likenesses only and not the use of any MLB team logos or marks. Examples of products licensed by the MLBPA include trading cards, video games, T-shirts, caps, a wide variety of other products such as pennants, posters, pins, action figures and advertising campaigns for a wide variety of products and services ["Frequently"].

The encroachment of MLB into Japanese stadiums, popular culture, and the Japanese economy can be seen as a complement to Nippon League play, with trans–Pacific players creating strong links between the fates of each enterprise. Yet, those same waters aren't completely placid. As Whiting brings up in his brief examination of the World Baseball Classic, potential animosity towards MLB and American baseball culture can spring up in the media and with fans, especially for those concerned about MLB's dominating economic power. Perhaps more likely, such animosity is at play more prominently at the ownership/management level of Nippon League interests. Team owners can view the movement of Japanese stars into MLB and the possible economic contention for the public's attention as a challenge to the vitality of NPB (Whiting *You* xx–xxi).

As maintained throughout this book, the studies contained within are seeking to neither inherently damn nor praise the "off the beaten baseball path" realities of MLB as an economic and cultural force, but rather to understand the complexity and extent that MLB exists in these regards and their use values. To better understand the Japanese life of MLB the authors spoke in 2011 to Jim Small, the managing director of MLB Japan. The following is a discussion of MLB's presence and life in Japan and on the international stage. Like other targets of study in this book, Small's interview reveals a significant arm of baseball that creates and maintains its economic and cultural life.

Interview with Jim Small

MATHEW BARTKOWIAK: We want to start out and get an idea about what kind of presence MLB has in Japan and what kind of relationship does MLB have with the Nippon League?

JIM SMALL: Well, our Japan office ... let me start out with a two-minute overview of what we do in the region and that may help as you're asking questions later on. Major League Baseball International is like the NFL or NBA and any other professional league. We have four areas of business and one of them, and our most profitable, is media: primarily television, cable, satellite, open-air traditional television. Then we have sponsorship which the difference between a — I'll explain what that is in a second — basically it is companies paying us for the right to pull brands. Their logos are our logos. I'll explain that in a second. Third is licensing. Licensing is just selling a cap and a t-shirt and things like that. A licensed product is simple. It's just, you know a Red Sox cap, it's like anything that you'd buy in Wisconsin. You know a Brewers cap and the same thing. But a sponsorship is [different]. So this is a deal we get with Kellogg's. Kellogg's Japan where you buy this box of, they call them Frosties here, but it's Kellogg's Corn Flakes. You would get a free baseball card inside of one of these players. So that's traditional stuff ... that at least I grew up with in the States but is kind of new to this market. So that's a sponsorship versus licensing. Then a fourth area is events. We've had I think three opening days here in Japan. We've had All Star series here and play around the region. And also in events is what we call grassroots marketing ... getting more people playing the game. So, I'm responsible for building all of those businesses throughout Asia, both here and in Japan and we have an office in Beijing that looks after our China market and then we have a series of partners, mostly agencies in Korea, Taiwan, India, places like that where we do business. So, what happened is that in 2001, Ichiro came to Major League Baseball. And prior to Ichiro we had a series of agents here that we sold our sponsorships through and we would sell our television rights to Dentsu and, there wasn't really a need for full-time people in this market. We would simply fly over from New York, conduct business for a week and then fly back. But after Ichiro, it became obvious that there was a lot of opportunity here that we weren't getting to. And so in 2002, basically, we decided it would be worth it to open an office here. And in 2003 I came to open the office. So, we have an office here. It's a small office. It's five people and our responsibility is to build our business and to try to grow the business of Major League Baseball. A lot of our business is directly connected to the fact that Ichiro, Matsui, Matsuzaka are playing in the Major Leagues. So many people, you know, in Japan want to be able to see their guy. They want to be able to watch Ichiro play on television and that creates a great business opportunity for us. Our relationship with the professional league here, I think in general, is good. I think we think it's good. I think we have a very healthy relationship with them. I'm not sure that everybody you talk to on the Japanese side would feel the same way. And I think the reason is, I think that there are still some, what I would call "old views" that exist in Japanese baseball that think that somehow we took away Ichiro, we took away Matsui, which nothing could be farther from the truth.... Every player that has left Japan to go and play in the Major Leagues has gone under a negotiated agreement between us and NPB. So, there's never been a case where a player was stolen or taken away that was a violation to our agreement. So it's a basic human right and it's within their rules of Japanese baseball that after a certain amount of time, after nine years, a player can be a free agent and sign with whatever team he wants to sign with and that's what Hideki Matsui did. It's also in the rules with us and them that if a player wants to go to the United States and play Major League Baseball that he can notify his club and that club can post him to our teams and a sealed bid is sent and if the club accepts that sealed bid, the player can negotiate with a Major League team. That's how Ichiro went and that's how Matsuzaka went. Now sometimes it doesn't work. Iwakuma, a pitcher for Rakuten last year, couldn't reach an agreement with Oakland on a contract, so he returned. So this old philosophy of, "boy, you're taking our players," which I have to say is a very, very small percentage, of the Japanese baseball establishment feels that way but, some of them do and it's not connected with any facts. So, that being said, we understand that if a player exercises his right and leaves for Major League Baseball that there can be some negative impact to the League here. Now, what I say as a sports marketer is that if I'm that club, I look for an opportunity. I look for the fact that, when Ichiro in 2004 set the hit record, George Sisler's hit record, that was an opportunity for Japanese baseball because so many people were focused on the game of baseball in Japan. My question is does "the rising tide raise all boats?" and they are not our competitor and we're not their competitor. The competitor is video games and it's maybe the NBA or soccer. You know, Japan's a big country so you can have a kid in Osaka that that has a Hanshin Tigers shirt and a Seattle Mariners cap. That's okay. It's still baseball. So there may be some short-term effects in some markets but I don't think there's been a negative long-term effect for these players going over. As a matter of fact, I would say that it might be the opposite. There might be more positives coming to the game because maybe people who are more casual fans of baseball became big fans when Ichiro went over.

BARTKOWIAK: Okay, so the role of diplomat doesn't have to be played too much by you in terms of players going out or even U.S. players coming into Japan then?

SMALL: No, it's still really important to be diplomatic. It's so very important to be respectful in this culture particularly; I've lived in it for eight years, and respect is very important. It goes both ways. We get a lot of respect from them and we try to give them a lot of respect as well. Being a diplomat is important but at the end of the day, it's business and it's also, you know, if a kid graduated from Keio University here and was offered a job at Microsoft and he was working with Fujitsu, nobody could stop him. Nobody would stop him. So it's technically the same thing. If a player has the ability to go against the best players in the world, and right now the best players in the world are in Major League Baseball....

BARTKOWIAK: So in terms of your experience, kind of building on the theme here, fans that you have encountered—I know we talked a little bit about perhaps general managers, etc.—but would you say that fans generally are embracing of Major League Baseball culture in Japan and in Asia?

SMALL: Yes, I do. Particularly in Japan. I think that, and I do say this with humility, it may not sound like a humble statement but I do mean it that we are very, very fortunate in that we are viewed by the Japanese baseball fan as the premier sports league, particularly baseball league, but I think also sports league in the world. And that they look at their guys going to play Major League Baseball, thinking "wow, our guy has made it." Because it is the highest level in the world.... And I need to explain that comment. There's great baseball players and the NPB has tremendous players in a great quality of baseball. But they restrict the number of foreign players to four per team. So I would say, if the United States did that, if the Milwaukee Brewers' twenty-one of their twenty-five players had to be U.S. citizens, then Major League Baseball wouldn't be the best in the world. Because you artificially restrict and you choke talent that should be coming and playing. So, we don't have that. We have twenty-five, depending upon the roster, 25 percent and 35 percent of the players on Major League teams are from outside of the United States on the Major League roster. So, we're taking the best in the world, and saying "come and play." We don't care where you're from, what language you speak; come and play Major League Baseball. We don't do that here and I don't think that the quality of baseball would be the same until they do that.

BARTKOWIAK: So, in your career, have you ever worked with Japanese players who have very much focused on getting to the majors or concurrently perhaps have stated that no matter what, they want to stay within the Nippon League play?

SMALL: You know that's a good question. That's one, as you mentioned, playing a diplomat. We don't contact players while they're on a contract with NPB teams and it's really not appropriate for us to have those conversations until that player is free and clear through the system: the posting system or the free agent system. That said, there have been several players' agents who approached us before the players went over and said, "Hey, can we talk to you about this; what can we expect?" Most of them are from a business standpoint and I've always been happy to work with them. But we try to keep our distance simply because we want to be respectful of the negotiated relationship we have with these guys. We're not going to go and pick off players. And the players, there is no "hidden talent." Either you can throw, you can hit, you can run, or you can't. And our scouts are here all the time. So our scouts know the players they can fit into a Major League system, and the ones that might not. So there is really no added value in us having a conversation with them before they declare their intent.

BARTKOWIAK: Now you mentioned some other international offices for MLB. From what you know, are there any offices in Latin America?

SMALL: There's not for Major League Baseball. So what we've done is, we have offices in London, Beijing, Sydney, and Tokyo. With Latin America, we looked closely at whether we should put boots on the ground in a country. There are four markets. They are: Puerto Rico which is considered an international territory for our purposes ... it's Puerto Rico, Venezuela, Dominican, and Mexico. And what we decided is we were better off continuing to manage those relationships out of New York. Because if we were to open an office in Dominican, that person is still traveling to Mexico, or still traveling to Puerto Rico or to

Venezuela. And the same thing if they're in Mexico. And there is a huge benefit from a business standpoint in just being closer to the mothership of New York. So, we have a staff of Spanish speakers that work out of our New York office, so all Latin America operations are handled out of New York.

BARTKOWIAK: I was just thinking of Ozzie Guillen's comments about translators within the majors and I just wondered if there was any kind of collaboration. Or did your office have to try to address anything. Did you work in conjunction with other offices to try to make sense of the reality of the situation?

SMALL: A couple things. One, Ozzie's comments were slightly out of context. I shouldn't say out of context. I would ask him to look at the type of player that's coming in from Latin America and the ones coming in from Asia. And because of what I explained, very few players come in from Asia at a young age and work their way up from the minor leagues. These are all established stars. Hideki Matsui played nine years in major [NPB] league baseball. So he's an established player that's coming down to the New York Yankees and needs to have an interpreter. That's an appropriate thing we provide. I think it's a little bit different with the Latin players in that they are not spending eight or nine years playing in the Dominican and then coming over. They are starting at a young age. And so what our teams have tried to do, and I think they've done a good job, is to prepare that player while he's in the minor leagues and moving up. Learn the ability to learn how to open a checking account, learn how to order food at restaurants and obviously speak English. So by the time that that Latin kid has made it into the Major Leagues he has probably been in the United States for three or four years at least or more. And he's probably more accustomed to the language and lifestyle than a player that's coming over from Japan at thirty years old. So they are a little bit different situations. That said, almost all of our clubs work with Latin players or other international players to try to help them assimilate to the lifestyle of going from San Pedro de Macorís to living in Beloit, Wisconsin. That's a big change and it's not easy to make. And I think a lot of our teams have done a good job in trying to help them with that transition.

BARTKOWIAK: What is your experience in the Tokyo office; how does your experience perhaps draw some similarities or differences between where you are and the other offices around the world? Are you dealing with different issues or do you all commonly deal with similar issues in different ways?

SMALL: One of the things that I've learned, I learned a while ago ... I used to work at Nike. At Nike they always talked about how you have to think globally but act locally and that means basically that every country is different and to say Asia, and it's easy to say well, look at Asia as a continent and one area. And it's not, it's just so different. And the mentality in each market is extremely different. Japan is so different than China. The way you do business, how you do business. Obviously the language, the food, everything is very, very different. And that's all different in Korea and India and Philippines and everywhere you go. You go beyond and you look at Europe, Latin America. You know every place is different so what we've tried to do is say, look where are we going and what road will take us there. We have a phrase, "if you don't know where you're going, any road will get you there." But what we need to do is figure out where we're going and how are we going to get there in that market. So, a place like China, for instance, we know that someday we want China to be very similar for our business as Japan, where people love Major League Baseball; they play the game heavily, they consume our sponsors' products, and it's an established business market. So to get there, we need to build the sport, because you can't have a business if you don't have a sport. So in China, everything that we are doing is really aimed at building the popularity and knowledge of baseball and hopefully create a great MLB player from China in the next five to ten years. And there are a lot of things that we're going to do for that. For instance, we have an academy in China, that I happened to be at last week, and we're taking these kids when they are twelve, or thirteen years old, brought them in and it's our instructors, our strengthening and conditioning coaches on health and nutrition. And these kids have grown big and strong and are very good baseball players now. And we needed to have them in that environment for them to flourish. Now hopefully they are going to grow up to be a Major League player; that's still difficult. You know there are a lot of good players in the United States that don't make it. I heard somewhere that in the draft, only 30 percent of first-round picks in the amateur draft of Major League Baseball ever make it to the Major Leagues. And that's the crème de la crème. So our work is cut out for us, but, even if we fail, and even if we don't get one kid in the Major Leagues, we've now turned out exceptional young, gifted, baseball players and they may go on and play in China, may become coaches, they may go on and become the sports marketing director of Coca-Cola, but they are baseball people. And so if we continue to do this, we are going to see in China a rising tide and eventually, hopefully, we are going to get baseball to be steeped in the culture of China.

BARTKOWIAK: One thing I found very interesting, and I apologize, perhaps this jumps away from the pre-submitted questions, but one of the things I was kind of marveling at when I was exploring the Hall of Fame this last month, was that I saw a program actually of a MLB/NPB game in Japan. And I was wondering if you could maybe briefly tell me a little bit about the history of how those interleague games kind of came into play. I'm reading a little bit about Albert Spalding right now and his international tours of baseball and am wondering how recently in our time have these things [formal developments] come into play?

SMALL: You're right. The Spalding tour was one of the first ones and they went around the world and played in Egypt in front of the pyramids. And there are some great pictures of them playing baseball in front of the pyramids. But it's funny, on that trip, they went to some very interesting places, but it was here [Japan] that there was actual, what I would say, baseball being played. Lefty O'Doul, when he was coming in the '20s and '30s and Babe Ruth who came here: it started then and it was important for Japan/U.S. relations. You know it was a very interesting time. One of the trips, I'm sure you're aware of this but, there was a catcher on the U.S. team named Moe Berg who actually spied on the Japanese and made plans of Tokyo Bay while he was here on one of those tours. I don't think we've had any spies on any of the recent tours but we don't really check. We don't ask our players about that [joking]. But we've kind of restarted that format and after the war, there were teams that would come over. So the Yankees would come over and play for two weeks and later the Baltimore Orioles came. You know Brooks Robinson and all those guys. Cincinnati came. The Brooklyn Dodgers came. So every few years we would bring over a team but they were here for weeks, sometimes twenty-one games and in the 1980s when salaries continued to escalate and players' time became more precious to them and they didn't need to go for two or three weeks and earn money, then we changed the format a little bit. And starting in 1986, we started with an all-star tour that would come and that's what we continue. So the fans here have gotten to see some amazing players. Barry Bonds loved to come here. Roger Clemens, Ozzie Smith. It's interesting and now that we say it, I'll bet if we go back and look at it, there were dozens of Hall of Famers since 1985 that have come to Japan to play. So it's something that the players want to do. They hear about it. And they hear about it from other players and think, "what a great opportunity." So we've been very fortunate to get those guys to come. And in addition to that we've done the Opening Day game in 2000, 2004 and 2008 and we're hoping to do it next year [2012] as well.

BARTKOWIAK: The reception and attendance has been quite encouraging I would imagine then if the plans are continuing?

SMALL: They have. And depending upon the year and the number of games, we average between 25,000 and 40,000 fans per game, depending upon the stadium and all that. We also have to be mindful, I would say, that we can't just do the same thing. The fans are very sophisticated. And Tokyo particularly is a world class international city and there's growing expectations of the types of events that they get. You know they've had the World Cup soccer tournament here. They have various international world championships. We've had three opening days here. So, we always have to be mindful of what kind of event we're bringing here and make sure it's something the fans want to see.

BARTKOWIAK: Okay. I'm wondering, based on the conversation before, if you have any thoughts on what the future relationship of the NPB and MLB will be in the coming years. Do you foresee it being as seemingly peaceful as you've described here, of course with some dissenting voices, but generally does the path look pretty clear at this point?

SMALL: I would hope that we're closer. What we've done over the past few years, we've done a lot of marketing exchanges. We bring over NPB marketing executives and just show them how we do business. There's a change that's going on in Japanese baseball which is very much to the positive and it's changed so much since I came here eight years ago. There is more focus put on marketing the game. And when I say marketing, it's really as simple as focusing on your fan base and giving them what they want. And believe it or not, that's just not been done here. I say that baseball is popular in Japan despite the marketing, not because of the marketing. There are really so many examples of teams not really focusing on their fans. And that's changing. You're seeing more and more emphasis put on that. It's led by the Pacific League teams. You know the guys up in Softbank in Fukuoka, Rakuten Eagles, Nippon Ham up at Sapporo, Chiba Lotte, when Bobby Valentine was here. All of them really focus on putting the fans first and understand what we learned a while ago which is: in Major League Baseball in the United States, we don't sell baseball. We sell a three-hour entertainment experience. And we have to do that because not everyone is a baseball fan. But almost everybody likes to go somewhere with their family, that's reasonably priced, has good food, and lets you forget about your struggles, you know, lets you forget about your worries, your job situation, your health situation, whatever it is. We offer three hours of entertainment where you can escape the problems that you might have. And that's a whole different way of thinking than Major League Baseball in the 1970s which was, hey, there's a game today. If you want to come, great. If not, don't worry about it. Our people have gotten much more sophisticated and we're just like the airline business, we're just like the hotel business. If the plane takes off today from Chicago and there is an empty seat on it, American Airlines can never make that money back. It's not like Kellogg's. If they don't sell you this box today, you might come in tomorrow and buy it and it's good. Its inventory and everything still is good. We're just like the airlines and if you don't buy your ticket today, we'll never be able to resell that ticket for that game again. So, it is essential that we get people coming through the gate every single night. And the way to do that is to give people an experience that they are happy with. Our guys will go and sit in ballparks. I know of five CEOs, and I'm sure there are more, that will go and sit in the stands once a homestand, once every three games to watch what's going on. To listen to what their fans are saying. I know CEOs that have gone and worked concession stands. It's all about trying to understand what that fan wants and then giving it to him. Because if we don't, fans are not going to come. We're not going to get their money. That is just starting to creep in here, in Japan. We would be delighted to continue to facilitate that. I think we play a role in that and I think a lot of this has come from their marketing people coming and seeing how we market it. I would love to facilitate that to continue, that growth, because if baseball here stays strong, the NPB stays strong, then we stay strong. We have a vested interest in NPB doing well, they're not the competition.

BARTKOWIAK: I suppose to continue the theme of questioning the relationships and diplomatic roles between the two countries, I'm wondering, with the knowledge that Major League Baseball plays a major role in the World Baseball Classic, has the World Baseball Classic, especially with the phenomenal success of it in Japan, changed the culture of baseball somewhat or perspectives towards MLB in Japan?

SMALL: Particularly in Japan, the World Baseball Classic obviously has been an overwhelming success, based highly on the fact that they won the first two events. In Japan, the Japanese team and the Japanese way of playing baseball is perfectly suited for a tournament like this. And so what has happened is, baseball, because of the WBC, I think has seen a resurgence here. And it definitely has in Korea. The same thing, the KBO is year after year setting attendance records since 2006, and they specifically cite their success in the World Baseball Classic. So, in the bigger countries it's been very obviously positive. Less in the smaller countries and one of the reasons why the effect of baseball being out of the Olympics has been softened in places like China, South Africa, places like that, is because of the WBC. We are able to inject funding into the China baseball system, and give them a chance to play in a platform that is, in baseball terms, much more impressive than the Olympics. The Olympics again were not the best players. World Baseball Classic is the best players.

BARTKOWIAK: Thank you so much for your time.

Respect for Global Expansion

What struck us about Jim Small's perspective in the conversation was the idea of respect. In his interview, he mentioned how to maintain a sense of respect between MLB and NPB, especially when there are undeniably some that believe MLB "stole" Japanese talents. Two chapters in this book, 7 and 10, discuss how some fans consider their talents have been stolen or taken advantage by MLB. This interview, however, argues that this has not been the case. There is an agreed-upon mechanism between two national offices. MLB's Small does not consider NPB as a competitor. It is possible to argue that it is the case simply because MLB is much larger than NPB and the American baseball enterprise does not need to worry about NPB having much impact on its business plans. The next chapter on MLB international expansion, however, seems to substantiate this claim, at least partially, that MLB might indeed be attempting to grow the sport, including in other leagues, in general, and not just MLB itself.

Of course, objective academic minds require critical investigation of Small's statement about "respect." This book will leave this responsibility to the next chapter on MLB's global expansion. We would rather like to consider what resonated in our minds when Small emphasized so much on collective development, growth, and expansion of baseball across the league boundary lines. What came to our minds first was the title for Robert Whiting's book on Japanese baseball, *You Gotta Have Wa*.

In that book, Whiting shows the cultural crush between Japanese and American baseball. In many parts of the book, the author introduces his reader to American players that abhorred how Japanese professional baseball worked from training to hierarchy. In a collectivism-based nation like Japan, individualism that many of these American ballplayers believed in was not well accepted. That is why they had to have *wa* [harmony]. To be culturally successful in Japan and to be accepted in its society, a player is expected to prioritize what is important to the team more than what is important to him. Failing to do so naturally results in fans being excited about the exotic nature of the players but not accepting them truly to their league. The same was true with many coaches and staff members. As Whiting states, these players were considered "foreign devils" and a "necessary evil" (*You* 263, 266)

Small very well understands this cultural background. When read side by side with the aforementioned two chapters, Small's interview shows the multi-faceted nature of recent MLB expansion. In many ways, even outside of Japan, there are many international projects that provide returns to the new market that the League explores. As business entities, MLB teams ultimately pursue revenue and profits. Small seems to reflect, however, that in the age of increased cultural exchange, a new form of soft-power is necessary. Joseph Nye in 1990 used the phrase "soft power" to distinguish cultural power and military power. In MLB's context, hard power is the traditional hard-sell approach. While it continues to work in many ways, more culturally sensitive soft power approaches that Small discusses also supplement MLB's expansion across the oceans.

10

The Globalization of MLB and Its Consequences

Major League Baseball, without a doubt, is a global enterprise. Over one-quarter of MLB players are from outside of the U.S. Over thirty countries are represented among MLB and minor league players. Its staff is also diverse in their national origin. On the one hand, this creates conflicts. As mentioned earlier in this book, White Sox Manager Ozzie Guillen once commented, "I say, why do we have Japanese interpreters and we don't have a Spanish one. I always say that. Why do they have that privilege and we don't?" On the other hand, what Guillen implied in this quote was that when a Japanese player comes to MLB he does not come alone. Behind new Japanese MLB players there are one or two more Japanese staff members that join the team. Consider the case of Matsuzaka. When he joined the Red Sox, a Japanese trainer who had been with the Red Sox's minor league team for a few years was moved up to the Majors. Since then, the Red Sox have added a few more Japanese staff.

What makes MLB a global entity and not just cross–Pacific or cross–Caribbean is its expansion schemes. Even if it is yet to be truly global, its scope is global. Some of its games take place outside of the U.S. as regular-season games have been played the last decade in Japan, Mexico, and Puerto Rico. MLB's official website is mostly free of national boundaries. MLB's merchandise is available in different corners of the world. MLB also goes abroad to teach children how to play baseball. Enumerating all the activities in which MLB has engaged itself would generate a long list. Such an exercise in itself is probably a worthy project. A more immediate fundamental question, however, is what all of these projects collectively mean. What are some of the motivations behind them, especially considering how costly some of the projects can be, at least in the short term? What does MLB gain in addition to financial revenue? How does globalization enrich MLB?

Alan M. Klein posed a thought-provoking question in his book *Growing the Game: The Globalization of Major League Baseball* when he asked: "The question is whether [MLB will engage itself in globalization] as a twentieth-century colonialist or as a twenty-first-century decentered global enterprise. The former strategy represents familiar ground but is doomed to slow growth and persistent resentment; the latter will at first feel uncomfortable but will aid the worldwide health of the sport" (1). Although the objective of this chapter is not to offer a direct answer to this question, it aims to discuss several case studies that Klein did not necessarily address in his book. In the years since Klein's work came out in 2006, much has changed. This chapter discusses some of the latest examples of globalization.

To answer these questions, this chapter first examines different international and global projects that MLB has been involved in. MLB's official publication *Major League Baseball: International Business Review* and its English version serve as the base for this section. The section to follow looks at the opinions that question MLB's expansion. Jim Small, the managing director of MLB Japan, recognized in his interview compiled in this book that there were fans and/or management that felt that MLB "stole" Japanese players. This section studies how these negative views about MLB surfaced, particularly in Japan. As discussed earlier in this book, Japan has been the latest nation that has produced many and successful MLB players. Many of these players were the most popular sports players in their respective countries. Additionally, their success has led many promising high school and amateur baseball players to consider playing in the U.S. without spending any time playing in their domestic professional league. Studying what MLB shows and how some fans react to this global expansion of MLB will reveal the complex nature of a global sport.

MLB-Driven Globalization of Baseball

Wider understanding of an MLB experience requires analyzing MLB in a global context. Discussing the relationship between sports and globalization, Toby Miller, et al., argue that "the sport experience, which links nationalism, public policy, the media, and contemporary cultural industrialization, must be considered in wider deliberations of globalization" (16). It is not difficult to observe the impact of global business exchanges that affect how fans experience baseball. Seeing non–American players on an MLB roster is another apparent example. Somewhat hidden underneath these obvious examples is the crush of culture. In other words, sports reflect "the process of competition, ranking, and nationalism inscribing a deep structure of Western culture" (Miller, et al., 23). This is why it is significant to understand the global and/or international environment in which MLB operates, in order to truly understand the League's dynamism.

Globalization of baseball brings various benefits to MLB. MLB continues to have over 200 non–U.S. born players. This, in many ways, secured the League's status as the most competitive league in the world, more media exposure and more marketing and licensing opportunities. MLB, however, is not simply the benefactor of this trend. It also is the driver. It constantly recruits players from abroad, seeks ways to put their games on air outside of the U.S., holds MLB-sponsored events, sells its licenses, and gathers sponsors. This section examines each of these MLB efforts to understand how exactly MLB tries to expand its scope outside of North America.

An apparent form of internationalization of MLB comes in team rosters. When MLB's season started in 2011, 27.7 percent of the ballplayers on the Opening Day rosters, or 234 out of 846 players, were born outside of the U.S. The numbers were similar in 2010 when 231 out of 833 listed players, or 27.7 percent of the players, were born outside of the fifty states. While this was a slight decline from the previous years, including 2005 when 29.3 percent of the players were non–U.S. born, it still shows an international presence. Out of the 234 international players in 2011, eighty-six players were from the Dominican Republic, sixty-two were from Venezuela and twenty were from Puerto Rico. It is no surprise that many of the international MLB players come from these Latin American nations and territories. Other nations had smaller numbers. Ten players were from Japan. Australia had five players. Three Taiwanese players were on rosters. In total, fourteen nations were represented on the 2011 Opening Day rosters ("2011 Opening Day"; "Non–U.S. Born").

This internationalization of players, of course, is not truly global. While the representation of fourteen nations shows that MLB is not played only by Americans, it also shows that the majority of nations do not have baseball players playing MLB. In 2006, even with the Minor Leagues taken into consideration there were only thirty-three countries represented, representing about 45 percent of its approximately 7,000-player rosters (Major League Baseball *Major League Baseball*). Additionally, some teams are more internationally-oriented than others. For example, the 2011 Opening Day roster of the New York Yankees included sixteen international players, an increase from ten in 2000. The Colorado Rockies, Detroit Tigers, Los Angeles Angels, and Los Angeles Dodgers each had eleven players. The Dodgers included players from eight different countries and territories. The roster diversity, however, varies from team to team ("2011 Opening Day").

A study on the relationship between international players and MLB ticket sale revenue seems to complicate the matter. On the one hand, almost one-third of MLB players were born outside of the fifty U.S. states. Teams include close to ten, if not close to twenty, non–U.S. players. Despite these numbers, fans seem to look at international players as a unique presence, allowing teams with more international players to generate more ticket sales. A study conducted at University of Michigan shows that "ticket revenue increases by roughly half of a million dollars for each international player added to a Major League Baseball team, showing a sharp swing in fan favoritism for internationally diverse teams." Jason Winfree argues that in 2000 "each international player added approximately $595,000 to ticket sales." The author speculates that this international player-driven increase in ticket revenue had little to do with the location of teams. Rather, he claims that this is a reflection of a non–U.S. born player still being considered as "a novelty" ("Baseball Teams").

With a strong presence of international players in the League, MLB and current immigration issues are often inseparable. Many critics commented on MLB's plan to host its 2011 All-Star Game in Arizona. The criticism came from the state's passing of the Support Our Law Enforcement and Safe Neighborhoods Act, also known as Arizona Senate Bill 1070, in April 2010, and its taking effect in July 2011. Mike Lupica wrote in the *New York Daily News* right after Arizona governor Jan Brewer signed the bill: "If [Arizona SB1070] can't be stopped, if it does go into effect three months from now, the Major League Baseball ought to announce that a sport in which 30 percent of the players are Hispanic will not hold the 2011 All-Star Game at Chase Field in Phoenix."

Mike Freeman, a columnist for CBS's online sports section, speculated on a possible impact of Arizona SB1070 in the following imaginary story:

> It's 2011 and the All-Star Game is just a few days away in Arizona. Albert Pujols decides to take a stroll in downtown Phoenix. A police officer drives by and doesn't realize that Pujols is a baseball icon. To the officer, he looks potentially like an illegal alien. He is, after all, brown skinned. Pujols is stopped by the police. "Papers please," the officer says. If Pujols somehow forgot to bring proof he's an American citizen on his walk, then potentially off to jail he'd go. (Freeman)

Although Commissioner Selig soon commented that the All-Star Game should be held in Arizona — and indeed it was — this controversy showed that MLB is a social institution that was strongly connected to issues concerning immigration.

MLB and Global Media

For many international fans, broadcasting is how they access many MLB games. A new phase of MLB broadcasting started in 2001 when MLB International broadcast the 2001 All-Star Game in high definition in Japan. This marked the beginning of the technology-heavy MLB broadcasting style. As of 2009, over 2,400 MLB games were broadcast globally in 233 countries and territories in seventeen different languages. During the postseason games, ESPN International, Fox Sports Latin America, Rogers Cable from Canada, CDN from the Dominican Republic, three stations from Japan (Fuji TV, NHK, and TBS), Xports from South Korea, Televisa from Mexico, Canal+ and NOS from the Netherlands, Channel 5 from England, and Meridiano from Venezuela collaborated with the MLB production team to feed live games internationally (Major League Baseball *Major League Baseball* 10; Major League Baseball "A Decade" 10–11).

MLB International (MLBI) produces game feeds independently from domestic broadcasters. It has its own cameras, production trucks, announcers and other crew. Their production is shared internationally. MLB explains this system by stating:

> The MLBI feed is the same all over the world. However, international rightholders have three styles in terms of audio that MLBI customizes for each partner: they can originate commentary on-site, where a fully-equipped broadcast booth is provided for any on-site announcers; they can use the English-only telecast of MLBI announcers Dave O'Brien and

Rick Sutcliffe; or they can receive "natural sound" (crowd and game noise only) and insert the voices of their own announcers at the studios in their country [Major League Baseball "A Decade" 14].

As MLB International expands its scope, the significance of advertisements changes. A new form of sports marketing becomes necessary. Bernard James Mullin, Stephen Hardy, and William A. Sutton explain that sports marketing "consists of all activities designed to meet the needs and wants of sports consumers through exchange processes. Sport marketing has developed two major thrusts: the marketing of sport products and services directly to consumers of sport, and the marketing of other consumer and industrial products or services through the use of sports promotions" (9). These authors argue that there are essentially two kinds of sports marketing. In the context of MLB, the first is selling game tickets and broadcasting rights. The second involves marketing apparel, accessories, and various other products that feature MLB or its teams. MLB has excelled in both of these categories.

One of MLB's ways of marketing to the global baseball audience is the use of technology to customize advertisements. When a game is put on air internationally, a traditional advertisement behind the home plate may lose its value outside of the domestic market. It makes better marketing sense if a Japanese company can have this advertisement space when the game is shown in Japan and an American company when in the U.S. Realizing this international marketing phenomenon, MLB started using virtual advertisements in 2005. These digitally imposed advertisements can target a geographically-specific audience. Sam Fullerton and G. Russell Merz explain:

> Virtual advertising technology can be used to place computer-generated signage at strategic locations during the broadcast of sports event. During the recent Major League Baseball post-season games, TV viewers were exposed to a sign for a new Gillette razor whereas the fans in the stands simply saw a blank green surface. An advantage of virtual signage is that it can be changed during the broadcast. The Gillette sign that TV viewers first saw became a sign for State Farm Insurance later in the broadcast. It can also be used to display different signage to viewers in different geographic markets. (97)

In 2009, thirty-one companies signed up as virtual advertising partners. For example, Japanese fans watching a game may see a Mizuno advertisement behind home plate whereas American fans watching the exact same game may see an advertisement for Pepsi. This has allowed many companies to be identified as "behind the plate advertisers" in their own targeted markets (Major League Baseball "A Decade" 15).

MLB's Business Expansion

MLB does not showcase its baseball via broadcast media alone. Obviously, one of its largest projects in recent years is the World Baseball Classic. Its financial and media success is irrefutable. This international tournament, as described earlier in his book, however, is not the only MLB presence outside of North America. MLB has its games abroad. The League has made trips to Latin America and Asia, especially Japan. While MLB's international game presence has been in existence since the late nineteenth century, there has been a rapid increase since 1990. Especially in the 2000s, MLB has had numerous exhibition and regular-season games outside of the U.S. In 2000, MLB had its first-season game in Tokyo between the New York Mets and the Chicago Cubs. Later in the same year, MLB returned to Japan to play the Japan All-Star Series in four different locations. In 2001, the Houston Astros and the Cleveland Indians played preseason games in Valencia, Venezuela. In 2002, MLB all-stars went back to Japan to play seven games against Japanese counterparts. In 2003, the New York Mets and the Los Angeles Dodgers played in Mexico City. Another season opener took place in Japan the following year when the Tampa Bay Rays and the New York Yankees played. After playing six preseason and in-season games, these teams attracted a total of over 300,000 fans. In 2008, the first MLB game was hosted in China, between the Los Angeles Dodgers and the San Diego Padres. After seeing the enthusiasm of Chinese fans at the very first MLB game in China, Joe Torre was quoted saying, "It felt more like a regular season game than a spring training game." (Major League Baseball "A Decade" 40–41, 50)

An increased amount of MLB exposure globally results in an increase in international licensing opportunities. Licensing no longer means, especially with international sports, just t-shirts and baseball caps. Anita M. Moorman and Marion E. Hambrick explain that "revenues from global licensed sports apparel and other goods grew by $3.1 billion in 2008 to $19.9 billion. MLB alone had $5.1 billion in global sales" (160). Between 2000 and 2006, MLB's international retail sales multiplied from $50 million to $800 million. Between 2005 and 2006 alone, the business grew by 30 percent, attributable to the Southeast Asian market growth by 66 percent and European market growth by 40 percent. This growth is not just because of the Internet. Although it is true that the tie-up between MLB and JD Sports, a British sports fashion retailer, for example, has expanded MLB's market both inside and outside of the U.S., it is also notable that stores and offices marketing MLB and team logos have increased. For example, New Era opened its flagship store in London and Toronto in 2007. However, even since 2000, New Era caps had been a popular icon among the youth in Europe. Similarly, after establishing its European hub in London, Majestic Athletic has expanded the value of MLB not only for traditional sporting apparel but also for regular street clothing. The MLB logo can also be found on brands that have traditionally been little associated with baseball. H&M, for example, carries apparel and accessories for both men and women featuring MLB team logos (Major League Baseball *Major League Baseball* 38, 43; Major League Baseball "A Decade" 16, 18, 19).

Licensing, of course, is a big business in Japan. MLB collaborated with Sports Authority in 2001 to launch MLB "Fan Zones" in Japan. But just as the European market witnessed MLB's reach outside of the sports business, MLB started its cooperation with Lala Plan which became MLB's first licensee for women's clothing. Probably one of the most untraditional licensing in Japan was the opening of MLB Café in Tokyo in 2009. It has a café space on the first floor and dining space on the second and third floors. The café has accommodated various needs of Japanese MLB fans, including hosting parties and weddings. Inside of the café, customers find diverse MLB memorabilia, ballpark-themed food, MLB games on TV, and other MLB experiences (Major League Baseball "A Decade" 16–17, 21).

Other Asian countries have also welcomed MLB. In China, Eversports has been the key importer of MLB. After becoming MLB's official partner in 2007, it has opened over eighty lifestyle and sport stores in Beijing, Shanghai, and other locations. When it hosted an MLB retail event in Shanghai in May 2009, over 70,000 fans appeared not only to buy MLB-licensed products but also to participate in baseball-related activities, live music concerts, and other events. Similarly, both in Taiwan and South Korea, MLB's presence is on its increase. In Taiwan, there are over 100 Pegasus Taiwan Ltd stores featuring MLB products. In South

Korea, an apparel company, F&F, worked with MTV and hosted MLB Club Parties where over 8,000 fans attended. These examples show how the dramatic market expansion in Asia, especially in Southeast Asia, has greatly affected MLB's global business plans (Major League Baseball *Major League Baseball* 41; Major League Baseball "A Decade" 22–23).

MLB licensing also brings big business opportunities in Latin America. In the Dominican Republic, tourists can visit Baseball Corner in the Las Americans Airport to purchase various MLB items. Similarly, in Mexico, its largest department store chain, Liverpool, collaborated with Majestic Athletic and New Era Cap Company to promote baseball in Mexico City and Monterey. They have co-hosted an event for fans to watch the 2006 National League Championship Series games between the New York Mets and the St. Louis Cardinals. Additionally, Sears, Deportes Marti, and other retail stores have begun to carry MLB-licensed products.

Similar to licensing, sponsorship is another area where globalization of MLB has taken place. Fullerton and Merz explain that in a traditional sense, sponsorship: "generally involves the acknowledgement of the sponsor by the sports property and the ability of the sponsor to use the property's trademarks and logos in its efforts to leverage the sponsorship and reinforce the relationship in the minds of members of the sponsor's target market" (95). In 2009, MLB explains that there were over forty sponsors from Asia, Australia, Europe, Latin America, and other parts of the world that supported MLB. Consequently, the League recorded a sponsorship revenue increase of 75 percent compared to 2000. Some of the sponsors are in the food and beverage business. Pepsi is a prominent example. In 2002, it became the official soft drink of MLB in Latin America. It has conducted various promotional activities including inviting consumers to the All-Star Game, the World Series, and other prime games. Gillette, Banco BHD, and Maltin Polar, and also have a strong presence as MLB sponsors in the Latin American nations. MasterCard, Budweiser, and many other global companies have participated in MLB as its international sponsors (Major League Baseball "A Decade" 26–27).

Jim Small, in his Chapter 9 interview, talked about Kellogg's sponsorship. Its boxes of cereal contain a special baseball card. MLB reports that Kellogg's sales in Japan rose by 22 percent during the MLB campaign, compared to the same period in previous years without the specially designed boxes with MLB players printed. In total, Kellogg has printed about 4,000,000 boxes using a total of twenty-six MLB players.

Koikeya, a Japanese chips company, has done something similar. Its special bags feature MLB players. It also is similar to a lottery ticket for MLB memorabilia. Komatsu, a Japanese heavy-duty construction equipment manufacturer similar to Caterpillar, also is a sponsor of MLB. Although it is almost counterintuitive that such a company would be interested in a baseball league, it has produced and shared calendars, towels, caps, shirts, cards, and other items as its promotional products. Such examples continue. NTT, a Japanese telephone company, distributes marketing materials to its existing and prospective customers. Ichiro frequently appears in the advertisement of Sato Pharmaceutical and Nikko Cordial, a financial services firm. The promotional project by ENEOS, a gas station, included a five-day trip for 100 customers to the game between the Seattle Mariners and the New York Yankees. Those who won the prize visited the stadium in Seattle, received an autographed ball by Ichiro, and had very rare MLB experiences. Thanks to this promotion, ENEOS's sales increased by 10 percent between 2005 and 2006 (Major League Baseball *Major League Baseball* 48; Major League Baseball "A Decade" 24–31).

All of these promotional efforts would be infertile without proper market development. Sponsorship, licensing, broadcasting, and other activities would not otherwise reach customers. MLB, therefore, invests many human and financial resources to grow its existing markets and explore new ones. Jim Small stated, in his interview, that expanding MLB to China would be an important task. Teaching Chinese school children how to play baseball might lead to only one successful MLB player. But it can also develop a new market for MLB. This is why the League has its market development presence in over sixty countries.

Some of the most prevalent market development programs by MLB deal with grassroots-level youth baseball. One of them is the Play Ball! Program. Started in 1999, MLB International supports international organizations that help develop or expand youth baseball. It has donated playing equipment, supplied MLB team-branded caps and t-shirts, offered coaching staff, and provided teaching materials. Since 1999, almost one million children in Australia, Germany, Italy, South Korea, Mexico, Puerto Rico, South Africa, and the U.K. have joined the program. Through Play Ball!, MLB has established partnerships with baseball associations in Europe and Africa. A similar project, the Pitch, Hit, & Run Program, started in 1994 to support school baseball programs. Over four million school children in Australia, Germany, Italy, Japan,

South Korea, Mexico, Puerto Rico, South Africa, and the U.K. participated in the project. For children in Puerto Rico, the winning prize of this project was a trip to the MLB All-Star Game. These leading projects offer children opportunities to play baseball and be aware of the values that MLB represents (Major League Baseball *Major League Baseball* 30–31; Major League Baseball "A Decade" 38).

Some other projects are more country-specific. In Canada, for example, Winterball is a nationally recognized program for physical education classes. This project started in 2004 when MLB and Baseball Canada signed their partnership. All ten of Canada's provinces participate in this project and teach the basics of baseball to students in "a fun, non-competitive" way. MLB had, of course, had some presence in Canada previously. It has used the Toronto Blue Jays in many of its promotional materials for the Canadian market. But Winterball became an even bigger success. During the first three years, the program was adopted by 1,100 schools. Over 200,000 students played baseball. In 2006 alone, almost 85,000 school children played the game thanks to Winterball. By 2009, this nine-week program had reached more than 400,000 students between the ages of eight and twelve in 1,600 schools (Major League Baseball *Major League Baseball* 35; Major League Baseball "A Decade" 38).

China has been one of the focus markets. MLB recognizes the country as "a fast-growing market for the game of baseball." The Play Ball! Program went to China for the first time in 2007. Over 120 elementary schools have adopted the program and MLB International was successful in reaching out to more than 120,000 children aged eight to twelve. At the completion of each session, MLB donates all the used equipment to the local communities for their future use. For school children in middle school and high school, MLB International offers the MLB Development Center. This reflects collaboration among the Wuxi Municipal Government, the Bureau of Sports Administration, and MLB. Opened in the eastern part of the region called Wuxi in September 2009, the Development Center is "the first full-time MLB training facility in China [that] provides professional baseball training ... within an academic school environment." This institution is unique in that it aspires to prepare its students athletes in three areas: academic education, baseball, and global opportunities. For this purpose, students take regular academic classes, receive baseball training by a professional coaching staff, and take classes in English (Major League Baseball "A Decade" 39).

South Africa is another part of the world with a strong MLB presence. Using the country as the foothold for the entire African continent, the League attempts to popularize baseball in African countries where few people have played baseball. This development program has offered financial assistance, sent coaches, and donated baseball equipment to the African Development Foundation. MLB has hosted baseball clinics and sent former players and executives to West African countries. Additionally, in cooperation with the Ugandan Little League, it helped build seven baseball fields (Major League Baseball *Major League Baseball* 37; "ADF Brings MLB").

MLB International is also invested in training elite players outside of the U.S. through its international academies. These academies, located in Tirrenia, Italy, Queensland, Australia, and Wuxi, China, offer intensive training camps to young talented players mostly between the ages of sixteen and eighteen. Players and coaches in these academies represent over thirty countries and territories including Nigeria, Uganda, Micronesia, Fiji, Papua New Guinea, Sweden, Slovenia, Denmark, and Bulgaria that are little associated with baseball. Each of approximately sixty to sixty-five players at each academy has a chance to be seen by MLB recruiters and scouts. Over 100 graduates so far have signed with MLB teams. Many others have been recruited to play at the collegiate level in the U.S. or played on their respective national team during the World Baseball Classic tournaments (Major League Baseball *Major League Baseball* 32–33; Major League Baseball "A Decade" 36).

MLB International has many other marketing development projects both for fans and coaches. For example, the MLB Festival was started in London in 1994. This is "a mobile, interactive fan experience that provides local baseball fans with a genuine MLB experience." It has over ten attractions such as batting cages, pitching tunnels, and official MLB stores. The festival has gone to Australia, the Dominican Republic, Germany, Puerto Rico, Mexico, and Venezuela. Some programs for coaches invite international coaches to the U.S. whereas some others send MLB-trained coaches abroad. The Coaching Development Program is one of the examples of the first category. It invites coaches from all around the world and teaches international coaches how to become better and more effective coaches. Fourteen MLB clubs have hosted close to 100 coaches from over ten countries during their Fall Instructional League. The Coaches in Resident Program sends full-time professional coaches abroad to share their expertise internationally. The U.K., South Africa, and Italy have taken advantage of this program. As of 2009, the program held over 550 training sessions and coached over 8,000 coaches in these three countries. (Major League Baseball *Major League Baseball* 34; Major League Baseball "A Decade" 37–38).

All of these examples show that from licensing and sponsorship to market development to recruiting international players to MLB, the League has a very holistic plan to internationalize and globalize its operation. As Alan Klein explains, an obvious example of globalization is the recent influx of Japanese players. But it is also to have baseball in a country where baseball previously had little presence. Klein discusses the life story of Maribel Alezondo, from Costa Rica. In a nation where soccer is much more popular than baseball, she is in the baseball business. She was one of the workers at the Rawlings factory where she hand-stitched MLB baseballs for eleven hours a day. She made thirty cents per ball. International MLB players come only from a limited number of nations and territories. This expansion model is not surprising. Putting MLB in parallel with other for-profit enterprises reveals that MLB's international business model is very similar to other international companies. These companies, as a result of their globalization attempts, often times face resistance. Think about Maribel Alezondo. She no longer works at the factory because her work deformed her fingers and arms. She is quoted, "It's an injustice that we kill ourselves to make these balls perfect, and with one home run, they're gone" (Klein 8–9).

From McDonald's to Nike to Wal-Mart, no international firms have avoided such predicaments in one way or another. MLB is not an exception. To focus on how MLB tries to expand globally and how it has been successful in many of its projects, therefore, is to draw an unfairly rosy picture of its operation without considering how their business is perceived abroad.

Reactions to MLB Expansion

There is no doubt that many fans appreciate and enjoy MLB. Simply looking at the TV ratings of MLB games, increasing global sales of MLB products, welcoming attitudes to international academies and coaches, and other evidence suggests that MLB is frequently accepted abroad very positively. Jim Small, in his interview, mentioned that there were some fans that were not entirely happy. He claimed that some felt that MLB was "stealing" Japan's talented players. This section investigates such negative reactions to complicate the matter of MLB globalization.

Latin America, without a doubt, is the largest exporter of MLB players. An article by Ben Badler in *Baseball America* featured more recent contracts signed by Latin American players. While MLB has opened up opportunities for many young, aspiring players to play in the U.S., many have reacted to this phenomenon as MLB's exploitation of Latin American talents. About 30 percent of the Opening Day rosters for the past several years have been filled by Latin American players. As for the Minor Leagues, the number goes up to close to 50 percent. Arturo J. Marcano and David P. Fidler explain that "Latin America has become ... a strategic asset for MLB." They argue that this is because Latin American players are not well protected by the League or other organizations so they can easily be taken advantage of. The authors write "North American amateurs are subject to the annual draft, which contains extensive protections for drafted players negotiated between the MLB Commissioner's Office and the Major League Baseball Players Association. MLB also has official rules protecting high school and college players in North America from unscrupulous behavior by teams." But Latin American players do not have the same kind of protection.

Marcano and Fidler also point out that while the idea of "strategic asset" also describes the Asian market, there is a distinct difference between the two:

> Asian players, such as those from Japan and Korea, typically enter MLB as free agents after their initial contracts with professional teams in their home countries have expired.... If a MLB team wants to recruit a Japanese player under contract with a Japanese professional club, it must go through an elaborate process agreed upon by MLB and the Japanese baseball commissioners. A similar agreement exists between MLB and the Korean professional league.

This means that both North American and Asian players do not get involved in the negotiation process alone. There is a structured negotiation system in place that makes sure that teams, the commissioner offices, MLB clubs, and other pertinent parties are equally involved.

In Latin America, negotiations between players and MLB clubs are not regulated as much. As Marcano and Fidler write, "The opposite [of what happens in North America and Asia] is true for Latin America, the biggest market for foreign baseball talent. Latin prospects are not subject to the amateur draft, nor do agreements exist between MLB and Latin professional leagues about talent transfers. MLB recruitment in Latin

America is a free-agency system that is essentially unregulated." Additionally, compared to prospective MLB players in North America and Asia, Latin American prospects tend to suffer from their lower socioeconomic contexts. As a result, they are more likely to be subjugated to labor exploitation.

The issues are more complex in Latin America because of the age of those prospective players. Players in Asia, for example, are usually well established as professional baseball players in their own domestic league. It is not as frequently the case with Latin American players. They are likely to be much younger than Asian or North American prospects. Examples are abundant in the past ten years. For example, the Astros signed two sixteen-year-olds, Luis Reynose from the Dominican Republic for $700,000 and Arturo Michelena from Venezuela for $220,000. The Twins similarly added another sixteen-year old, Miguel Gonzales, for $650,000. The Padres signed Jose Ruiz from Venezuela for $1.1 million. The Blue Jays signed Wilmer Becerra and Jesus Gonzalez from Venezuela, and Dawel Lugo, a Dominican shortstop. The Royals added Eller Hernandez. The Rangers signed Ronald Guzman from the Dominican Republic. All of these players were sixteen-year-olds. Few sixteen-year-olds in Asia are exposed to MLB recruiters' eyes (Badler; Marcano and Fidler).

Marcano and Fidler explain that these young players are brought to the U.S. because "MLB's recruitment system is intentionally designed to access baseball talent as young and as cheaply as possible." They continue:

> Without question, recruitment practices in Latin America target children, defined in international law as persons under 18-years of age. The only official rule MLB has adopted to regulate Latin recruitment is the so-called 17-year-old rule, which teams have routinely violated since the rule was implemented in the mid-1980s and the Commissioner's Office has refused to enforce effectively. Latin prospects who are of age but pretend to be younger than they really are, also serve as evidence that MLB teams prefer signing younger players. Teams also routinely scout and make contract with players well under 16, sometimes looking for talent among 10-, 11- and 12-year-olds. Often, teams recruit players too young to sign in their "baseball academies" to hide them from other teams and to begin the prospect's training as early as possible.

It is, however, not just the recruitment system that encourages MLB to exploit young talents in Latin America. Kyle Tana writes that MLB actively invests in this region to further enhance its involvement: "Major League Baseball invests upwards of $76 million annually in the Dominican Republic, of which $16 million is used in the operation of official MLB baseball academies, which turn out to be million dollar 'training facilities.'" There are only two MLB teams that do not have an academy in the Dominican Republic. MLB's attitude of looking at the Latin American region as the harvest land of talents is obvious. Tana even introduces a common joke among general managers of MLB clubs that states that they would rather have "twenty Dominicans at $5,000 a piece rather than 2 Americans at $50,000 each." Recruited players, however, have little guarantee that they would make it to MLB. Usually, only one out of forty applicants to an academy is admitted in the Dominican Republic. Out of these promising players, less than 1 percent will play in MLB.

These examples show that MLB's expansion to Latin America caused some concerns about the League's treatment of young players. Ideas such as labor, human rights, children's rights, and protection of the youth frequently surface in the analyses of MLB and Latin America. Although the situation is vastly different, Japanese fans also express their concerns about MLB's presence. On the one hand, the negotiations between a Japanese player and an MLB club are extremely regulated. Jim Small touched upon this in his interview. However, this is nothing similar to what happens in Latin America, as described above. Alexander Blenkinsopp explains:

> While no restrictions prohibit players from Puerto Rico, the Dominican Republic, Mexico, or most other Latin American nations from playing for U.S. major league teams (Cuba is a notable exception), Asian players face several limitations. In Japan, players are bound to their clubs for a full nine years — most often encompassing the prime of their careers — before they can see employment with U.S. or Canadian teams. Korean players must complete two years of military service before they turn 27 years old, binding them to their countries until they complete their stints in the armed forces and depriving them of two seasons of experience.

Therefore, Japanese fans are not worried about MLB's exploitation of Japanese youth. But they are more concerned about the outgoing flow of top-level baseball players to the U.S. and losing Japanese talents in the domestic league.

A common cause of concerns regarding MLB's presence in Japan is that MLB will import most of talented Nippon Professional League

(NPB) players and the NPB will be left with second-tier players is a popular one. Although a very restrictive negotiation framework is in place between the NPB and MLB, so that the NPB would not be a farm ground of MLB, many fans and those in the baseball business still express their concerns in many occasions. Katsuya Nomura, a former head coach of the Rakuten and one of the NPB icons, is one of the most influential figures to share such concerns publicly. He stated:

> If you let me complain about anything today, let me tell you that what upsets me the most. It is everyone is talking only about going to play in MLB. NPB is going to suffer from a chaotic condition if this trend continues. I understand there are pros and cons in playing in MLB. You can only live once. It is admirable that you want to challenge yourself to achieve your dream. But NPB has taken care of us. We would not be where we are now without NPB. So we are worried more about what will happen to NPB. You can only have a top-notch player once every ten years, if not less frequent. Think about this. Ichiro is gone. Matsui is gone. Do we have anyone in Japan that is as good? The answer is no ["Nomu-san"].

Nomura's comment reflects his widely-shared concern about the future of NPB. As he states, he understands and even respects the fact that players aspire to play in MLB. His worry, however, is the possible void of talent in NPB.

Nomura's concern is not out of context. When Daisuke Matsuzaka debuted as a Red Sox pitcher against the Kansas City Royals in 2007, almost 200 journalists and media crew from Japan showed up at the game site. However, when the NPB season started just a week prior, no opening game received as much media attention (White "Japan Frets"). Player agents such as Don Nomura, responsible for Hideo Nomo's move to the Dodgers in 1995, are trying to convince young players to consider playing in the U.S. without committing themselves to NPB (White "Japan Frets"). The controversies around Tsuyoshi Nishioka at the end of the 2010 season also caused similar concerns. After Nishioka contributed to his team's winning of the Japanese championship in 2010 and showed his performance at WBC, he stated that after achieving his dream for the team, he was hoping to try to achieve his person dream by playing in MLB ("Nishioka").

Critics argue that the environment surrounding NPB is getting worse. While MLB was mostly interested in well-established talents in the NPB during the late 1990s and 2000s, it has realized that it would make more economic sense to invest in amateur players. For example, the Orioles spent $10 million for the two-year contract with Uehara. The Braves spent $24 million for the three-year contact with Kawakami ("Nihon Kyukaiwa"). The Red Sox spent $52 million for the six-year contract with Matsuzaka, in addition to over $50 million for the rights to negotiate with him ("Matsuzaka"). Instead, amateur players will cost substantially less to MLB clubs. For example, Junichi Tazawa cost the Red Sox only $3 million for its three-year contract (Browne). Tazawa played for Nippon Oil, a corporate-sponsored amateur team. When he announced his interests in playing in MLB, he asked NPB teams not to select him in their draft. When all the teams agreed to do so, he was, for this particular reason, not restricted by NPB's regulations regarding negotiating with MLB clubs (Whitehouse). Born in 1986, he was only a twenty-two-year-old when he signed with the Red Sox, five years younger than Matsuzaka at the signing of his contract with the Red Sox. Tazawa's example showed that an MLB club could not only obtain a promising Japanese player for lower cost but also for a longer period in their career.

The fear of young talent drain became imminent in the summer of 2009 when Yusei Kikuchi, then an eighteen-year-old high school star pitcher expressed his interests in MLB. When he pitched in a game at a National Athletic Meet qualifier on September 28, 2009, scouts from all twelve NPB clubs and eight MLB clubs gathered. The MLB clubs present at the game included the Dodgers, the Cubs, and the Giants. The NPB regulation states that the maximum payment to a high school graduate player is limited to 150 million yen, including bonus. MLB has no such restrictions. When Stephen Strasburg signed a four-year contract with the Nationals, it cost the team $15.1 million, approximately ten times the amount of the NPB limit ("Nihon Kyukaini").

Although Kikuchi agreed to remain in Japan and play for the Seibu Lions, this caused frustrations among MLB scouts without alleviating the concerns of NPB supporters. On the one hand, the aforementioned clubs that showed interests in acquiring Kikuchi and others, including the Red Sox and the Mariners, in general agreed that NPB unfairly influenced Kikuchi despite his true interests in and aspiration to play in the U.S. By signing with a NPB club, Kikuchi is now required to play nine seasons in Japan until he can become a free agent. On the other hand, the Lions' signing with Kikuchi did little to convince NPB that prospective players were more interested in the domestic league than in

MLB. Also on the other hand, the success of young MLB players from Japan including Tazawa attracts many high school age players. Kikuchi needs to wait nine seasons until he is eligible to become a free agent to play in MLB. It may take him at least five or six years until he can take advantage of the posting system. But every summer, at the end of the national high school championship, new stars are born. NPB does not have much advantage over MLB despite the language, cultural, and other barriers that nineteen-year-olds will have to face in the U.S. ("Nihon Kyukaini"; White "Japan Prep").

For fear that NPB will be a minor league for MLB, NPB has implemented various regulations. As stated earlier, in order for an NPB player to become a free agent to negotiate with an MLB club, he needs to play nine seasons. This means for many players that their prime may be over before they obtain the right to be considered for MLB. Even if that is not the case, MLB teams may consider that their prime may be over soon, making them less attractive as investments. There is a way for a Japanese NPB player to play in MLB without waiting nine seasons. It is the posting system that Ichiro and Matsuzaka have taken advantage of. There are, however, disadvantages. While it allows less experienced players to be at the negotiating table with an MLB club, his home club in Japan can unilaterally disallow the continuation of the negotiation regardless of the player's will. Jeff Passan argues that with the posting system, only the NPB teams win from it. Its players and MLB teams are heavily disadvantaged. Although he analyzes that the posting system no longer works as well as it used to, especially after the Rakuten Eagles had to return the $19.1 million posting fee to the Oakland Athletics after failing to reach an agreement in 2010, it continues to restrict the flow of talents across the Pacific. (Japan Professional "Transfer"; Japan Professional "Other"; Passan "Will Yu").

These rules favor clubs' interests over those of individuals. It is natural that the Japanese Professional Baseball Players Association (JPBPA) considers the framework in place between NPB and MLB to be highly detrimental to the development of the sport. If a player refused to be considered for the domestic draft as Tazawa did, that player is not eligible to play in NPB for two years after leaving the club outside of Japan. If a player directly went to play abroad after graduating from high school, this no-return-to-NPB period is extended to three years. This rule has led many players to stay in Japan for fear that they would not be able to play in NPB after they stop playing abroad. JPBPA considers that it is necessary to make NPB more attractive to players so that they would rather stay in Japan to play. It argues, "instead of creating rules and restrictions ... we need to reform NPB so that prospective players will find it an ideal place to play" (Japan Professional "Transfer"; Japan Professional "Other").

The Way Through Wa

Globalization of MLB has impacted many. This chapter opened with an obvious example of MLB globalization: Matsuzaka. But it has also introduced an unfortunate life story of Maribel Alezondo. The global presence of MLB has brought many consequences. MLB has benefited from expanding media exposure and licensing and sponsorship opportunities. International players continue to attract many fans. WBC is slowly but surely taking off. Its market development efforts have been successful. There is little doubt that it is a highly successful enterprise that centers its business in selling a few hours of entertainment in a stadium and even more on TV, online, and through t-shirts.

Globalization of MLB has also negatively impacted those involved. On the other side of the spectrum from Matsuzaka, there are numerous young players from Latin America that seem to partake in what Kyle Tana called a "cheap labor bazaar." Aspiring talents in Japan are blocked from pursuing their dreams because of restrictions imposed by NPB that consider MLB as a rival. As Jim Small repeatedly mentioned in his interview, a sense of respect is significant. In the lexicon of the Japanese, it is the idea of *wa*. MLB has been an international enterprise for decades. It has globalized itself even more and at faster speed since 2000. To maintain its status and to further grow as a global enterprise, MLB's task perhaps is to remember: "You Gotta Have *Wa*."

Conclusion

Major League Baseball is a complex entity. As popular culture theorists Jack Nachbar and Kevin Lause argue, popular culture including baseball and its American professional league carry "the underlying cultural mindset which those [popular cultural] artifacts and events both reflect and mold" (32). We have demonstrated how MLB exists within a very high-context environment intertwined with contemporary American and international experiences.

The arrival of Matsuzaka, the success of Ichiro, an increasing presence of Japanese MLB players, and other trans–Pacific developments in the past decade launched this book. All of these examples reflect global capitalism. Every tenet of Appadurai's globalscapes explains this exchange over 6,000 miles. The voices of Latin American MLB players as well as Maribel Alezondo, the Costa Rican worker, also represent different aspects of globalization of baseball. Therefore, MLB globally means not simply expanded business opportunities, an increased exposure, or a concentration of talents, but also a disparity in baseball experiences, cultural colonization, and reinforced national identities.

Within the U.S., MLB showcases an integration of various cultural expressions. Ballparks today are filled not only with visual stimulations but also with audio stimulations. Music is an indispensable part of the game, from advertisements to walk-on music, and to the cheering by fans. To listen and to sing along both enhances the experience at a ballpark. Similarly, giveaways, memorabilia, and team logos all have symbolic values and represent and formulate fan identities. Free giveaways, including bobbleheads, allow fans to be a part of the game more than just as an attendant. Memorabilia allows them to share a piece of MLB history privately. Fans have eloquently expressed sentimental values that they saw in old team logos. All of these examples clearly show that MLB is more than an athletic entity. It is a way of living and participating in America's national pastime.

Of course, the dividing line between MLB experiences in the U.S. and those abroad is far from clear. The difficult questions about cultural power, identity struggles, and dominance of certain economic powers exist both inside and outside of the U.S. Similarly, fans in Europe, Asia, and the rest of the world also partake in generating an MLB culture by attending games, visiting the National Baseball Hall of Fame, and frequenting MLB's website.

Although this book has only examined a very small part of MLB happening outside of the field of play, it is evident that what happens between the two white lines is nothing but one of the many embodiments of MLB's symbolism. This is to say that MLB is not monolithic. We experience the game in countless different ways. It carries as many diverse meanings. Sometimes, MLB is as real as hearing the noise, smelling hot dogs, and seeing world-class play just a few yards (if you are lucky enough to have one of those seats) ahead. Other times, it is as emotional as what the Red Sox fans felt at the end of the 2004 season, or reminiscing about childhood days watching the game with a parent or grandparent. Many other times, it is as virtual and digital as the superimposed advertisements found in World Series or WBC games. Many of the highly avid MLB fans exist outside of the U.S. without having the chance to actually visit a ballpark. However, they enjoy the game online.

Understanding the essence of MLB necessitates shedding light on what happens outside of those two white lines at the ballpark. Examining the nature of technology, Martin Heidegger argues that in order to understand its essence, we should not directly look at it, but rather, we should examine "Gestell" or the "framing" which generates the Zeitgeist (311–41). Our approach was similar. While statistics, player performance analysis, and other data and figures can very well showcase a part of MLB, it does not fully reveal what MLB really is. Despite seeming like there is an overabundance of MLB in today's popular media, it is clear that it is an entity that requires more scholarly investigations. It can tell so much about what American and international cultures are, where they are headed, how they interact with each other, and possibly how Walter LaFeber's prediction on the clash between culture and the capital may or may not be realized in the coming future.

Afterword

As the opening of this book shared with its readers, the origin of the book exists in one afternoon that Mat and I spent in Linton Hall at Michigan State University. Over the following five years, we have discussed MLB and its unbeaten path on numerous different occasions. What stands intriguing about these five years is that while we conducted our research we lived many of these MLB experiences ourselves.

Visiting the National Baseball Hall of Fame in upstate New York was, as Brad Horn stated, a journey. After getting off at the airport in Albany, NY, the car ride was over an hour and a half through the countryside. Although the Hall would, without a doubt, attract more visitors if it existed in New York City or elsewhere, the Hall experience started en route. The agrarian idealism that baseball in American history has represented is a part of what visitors live as they walk in the neighborhood of the Hall.

As an avid baseball and MLB fan, Mat was enthralled by the discoveries on memorabilia and giveaways. Now each of us has a Matsuzaka bobblehead, a proper popular cultural representation of our work, in our respective offices. When we visited Busch Stadium in St. Louis, he was adorned with a baseball hat of an old Milwaukee Brewers logo. Many of us live these MLB and baseball experiences without truly questioning how they can reveal its essence.

This project has offered us opportunities to conduct research in the U.S. and in Japan. Some of the preliminary sources existed outside of these two countries. We have touched upon countries in Europe, Africa, the Americas, Asia, and Oceania. It is, therefore, probably proper that I write this concluding section of the book in Amsterdam's Schophol Airport on my way back from France with almost a half-day delay. Amsterdam this morning is chaotic. The dense fog has allowed few flights to leave or arrive even close to the scheduled times. Frustrated passengers are inquiring what is happening. More experienced passengers seem to be more relaxed and deal with the unforeseen and the unpredictable in most flexible ways.

Probably we experience MLB in a very similar way with chaos and order. As this book has shown, MLB is intertwined with so many different factors. Where the league and its culture are headed has little to do with where it hopes to go. Rather, unforeseeable and unpredictable external factors from international business to politics to economics affect the framing of MLB and how MLB frames our lives. In other words, we interact with MLB in a very chaotic environment while making the best sense out of such experiences. It is our sincere hope that our readers see this chaos and order more clearly than before.

Works Cited

Adams, Russell. "Is Ichiro's Annual Salary Too Much or Too Little? New Scoring Method to Evaluate Players Based on Profits." Translated in *Courrier Japon* July 2007: 56–58. Print.
"ADF Brings MLB Envoy Program to Ghana." *African Development Foundation*. African Development Foundation, n.d. Web. 11 Nov. 2011.
Alexomanolaki, Margarita, Catherine Loveday, and Chris Kennett. "Music and Memory in Advertising: Music as a Device of Implicit Learning and Recall." *Music, Sound & the Moving Image* 1.1 (2007): 51–71. Print.
Anderson, Ben. "A Principle of Hope: Recorded Music, Listening Practices and the Immanence of Utopia."*Georgrafiska Annaler: Series B, Human Geography* 84.3–4 (2002): 211–27. Print.
Anderson, Chris. *Free: The Future of A Radical Price*. New York: Hyperion, 2009. Print.
Appadurai, Arjun. *Modernity at Large: Cultural Dimensions of Globalization*. Minneapolis: University of Minnesota Press, 1996. Print.
Aristotle. *The Politics*. New York: Penguin, 1992. Print.
Associated Press. "Guillen Says Latinos at a Disadvantage." *ESPN.com*. ESPN, 3 Aug. 2010. Web. 11 Nov. 2011.
———. "Lasorda Says U.S. Can't Allow Loss." *ESPN.com*. ESPN, 5 Mar. 2009. Web. 11 Nov. 2011.
———. "Secret Ballot Eliminates Baseball, Softball." *ESPN.com*. ESPN. 8 July 2005. Web. 11 Nov. 2011.
———. "Woman Says Complaint Got Her Fired." *ESPN.com*. ESPN, 17 Oct. 2003. Web. 11 Nov. 2011.
Astleford, Andrew. "U.S. Baseball Team Hopes Beijing Isn't the Last Out." *Washington Post* 4 Aug. 2008: E1. Print.
Badler, Ben. "Teams Spend Aggressively for Latin Players." *Baseball America*. Baseball America, 25 July 2011. Web. 11 Aug. 2011.
"Baseball and Softball Strike Out with IOC." *China Daily*. China Daily, 25 Aug. 2008. Web. 11 Nov. 2011.
The Baseball Hall of Fame and Museum Japan. *The Baseball Hall of Fame and Museum*. Tokyo: The Baseball Hall of Fame and Museum Japan, 2011. Print.
"Baseball Teams with More International Players Draw More Fans, Profits." *University of Michigan News Service*. University of Michigan, 9 Feb. 2010. Web. 11 Nov. 2011.
Bashford, Suzy. "Give and Take." *Marketing* 13 Dec. 2006: 26–27. *ProQuest*. Web. 11 Nov. 2011.
Beaton, Rod. "Fan's Internet Sites, MLB Clash Over Copyright." *USA Today* 21 Aug. 2002, Final ed.: 6C. Print.
Beck, Jason. "Tiger Fans Will Get Their Rally Towels: Fans Demand Prompts Additional

Giveaway at Comerica." MLB.com. Major League Baseball, 20 Oct. 2006. Web. 11 Nov. 2011.

Becker, Michael. "Matsui Brings Bat, New Audience to Angels." *Press-Enterprise* [Riverside, CA]. Press-Enterprise, 31 Mar. 2010. Web. 11 Nov. 2011.

Beggy, Carol, and Mark Shanahan. "'Sweet Caroline' Revealed." *Boston Globe*. Boston Globe, 21 Nov. 2007. Web. 11 Nov. 2011.

Belson, Ken. "Teams Looking for a Little More Bounce from Bobbleheads." *New York Times* 11 July 2010, sec. SP: 2. Print.

Bishop, Ron. "Stealing the Signs: A Semiotic Analysis of the Changing Nature of Professional Sports Logos."*Social Semiotics* 11.1 (2001): 23–40. Print.

Blackwood, Thomas. "Bushido Baseball? Three 'Fathers' and the Invention of a Tradition." *Social Science Japan Journal* 11.2 (2008): 223–40. Print.

Blair, Jeff. "Major League Baseball and the Olympics Just Don't Need Each Other." *The Globe and Mail* [Toronto] 12 Aug. 2008: S11. Print.

Blenkinsopp, Alexander. "Asian Invasion: Baseball's Ambassadors." *Harvard International Review* 24.1 (2002): 12–13. Web. 11 Nov. 2011.

Bloom, Barry M. "Obama May Help Bid for Olympic Return." MLB.com. Major League Baseball, 6 Nov. 2008. Web. 11 Nov. 2011.

Boaz, David. "Yellow Peril Reinfects America: U.S. Hostility Turns to Japan." *Wall Street Journal* 7 Apr. 1989: 14. *LexisNexis*. Web. 11 Nov. 2011.

Bodley, Hal. "Cooperstown's Diamond Anniversary." *2011 National Baseball Hall of Fame and Museum*. Cooperstown, NY: National Baseball Hall of Fame and Museum, 2011. Print.

Bogard, Leo. *The Age of Television: A Study of Viewing Habits and the Impact of Television on American Life*. 1956. New York: Frederick Ungar, 1972. Print.

Bondy, Filip. "U.S. Mastery on Diamond Is Long Gone." *New York Daily News* 24 Mar. 2009, final ed.: 46. *LexisNexis*. Web. 11 Nov. 2011.

Bowe, John. "The Copyright Enforcers." *New York Times* 6 Aug. 2010, final ed., sec. M: 38. *LexisNexis*. Web. 11 Nov. 2011.

"Brewsfan.net Net Forum."*Brewersfan.net*. Yuku, 16 Nov. 2010. Web. 11 Nov. 2011.

Brewster, Mike. "Bill Veeck: A Baseball Mastermind." *Bloomberg Businessweek*. Bloomberg, 27 Oct. 2004. Web. 11 Nov. 2011.

Brown, Maury. "Interview: Bob Bowman — President and CEO — MLBAM." *The Biz of Baseball*. Business of Sports Network, 1 Jan. 2008. Web. 11 Nov. 2011.

_____. "MLB Advanced Media Wins '2010 Best in Digital Sports Media Award.'" *The Biz of Baseball*. Business of Sports Network, 20 May 2010. Web. 11 Nov. 2011.

_____. "MLBAM: The Stealthy Money Machine." *Hardball Times*. Hardball Times, 5 Dec. 2005. Web. 11 Nov. 2011.

_____. "Understanding the Real Value of MLBAM and MLB Network." *The Biz of Baseball*. Business of Sports Network, 19 Jan. 2009. Web. 11 Nov. 2011.

Browne, Ian. "Tazawa Officially in Fold for Red Sox." MLB.com. Major League Baseball, 4 Dec. 2008. Web. 11. Nov. 2011.

Buccigross, John. "Every Sport Is Music to My Ears." *ESPN.com*. ESPN, 2 Aug. 2004. Web. 11 Nov. 2011.

"Can Baseball Bounce Back? After Economic Downturn Threw the Sport a Curve, MLB is Hoping Revenue Will Increase This Season." *Toronto Star* 2 Apr. 2010. sec. Business: B3. *LexisNexis*. Web. 11 Nov. 2011.

Caple, Jim. "Bobbleheads Are Bigger Than Ever." *ESPN.com*. ESPN, 13 May 2010. Web. 11 Nov. 2011.

_____. "What Happened to Cartoon Logos?" *ESPN.com*. ESPN, 19 Jan. 2011. Web. 10 June 2011.

Castle, George. *Baseball and the Media: How Fans Lose in Today's Coverage of the Game*. Lincoln: University of Nebraska Press, 2006. Print.

Chacar, Aya, and William Hesterly. "Innovations and Value Creation in Major League Baseball, 1860–2000." *Business History* 46.3 (2004): 407–38. Print

Chidester, David. "The Church of Baseball, the Fetish of Coca-Cola, and the Potlatch of Rock 'n' Roll: Theoretical Models for the Study of Religion in American Popular Culture." *Journal of the American Academy of Religion* 64 (1996): 743–65. Print.
Chisox73. "Help Bring Back Old Brewers Logo!!" *Baseball Fever*. Baseball Fever, 5 Dec. 2004. Web. 11 Nov. 2011.
Cohen, Jeff. "Burr Ridge Auctioneers Subpoenaed in Sports Memorabilia Fraud Probe, Sources Say: Authorities Said to be Investigating Possible 'Shill Bidding' to Drive up Prices on Collectibles." *Chicago Tribune*. Chicago Tribune, 5 Aug. 2008. Web. 11 Nov. 2011.
Cook, Kevin, and Richard O'Brien. "Foul Balls." *Sports Illustrated* 89.20 (1998): 36. *Academic Search Premier*. Web. 8 Dec. 2010.
Costa, Brian. "MLB Authenticators Ready for A-Rod's 600th Homer." *Wall Street Journal*. Wall Street Journal, 21 July 2010. Web. 11 Nov. 2011.
"Cowboys, NFL Big Winners at 3rd Annual Sports Business Awards." *Sports Business Daily*. Street and Smith's Sports Group, 21 May 2010. Web. 11 Nov. 2011.
Creamer, Chris. "Houston Astros Logo (2000)." *Sportslogos.net*. Chris Creamer, 17 Mar. 2008. Web. 11 Nov. 2011.
———. "St. Louis Cardinals Logo (1967–1997)." *Sportslogos.net*. Chris Creamer, 16 July 2008. Web. 11. Nov. 2011.
Cryns, Jim."At Bat Music."*ExpressMilwaukee.com*. Express Milwaukee, 14 Aug. 2008. Web. 11 Nov. 2011.
Dall, Steve. Personal interview. 24 January 2011.
Dachman, Jason. "MLBAM's Inzerillo on the Future of Live Video Streaming." *Sports Video Group*. Sports Video Group, 17 May 2010. Web. 11 Nov. 2011.
D'Angelo, Tom. "Opinions Mixed on Florida Marlins' Vuvuzela Giveaway." *Palm Beach Post*. Palm Beach Post, 20 June 2010. Web. 24 Sep. 2010.
Danesi, Marcel. *Why It Sells: Decoding the Meanings of Brand Names, Logos, Ads, and Other Marketing and Advertising Ploys*. New York: Rowman & Littlefield, 2008. Print.
Davis, Jessica. "Sports Memorabilia Lawsuit Against eBay Moves Forward." *Infoworld* 23 Oct. 2000: 20. Print.
Dawidoff, Nicholas. "Field of Kitsch: Is Nostalgia Wrecking Baseball?" *The New Republic*. Byliner, 17 & 24 Aug. 2004: 22–24. Web. 11 Nov. 2011.
DeMarco, Tony. "Angels' Method Proving a Consistent Winner." *NBC Sports*. MSNBC, 6 Mar. 2010. Web. 11 Nov. 2011.
"DL Starting List Drops from 106 to 69." *ESPN.com*. ESPN, 6 Apr. 2009. Web. 11 Nov. 2011.
Dunkin, Amy. "Sports Memorabilia: A Way to Field Some Dreams." *Business Week* 13 Aug. 1990: 122. Print.
Ehrenreich, Barbara. *Dancing in the Streets: A History of Collective Joy*. New York: Henry Holt, 2006. Print.
"ESPN360.com Taps MLB Advanced Media for ESPN3.com." *ESPNMediaZone3.com*. ESPN, 8 Mar. 2010. Web. 11 Nov. 2011.
"ESPN's 20th MLB Season of Chronicling the Moments." *Sports Media News*. Sports Media News, 17 Mar. 2009. Web. 11 Nov. 2011.
"ESPN Fact Sheet." *ESPN Media Zone*. ESPN, 10 Jan. 2010. Web. 11 Nov. 2011.
Etoh, Mitsumasa. "WBC-Uneijou no Kadai [WBC: Operational Issues]" *Sports Navi Plus*, 24 Feb. 2009. Web. 30 Nov. 2010.
Fatsis, Stefan. "Living Dolls: Collectors Clamor for Bobbleheads of Beloved Sports Figures; Head-Wagging Game Premiums Given Free to Fans Have More Than Sentimental Value." *Wall Street Journal* 14 Mar. 2001, Eastern ed.: A1. Print.
Federal Bureau of Investigation San Diego. "Operation Bullpen." *Federal Bureau of Investigation, San Diego*. Federal Bureau of Investigation, April 2000. Web. 11 Nov. 2011.
"Fewer Sports for London Olympics." *BBC Sport*. BBC, 8 July 2005. Web. 11 Nov. 2011.
Fisher, Eric. "Baseball Adopts Nationals Name." *Washington Times* 23 Nov. 2004: A1. *LexisNexis*. Web. 11 Nov. 2011.

_____. "MLB Pays $66M for Tickets.com." *Washington Times* 16 Feb. 2005. sec. Sports: C3. *LexisNexis*. Web. 11 Nov. 2011.
_____. "MLBAM Close to Deal for HOF Site." *Sports Business Journal Daily*. Street and Smith's Sports Group, 29 Aug. 2005. Web. 11 Nov. 2011.
_____. "Ten Years Later, MLBAM Still Evolving." *Sports Business Journal Daily*. Street and Smith's Sports Group, 21 Mar. 2011. Web. 11 Nov. 2011.
Fitzpatrick, Frank. "Phils Prospect: Keep Baseball in Olympics." *Philadelphia Inquirer* 24 Aug. 2008, City-D ed: E12. Print.
"FOX Hits Three-Year Ratings High for Primetime MLB." *Sports Media Watch*. Sports Media Watch. 29 May 2011. Web. 11 Nov. 2011.
Fraley, Gerry. "Reversed Call Boots U.S.: United States 4, Japan 3." *Dallas Morning News* 13 Mar. 2006. 1st ed.: 2C. Print.
Freeman, Mike. "MLB All-Star Game Should Emigrate from Arizona over Immigration." *CBS Sports*. CBS, 28 Apr. 2010. Web. 11 Nov. 2011.
"Frequently Asked Questions." *MLBPA Info*. MLBPA, n.d. Web. 11 Nov. 2011.
Fullerton, Sam, and G. Russell Merz. "The Four Domains of Sports Marketing: A Conceptual Framework." *Sport Marketing Quarterly* 17.2 (2008): 90–108. Print.
Furuuchi, Yoshiaki. *MLB's Global Strategy through the WBC: The Background of the 600-Billion Yen Business*. Tokyo: PHP, 2009. Print.
Gallo, DJ. "Give Me Free Stuff, or Give Me Death." *ESPN.com*. ESPN, 9 Apr. 2010. Web. 11 Nov. 2011.
"Game-Used Community Protects Collectors." *Sports Collectors Daily*. Sports Collectors Daily, 30 Oct. 2006. Web. 11 Nov. 2011.
Glanville, Doug. "The World in One Game." *New York Times*. New York Times, 2 Apr. 2009. Web. 11 Nov. 2011.
Grant, Evan. "Uniform, Logo Changing Again? Team Petitions MLB to Alter Look for Third Time Since End of '99 Season." *Dallas Morning News* 26 May 2002, Sports Day sec.: 10B. *LexisNexis*. Web. 11 Nov. 2011.
Green, David, and Valerie Loveluck. "Understanding a Corporate Symbol." *Applied Cognitive Psychology* 8 (1994): 37–47. Print.
Gregor, Scot. "Setting Sun?" *Sporting News: Baseball 2010* (2010): 16–20. Print.
Grotticelli, Michael. "MLB's Advanced Media Group to Stream ESPN Events Online." *Broadcasting Engineering*. Penton Media, 12 Mar. 2010. Web. 11 Nov. 2011.
Grover, Ronald. "Watching the World Cup via MLB." *Bloomberg Businessweek*. Bloomberg, 3 June 2010. Web. 11 Nov. 2011.
_____. "The World Cup Online, Brought to You by Major League Baseball." *Bloomberg Businessweek*. Bloomberg, 3 June 2010. Web. 11 Nov, 2011.
Guevara, Marcano, and David P. Fidler. *Stealing Lives: The Globalization of Baseball and the Tragic Story of Alexis Quiroz*. Bloomington: Indiana University Press, 2002. Print.
Hansell, Saul. "Technology: Baseball Test May Soon Show if Time Is Right for Web Video." *New York Times*. New York Times, 27 Jan. 2003. Web. 11 Nov. 2011.
Hayashi, Yuka. "Japanese Nervously Await Testimony of Toyota's President." *Wall Street Journal*. Wall Street Journal, 22 Feb. 2010. Web. 11 Nov. 2011.
Hayes, Dan. "Shooting the Breeze with ... Baseball Hall of Fame Official Brad Horn." *North County Times*. North County Times, 30 Oct. 2010. Web. 11 Nov. 2011.
Heidegger, Martin. "Questions Concerning Technology." *Martin Heidegger: Basic Writings*. Ed. David Farrell Krell. New York: Harper & Row, 2008. Print.
Hiestand, Michael. "Baseball on Fox: A Thing of the Future." *USA Today*. USA Today, 3 May 2005. Web. 11 Nov. 2011.
_____. "MLB Takes Hardball Stance on Web Sites' Use of Its Data." *USA Today*. USA Today, 23 Oct. 2003. Web. 11 Nov. 2011.
Henderson, Pamela W., and Joseph A. Cote. "Guidelines for Selecting or Modifying Logos." *Journal of Marketing* 62 (1998): 14–30. Print.
Horn, Brad. Personal interview. 13 May 2011.

Hutton, Brian P. "Baseball in the Digital Age: The Role of Online and Mobile Content in Major League Baseball's Media Product Portfolio." MA thesis. University of North Texas, 2010. Print.
Hyle, Robert Regis. "Memorabilia Boom Spurs Coverage Gains." *National Underwriter/ Property & Casualty Risk & Benefits Management* 102.42 (1998): 17. Print.
Iijima, Tomonori. "Stop Broadcasting the Major Games." *Nikkan Sports*. Nikkan Sports, 19 July 2007. Web. 11 Nov. 2011.
"Important Enough to Collect?" *gameuseduniverse.com*. Game-Used Universe, 2 Jan. 2011. Web. 11 Nov. 2011.
"IOC Decision Tough on Baseball, Softball." *Daily Yomiuri* 16 Aug. 2009: 4. Print.
Irwin, Richard L., William A. Sutton, and Larry McCarthy. *Sport Promotion and Sales Management*. 2nd. Champaign, IL: Human Kinetics, 2008.
Iseman, Ellen M. "A Spring Training Pilgrimage Amid Changing Times." *New York Times* 7 Mar. 2010. Sports sec.: 2.*LexisNexis*. Web. 11 Nov. 2011.
Japan Professional Baseball Players' Association. "Other." *Japan Professional Baseball Players' Association*. Japan Professional Baseball Players' Association, n.d. Web. 11 Nov. 2011.
_____. "Transfer."*Japan Professional Baseball Players' Association*. Japan Professional Baseball Players' Association, n.d. Web. 11 Nov. 2011.
Jenkins, Lee. "Disputed Call Overshadows U.S. Victory over Japan." *New York Times* 13 Mar. 2006, late ed.: 1. Print.
Kadlec, Daniel. "Back in the Game." *Time* 16 Aug. 1999: 74. Print.
"Kansas City Promotion Guidelines." MLB.com. Major League Baseball, n.d. Web. 11 Nov. 2011.
Kass, Mark. "At Miller Park, It's Not Always about the Game: Aleta Mercer a Key Player in Team's Entertainment Lineup." *Business Journal of Milwaukee*. American City Business Journal, 23 Mar. 2007. Web. 15 Dec. 2009.
Kato, Hiroko. Personal interview. 3 Aug. 2007.
Katz, Harry, Frank Ceresi, Phil Michel, Wilson McBee, and Susan Reyburn. *Baseball Americana: Treasures from the Library of Congress*. New York: HarperCollins, 2009. Print.
Katz, Jeffery. "Take Me Out to the Rock Concert: Baseball Now Part of a Multimedia Experience." *NPR.org*. NPR, 23 July 2001. Web. 11 Nov. 2011.
Kiuchi, Yuya. "Obama for Obama: Barack Obama in Japanese Popular Culture." *The Iconic Obama, 2007–2009*. Eds. Derrais Carter and Nicholas Yanes. Jefferson, NC: McFarland, 2012. Print.
Klayman, Ben. "Analysis: No Perfect Game but MLB to Post Record Revenue." *Reuters*. Reuters, 25 Oct. 2010. Web. 30 Nov. 2010.
Klein, Alan M. *Growing the Game: The Globalization of Major League Baseball*. New Haven: Yale University Press, 2006. Print.
Klein, Jeff. "I.O.C. Decision Draws Cheers and Complaints from Athletes." *New York Times*. New York Times, 13 Aug. 2009. Web. 11 Nov. 2011.
Kohl's. Kohls, n.d. Web. 12 Aug. 2011.
LaFeber, Walter. *Michael Jordan and the New Global Capitalism*. New York: W. W. Norton, 2002. Print.
Lauer, John. "Traces of the Real: Autographomania and the Cult of the Signers in Nineteenth-Century America." *Text and Performance Quarterly* 27.2 (2007): 143–63. Print.
Lee, Soohwan, and Hyosung Chun. "Economic Values of Professional Sport Franchises in the United States." *The Sport Journal*. United States Sports Academy, n.d. Web. 11 Nov. 2011.
Lemire, Joe. "Inside the Prank-Filled, Thoroughly-Researched World of At-Bat Music." SI.com. Turner-SI Digital, 31 Jan. 2011. Web. 11 Nov. 2011.
Lemke, Tim. "A Different World: WBC Draws Bigger Buzz, Record Ratings." *Washington Times* 26 Mar. 2009: C05. *LexisNexis*. Web. 11 Nov. 2011.

_____. "Bite-Sized Fantasy Baseball: MLB.com Seeks to Lessen Amount of Time Required to Play." *Washington Times* 19 Mar. 2008: C02. *LexisNexis*. Web. 11 Nov. 2011.
Lengel, David. "Baseball and Softball Deserve to Remain Olympic Sports." *The Guardian* [London]. Guardian News and Media, 14 Aug. 2008. Web. 11 Nov. 2011.
Levy, Steven. "Covering All the Online Bases: The Digital Business of Major League Baseball Started out As a Mess. Now It Has $400 Million in Revenue and May Revolutionize the Economics of the Sport." *Newsweek*. Newsweek, 25 June 2007. Web. 11 Nov. 2011.
Liscio, Stephanie. "Cap Week: Time to Retire Chief Wahoo." *ESPN.com*. ESPN, 13 May 2011. Web. 11 Nov. 2011.
Long, Mary M., and Leon G. Schiffman. "Swatch Fever: An Allegory for Understanding the Paradox of Collecting." *Psychology & Marketing* 14.5 (1997): 495–509. Print.
Longman, Jere. "In Bottom of 9th, Baseball Plots Return to the Games." *New York Times* 17 July 2008, sec D: 5. Print.
Lupica, Mike. "Bud Selig Should Move 2011 MLB All-Star Game Out of Arizona if New Immigration Law Isn't Stopped." *New York Daily News*. New York Daily News, 29 Apr. 2010. Web. 11 Nov. 2011.
Machida, Akira. "MLB Targets Japanese Market." *SendenKaigi* 1 June 2007: 53. Print.
Major League Baseball. *Former Yankee Don Mattingly Gets Behind the MLB Authentication Program*. 9 July 2001. New York: Major League Baseball. Print.
_____. *Major League Baseball: International Business Review*. Tokyo: Major League Baseball Japan, 2006. Print.
_____. "A Decade of Growth." *Major League Baseball: International Business Review*. New York: Major League Baseball, 2009. Print.
"Major League Baseball Has Never Been More Popular." *Wall Street Journal* 10 Apr. 2010: A12. Print.
"Major League Baseball International Renews Four Broadcast Agreements and Signs One New Television Deal." MLB.com. Major League Baseball, 1 June 2009. Web. 11 Nov. 2011.
Major League Baseball Japan. *MLB in Japan*. Tokyo: Major League Baseball Japan, 2007.
"Mantle Memorabilia: Foul Balls." SI.com. Turner-SI Digital, 16 Nov. 1998. Web. 11 Nov. 2011.
Marcano, Arturo J., and David P. Fidler. "Baseball's Exploitation of Latin Talent." *NACLA Report on the Americas* 37.5 (2004): 14–18. ProQuest. Web. 11 Nov. 2011.
"Mark McGwire 50th Homerun Baseball." *Christies*. Christies, n.d. Web. 11 Nov. 2011.
"MasterCard and Major League Baseball Advanced Media Reward Fans for Loyalty with Priceless Perks." *MasterCard News Release*. MasterCard Worldwide, 15 July 2010. Web. 11 Nov. 2011.
Matsushita, Shigenori. "Individualist Ichiro and Collectivist Matsui." *President* 3 Sept. 2007: 21. Print.
"Matsuzaka, Red Sox Reach Agreement on Six-Year Deal." *ESPN.com*. ESPN, 23 Feb. 2007.Web.11 Nov. 2011.
Mayeda, David Tokiharu. "From Model Minority to Economic Threat: Media Portrayals of Major League Baseball: Pitchers Hideo Nomo and Hideki Irabu." *Journal of Sport & Social Issues* 23.2 (1999): 203–17. Print.
McCallum, Jack. "Will You Please Sign This?" SI.com. Turner-SI Digital, 14 Nov. 2005. Web. 11 Nov. 2011.
McCarron, Anthony. "It's Risky Business Yankees May Lose Yen if They Let Godzilla Go." *New York Daily News* 21 Nov. 2009, sports final ed., sec. Sports: 47. *LexisNexis*. Web. 11 Nov. 2011.
McCoy, Adrian. "Speculation Mounts on KDKA Radio Sale." *Pittsburgh Post-Gazette*. PG Publishing, 1 Aug. 2008. Web. 11 Nov. 2011.
McDonald, Mark, and Daniel Rascher. "Does Bat Day Make Cents? The Effect of Promotions on the Demand for Major League Baseball." *Journal of Sport Management* 14 (2000): 8–27. Print.

McGray, Douglas. "Japan's Gross National Cool." *Foreign Policy* 130 (2002): 44–54. Print.
McIntosh, William D., and Brandon Schmeichel. "Collectors and Collecting: A Social Psychological Perspective." *Leisure Sciences* 26 (2004): 85–97. Print.
McLeod, Ken. "The Construction of Masculinity in African American Music and Sports." *American Music* 27.2 (2009): 204–26. Print.
Mickle, Tripp. "MLS Leaving MLBAM, Taking Sites In-House." *Sports Business Journal Daily*. Street and Smith's Sports Group, 5 Oct. 2009. Web. 11 Nov. 2011.
Mihoces, Gary. "Logos Go One Better: Teams Alter Image, Sales with Changes." *USA Today* 18 July 1995: 3C. Print.
Miller, Doug. "@-Bat Music: Oakland Athletics." MLB.com. Major League Baseball, 26 Sept. 2008. Web. 11 Nov. 2011.
Miller, Doug, and Mike Krise. "@-Bat Music: Pittsburgh Pirates." MLB.com. Major League Baseball, 12 Aug. 2008. Web. 11 Nov. 2011. jor League BaseballAthletics" in African American Music and Sports."
———. "@-Bat Music: Los Angeles Dodgers." MLB.com. Major League Baseball, 25 Apr. 2008. Web. 11 Nov. 2011.
Miller, John R. "Our Fading National Pastime." *Wall Street Journal* 6 Apr. 2010: A17. Print.
Miller, Toby, Geoffrey Lawrence, Jim McKay, and David Rowe. "Modifying the Sign: Sport and Globalization." *Social Text* 60 (1999): 15–33. Print.
Milwaukee Brewers. *2010 Guest Information Guide*. 2010. Print.
"MLB Advanced Media." MLB.com. Major League Baseball, n.d. Web. 11. Nov. 2011.
"MLB Advanced Media Plays Ball with World Championship Sports Network in a Strategic Partnership and Equity Position." *MLB*.com. Major League Baseball, 29 Nov. 2005. Web. 11 Nov. 2011.
"MLB Authentication Program."MLB.com. Major League Baseball, n.d. Web. 11 Nov. 2011.
"MLB Ballpark Rankings: Promotions." SI.com. Turner-Si Digital, n.d. Web. 11 Nov. 2010.
"MLB, FOX, and Turner Reach New Television Agreements." MLB.com. Major League Baseball, 11 July 2006. Web. 11 Nov. 2011.
"MLB, Players Announce Internet Deal." *Washington Post* 20 Jan. 2005, final ed., sec. Sports: D09. LexisNexis. Web. 11 Nov. 2011.
Moorman, Anita M., and Marion E. Hambrick. "To License or Not to License: That Is the Question for Professional Sport Leagues and the NCAA." *Sport Marketing Quarterly* 18.3 (2009): 160–64. Print.
Muensterberger, Werner. *Collecting: An Unruly Passion*. Princeton: Princeton University Press, 1994. Print.
Mulligan, Robert F., and A.J. Grube. "Modeling Markets for Sports Memorabilia." *Journal of Economics and Economic Education Research* 7.2 (2006): 75–102. Print.
Mullin, Bernard James, Stephen Hardy, and William Sutton. *Sport Marketing*. Champaign, IL: Human Kinetics Publishers, 2000. Print.
"Music in the Market Place." *Better Business Bureau*. Better Business Bureau, 14 Dec. 2007. Web. 11 Nov. 2011.
"Name That Tune in MLB." *ESPN.com*..ESPN, 5 Aug. 2004. Web. 11 Nov. 2011.
Nachbar, Jack, and Kevin Lause. "An Introduction to the Study of Popular Culture: What Is This Stuff that Dreams Are Made of?" *Popular Culture: An Introductory Text*. Eds. Jack Nachbar, and Kevin Lause. Madison: University of Wisconsin Press, 1992. Print.
Nauright, John. "Global Games: Culture, Political Economy and Sport in the Globalised World of the 21st Century." *Third World Quarterly* 25.7(2004): 1325–36. Print.
NESN. "About." *NESN*. New England Sports Network, n.d. Web. 11 Nov. 2011.
"Nihon Kyukaiwa Dai Koukyou Jidaiwo Norikoerarerunoka?" [Can NPB Survive the Great Depression Era?]. *The Real Live Web*. Real Live 26. Dec. 2009. Web. 11 Nov. 2011.
"Nihon Kyukaini Kachimewa?" [Can the Japanese Baseball World Win?]. *ZAKZAK*. Sankei Digital, 29 Sept. 2009. Web. 11 Nov. 2011.

Nipps, Emily. "Free Rings Go For $125." *St. Petersburg Times* 16 Apr. 2009: 1B. Print.
"Nishioka Major Chousene" [Nishioka Challenges Himself in the Major]. *Sponichi*. 21 Oct. 2010. Web. 11 Nov. 2011.
"Nittere Major Leaguer Kirisute" [Nippon Television Gives up on the Major League Players]. *ZAKZAK*. Sankei Digital, 7 Apr. 2009. Web. 11 Nov. 2011.
"Nomu-san: Nihon-jin Major" [Coach Nomu on Japanese MLB Players]. *Sports Watch*. Sports Watch, 15 Nov. 2010. Web. 11 Nov. 2011.
"Non-U.S. Born MLB Players at Lowest Level Since 2006."*Reuters*. Reuters. 6 Apr. 2010. Web. 11 Nov. 2011.
Novak, Ralph. "The Fans Welcome Back Bill Veeck — as in Pain in the Neck for Baseball's Establishment." *People*. People Magazine, 19 Apr. 1976. Web. 11 Nov. 2010.
O'Keeffe, Michael. "Expensive Dirt: Steiner Sports Helps Yanks, Mets Cash in on Game-Used Equipment." *New York Daily News* 26 Nov. 2006, sports final ed., sec. Sports: 62. *LexisNexis*. Web. 11 Nov. 2011.
Olson, Catherine Applefeld. "Pro Sports Marketing Pitches Hits for Athletic Events." *Allbusiness.com*. Allbusiness.com, 28 Sept. 2002. Web. 11 Nov. 2011.
"Orioles Uniforms and Logos." MLB.com. Major League Baseball, n.d. Web. 11 Nov. 2011.
Ortiz, Jorge L. "MLB's Advanced Media Arm Pulls in Profits." *USA Today*. USA Today, 5 Dec. 2007. Web. 11 Nov. 2011.
_____. "With Ticket Sales Down, MLB Banks on Bargains." *USA Today*. USA Today, 2 Apr. 2009. Web. 11 Nov. 2011.
Passan, Jeff. "Future Is Now for the WBC." *Yahoo!Sports*. Yahoo, 6 Mar. 2009. Web. 11 Nov. 2011.
_____. "Team USA, WBC in World of Hurt." *Yahoo!Sports*. Yahoo, 16 Mar. 2009. Web. 11 Nov. 2011.
_____. "Will Yu Darvish Cross the Pacific to Pitch?" *Yahoo!Sports*. Yahoo, 15 Nov. 2011. Web. 18 Nov. 2011.
"Post Your Photo-Matched Game-Used Items Here." *gameuseduniverse.com*. Game-Used Universe, n.d. Web. 28 Jan. 2011.
"Primetime MLB on Fox Down from Last Year, but Hits Season-High." *Sports Media Watch*. Sports Media Watch, 20 May 2011. Web. 11 Nov. 2011.
"Product Overview" *Click Effects*. Click Effects. 14 Jan. 2010. Web. 14 Jan. 2010.
"Promotional Products Reach Efficiently, Don't Annoy: Survey." *Promo Magazine*. Promo Magazine, 16 Dec. 2009. Web. 11 Nov. 2011.
"Promotions and Giveaways." *Philadelphia Phillies*. Major League Baseball, n.d. Web. 27 Sept. 2010.
Purcell, Kristen, Lee Raine, Amy Mitchell, Tom Rosenstiel, and Kenny Olmstead. "Understanding the Participatory News Consumer." *Pew Internet & American Life Project*. Pew Research Center, 1 Mar. 2010. Web. 11 Nov. 2011.
"Questions re: Steiner & MLB Authentication." *gameuseduniverse.com*. Game-Used Universe, 18 Mar. 2008. Web. 28 Jan. 2011.
"Rays Schedule." *Tampa Bay Rays*. Major League Baseball, n.d. Web. 6 June 2010.
Reed, Keith."Dice-K Is Already Pitching for Sox — in Japanese Ads." *Tribune Business News* 30 Dec. 2006. *ProQuest*. Web. 11 Nov. 2011.
_____."Sox Have Dice-K, but Rivals Reaping Ad Dollars." *Tribune Business News* 25 Apr. 2007. *ProQuest*. Web. 11 Nov. 2011.
Rein, Irving, Philip Kotler, and Ben Shields. *The Elusive Fan: Reinventing Sports in a Crowded Marketplace*. Chicago: McGraw-Hill, 2006. Print.
Rivenburg, Roy. "Ballpark Organists: They're Out." *Los Angeles Times*. Los Angeles Times. 11 June 2005. Web. 11 Nov. 2011.
Sacraceno, Jon. "Ichiro Changes Perspective: Mariners Star Is Trying to Fulfill His Needs." *USA Today* 16 May 2007, final ed., sec. Sports: 1C. *LexisNexis*. Web. 11 Nov. 2011.
Sage, George H. "Patriotic Images and Capitalist Profit: Contradictions of Professional

Team Sports Licensed Merchandise." *Sociology of Sport Journal* 13.1 (1996): 1–11. Print.
Sandomir, Richard. "Baseball's Web Site Is Big Business." *New York Times*. New York Times, 2 Apr. 2006. Web. 11 Nov. 2011.
———. "Miller Says Hall Is 'Trying to Rewrite History." *New York Times*. New York Times, 6 Dec. 2010. Web. 11 Nov. 2011.
Savran, Stan. "Stadium Music Has Gone to Dogs." *Pittsburgh Post-Gazette*. PG Publishing, 22 Oct. 2000. Web. 11 Nov. 2011.
Schwartz, Alan. "Take Me Out to the Web Site!" *Newsweek*. Newsweek 14 Oct. 2002. Web. 11 Nov. 2011.
Seideman, David, and John F. Dickerson. "And a Fan Gets a Souvenir." *Time* 6 Dec. 1993: 24. Print.
Shapiro, Walter, John Dickerson, Janet I-Chin Tu, and David S. Jackson. "Bummer of '94." *Time*. Time Inc. 22 Aug. 1994. Web. 11 Nov. 2011.
Sheinin, Dave. "Memorabilia Swings Toward Authenticity." *Washington Post* 11 Jan. 2001, final ed., Sports sec.: D2. Print.
Shelton, William E. "Higher Education, Higher Values: The Anatomy of a Logo Decision." *Educational Record* 72.3 (1991): 36–38. Print.
Silva, Steve. "Red Sox Unveil New Club Logos and Uniforms." *Boston Globe*. Boston Globe, 11 Dec. 2008. Web. 11 Nov. 2011.
Small, Jim. Personal interview. 23 June 2011.
"Small Catalog/Web Merchant."*Multichannel Merchant*. 2006: 52. Print.
Smeltz, Nate. "Baseball Tonight Viewership Up 61 Percent During MLB Division Series." *ESPN Media Zone*. ESPN, 15 Oct. 2010. Web. 11 Nov. 2011.
Snyder, Matt. "Injuries Not Isolated to WBC." *AOL News*. AOL, 18 Mar. 2009. Web. 11 Nov. 2011.
Spangler, Todd. "MLBAM Inks Ad Deal with Auditude: Major League Baseball Advanced Media Previously Had Advertising Deal with Yahoo." *Multichannel News*. New Bay Media, 6 Apr. 2011. Web. 11 Nov. 2011.
"Sports Digest." *Irish Times* 21 Oct. 2009, sec. Sport: 8. Print.
Sports & Retail Editors/Baseball Writers & Columnists. "MLB Names Retail Partners for MLB Authentication Program Memorabilia." *Business Wire* 5 Mar. 2001: 1. *ProQuest*. Web. 11 Nov. 2011.
Stack, Kyle. "Behind the Scenes with Baseball's Authentication Process." *SI.com*. Turner-SI Digital, 17 Dec. 2010. Web. 11 Nov. 2011.
Stars_Rangers_82. "Which Is the Best Current MLB Team Logo—Poll #3." *Baseballnation.net*. Baseball Nation, 30 Mar. 2011. Web. 11 Nov. 2011.
Steinberg, Dan. "Authenticating Strasburg Balls and Dirt." *Washington Post* 15 June 2010, Met 2 ed., sec. Sports: D02. *LexisNexis*. Web. 11 Nov. 2011.
———. "USA Baseball Wins, Bizarrely." *Washington Post*. Washington Post. 14 Aug. 2008. Web. 11 Nov. 2011.
Stone, Brad. "Major League Baseball to Stream ESPN Events." *New York Times* 8 Mar. 2010, Late ed., sec. B: 4. *LexisNexis*. Web. 11 Nov. 2011.
Street, Jim. "Ichiro Keeps Hits Coming, Year after Year," MLB.com. Major League Baseball, 21 July 2009. Web. 11 Nov. 2011.
Szymanski, Stefan, and Andrew Zimbalist. *National Pastime: How Americans Play Baseball and the Rest of the World Plays Soccer*. Washington: Brookings Institution Press, 2005. Print.
Tana, Kyle. "Realities Behind America's Favorite Pastime: The Dominica Republic's Cheap Labor Bazaar." *Washington Report on the Hemisphere* 30. 9 (2010). Web.
Tarnoff, Andy. "Brewers Ponder Old-School Logo." *OnMilwaukee.com*. On Milwaukee, 29 June 2005. Web. 11 Nov. 2011.
Taylor, Rod. "Boosting Head Count."*Promo Magazine*. Promo Magazine, 1 Oct. 2004. Web. 11 Nov. 2011.

Tazzi, Ed. "Just Whose Team Is It Anyway?" *Brandweek* 45.21 (2004): 22. *Business Source Premier*. Web. 8 Mar. 2011.

"Team-by-Team Information." MLB.com. Major League Baseball. n.d. Web. 11 Nov. 2011.

Tedesco, Richard. "Shakin' It Up." *Promo Magazine*. Promo Magazine, 1 Aug. 2008. Web. 1 Nov. 2011.

"There Is More to the American Dream Than Money." *ZAKZAK*. Sankei Digital, 21 Jan. 2007. Web. 10 Mar. 2008.

"They'rrre Out! Olympics Drop Baseball, Softball." *NBC Sports*. MSNBC, 9 July 2005. Web. 11 Nov. 2011.

Tully, Judd. "Take Me Out to the Sports Memorabilia Dealer." *Cigar Aficionado* 9.4 (2001): 189–92. Print.

"2011 Opening Day MLB Rosters Feature 234 Foreign-Born Players: 27.7 Percent of Players Are Foreign-Born, Spanning 14 Countries and Territories." MLB.com. Major League Baseball, 1 Apr. 2011. Web. 11. Nov. 2011.

"Upper Deck Fights Against Unauthorized Memorabilia." *Amusement Business* 107.10 (1995): 24. Print.

Van Riel, Ceess B.M. "The Added Value of Corporate Logos—An Empirical Study." *European Journal of Marketing* 35 (2001): 428–40. *ProQuest*. Web. 11 Nov. 2011.

Van Riper, Tom. "Baseball Looks at the Small Picture." *Forbes*. Forbes, 17 Mar. 2009. Web. 11 Nov. 2011.

Vecsey, George. *Baseball: A History of America's Favorite Game*. New York: Modern Library, 2008. Print.

_____. "Olympics Are Only Spotlight for Some Sports." *New York Times* 16 Aug. 2009: SP8. Print.

Vrooman, John. "Theory of the Perfect Game: Competitive Balance in Monopoly Sports Leagues." *Review of Industrial Organization* 34.1 (2009): 5–44. Print.

Walker, Ben."Red Sox Sweep World Series." *Toronto Star*. Toronto Star, 29 Oct. 2007. Web. 27 Oct. 2011.

Walker, Don. "Brewers Announce Fan Giveaways." *Milwaukee Journal Sentinel*. Milwaukee Journal Sentinel, 21 Feb. 2008. Web. 11 Nov. 2010.

_____. "Brewers Hope to Add Fun to Ol' Ball Game." *Milwaukee Journal Sentinel* 24 Mar. 2003: 3c, 5c. Print.

_____. "MLB Setting the New Media Pace: Web Site Hits Increase Steadily." *Milwaukee Journal Sentinel*. Milwaukee Journal Sentinel, 11 Apr. 2008. Web. 11 Nov. 2011.

Walker, Rob. "Music to Score By: Why Does Stadium Rock All Sound the Same?" *Slate Magazine*. The Slate Group, 12 Feb. 2003. Web. 11 Nov. 2011.

Wendel, Tim. *The New Face of Baseball: The One-Hundred-Year Rise and Triumph of Latinos in America's Favorite Sport*. New York: Philip Lief Group, 2003. Print.

White, Paul. "Japan Frets Over Talent Exodus to North America." *USA Today*. USA Today, 30 Mar. 2007. Web. 11 Nov. 2011.

_____. "Japan Prep Star to MLB?" *USA Today* 29 Sep. 2009, final ed., sec. Sports: 5C. *LexisNexis*. Web. 11 Nov. 2011.

Whitehouse, Randy. "Coming to America: Tazawa Begins His Career with Dogs." *Sun Journal* [Lewiston, ME]. Sun Journal, 12 Apr. 2009. Web. 11 Nov. 2011.

Whiting, Robert. *You Gotta Have Wa*. New York: Vintage, 2009. Print.

_____.*The Meaning of Ichiro: The New Wave From Japan and the Transformation of Our National Pastime*. New York: Warner, 2004.

Williams, Pete. "Clubs Change Face of Freebies." *Sports Business Journal*. Street& Smith's Sports Business Journal, 26 June 2006. Web. 11 Nov. 2011.

Winfree, Jason A., Jill J. McCluskey, Ron C. Mittelhammer, and Rodney Fort. "Location and Attendance in Major League Baseball." *Applied Economics* 36 (2004): 2117–24. Print.

Wingfield, Nick. "Baseball Plans New Web Pitch for Fantasy Games." *Wall Street Journal*. 20 Jan. 2005: D3. *ProQuest*. Web. 11 Nov. 2011.

Womack, Graham. "A Note on Walk-Up Music." *Baseball: Past and Present*. Baseball: Past and Present, 19 Jan. 2010. Web. 11 Nov. 2011.

Wood, Anthony R. "Memorabilia Cop Calls 'Em As He Sees 'Em: Baseball Fighting Fakery with a Seal of Approval." *Philadelphia Inquirer* 11 Oct 2009, city-C ed., News Local sec.: B01. *LexisNexis*. Web. 11 Nov. 2011.

World Baseball Classic. International Baseball Federation, 30 Nov. 2010. Web. 11 Nov. 2011.

Yamaguchi, Mari. "Is Japan-Bashing Behind Toyota's U.S. Woes?" *Japan Times*. Japan Times, 9 Feb. 2010. Web. 11 Nov. 2011.

Yusem, Seymour. "Letter to the Editor." *Wall Street Journal* 13 Apr. 2010: A18. Print.

Zinser, Lynn. "Leading Off: Japan Shows the Way in Baseball." *New York Times*. New York Times, 25 Mar. 2009. Web. 11 Nov. 2011.

Zuckerman, Mark. "Making a Pitch to Return: IBAF Seeking Support to Get Sport Back in Olympics." *Washington Times* 26 May 2009: C02. Print.

_____. "No Use Crying Over Olympic Baseball End." *Washington Times* 12 Aug. 2008: C06. Print.

Index

ABC 81–2, 89
advertisement 9, 10, 21, 40, 43, 63, 82–3, 86, 89, 98, 115, 116, 120, 121, 154, 171–2, 175, 186–7
African Americans 13, 29; *see also* Negro League
All Star Game 85, 124, 169–70, 174, 176
All Star Series 120, 155, 172
All Star tour 152, 161, 172
Alvarado, Robert 32
American culture 111–3, 129, 150
American League 29, 85
Americanism 64, 143
Arizona Diamondbacks 65, 102
ASCAP 12–3, 22
Asia 119, 123, 133, 151, 152, 160, 173, 186, 188; baseball in 136, 139, 152, 157, 172; market in 120, 155, 173–4, 179; players from 119, 123, 154, 159, 179–80, 181
Atlanta Braves 4, 65, 69, 70, 84, 183
attendance 3, 4, 23, 24, 27, 30, 31, 122, 150, 162, 164
auction 4, 39, 45–6, 50, 54
Australia 91, 144, 152, 168, 174, 175, 177
authentication program 43, 44, 46, 47–52, 57–8
autograph 4, 43, 44, 47–8, 49, 52, 55–6, 89, 112, 175; *see also* sweet spot

Baltimore Orioles 19, 61, 65, 83, 127, 161, 183
baseball card 4, 44, 45, 47, 50–1, 121, 154, 155, 174–5
Baseball Tonight 83–4
Beijing 143, 147, 155, 158, 173
blog 18, 36, 38, 128
blues music 13
BMI 12, 13, 22–3
bobbleheads 4, 26–7, 30–1, 33, 34, 35–9, 31, 121, 186, 181

Bonds, Barry 161
Boston Red Sox 14, 31, 63–4, 68–9, 72, 84–5, 89, 97, 102, 114–6, 119, 121, 126–7, 130, 139, 153, 155, 166, 182–3, 186
broadcasting 2, 5, 11, 17, 30, 68, 69, 77–85, 93, 115, 116, 120–7, 136, 140–1, 151, 170–2, 175
Bronx 43, 121
Busch Stadium 188

cable television 5, 77, 81, 83, 84, 85
Canada 138, 170, 176
capitalism 1, 16, 18, 112, 115–6, 117–8, 123, 128, 130–1, 132, 135, 140, 150, 186
cards *see* baseball cards
Catalanotto, Frank 24
CBS 82, 91, 92, 170
cell phones 90, 91
Chase Field 169
Chicago 47, 69, 148, 163
Chicago Cubs 31, 36, 69, 172, 183
Chicago White Sox 19, 36, 64, 102, 145, 151, 166
Chief Wahoo 65, 69–70
Cincinnati Reds 29, 91
Clemente, Roberto 99–100, 152
Cleveland Indians 65, 69–70, 172
click effects 13, 22
coaches in resident 177
Coaching Development Program 177
Colorado Rockies 75, 169
Comerica Park 39
consumer 5, 7, 28, 32, 35, 37, 41, 64, 69, 71, 72, 115, 118, 128, 142, 153, 171, 174
Cooperstown 5–6, 89, 94–6, 104–9, 111–2
Cuba 83, 100, 138, 145, 146, 181
cultural capital 57

Dall, Steve 44, 48, 54, 57
Davidson, Bob 137

design 59, 61, 62–5, 67–8, 72–5
Detroit Tigers 37, 39, 60, 64, 149, 157
DirecTV Latin America 126
doping 138, 143–4, 148–9, 150
Dream Team 138, 144

economics 73, 189
education 5, 69, 75, 98, 101, 110, 176
ESPN 18, 35–6, 70, 81–5, 90, 92, 141, 142
ESPN.com 18, 36, 65, 84, 127, 149
ESPNHD 84
ESPN International 170
ESPN Radio 84
ESPN The Magazine 84
ESPN2 84
ESPN2HD 84
ESPN3.com 84, 87, 92
ESPN3D 84
ESPN360 92

fantasy 87, 90
FBI 46, 47–8, 51
FCC 85
Fehr, Donald 133, 145–6, 148
Fenway Park 14, 85, 94, 120
Fenway Sports Group 85, 115
Field of Dreams 112
Field of Dreams 44, 45, 54
Fielder, Prince 12, 20
film 3, 9, 11, 15, 19, 71, 112
FOX 81–5, 170
FOX Saturday Baseball Game of the Week 85

"Game of the Week" 89
game-used 4, 43–56
Gameday Audio 80
Gehrig, Lou 99–100
Germany 175–6, 177
giveaways 2, 4, 26–41, 4, 67, 68, 93, 121, 186, 188
globalization 6–7, 97–8, 99, 115, 131, 139–40, 151, 167–8, 174, 178, 185–6

Hall of Fame *see* National Baseball Hall of Fame and Museum
high school 13, 97, 134, 167, 176, 179, 183–4
history 33, 44, 53–5, 75, 76, 100, 188; baseball and 5, 10, 13, 16, 19, 21, 40, 41, 53–4, 61, 65, 94–6, 99–102, 104–6, 108–9, 111–2, 126, 144; giveaways and 28; logos and 60, 61, 67, 68–70, 71, 76; media and 79, 83; memorabilia and 44; MLB and 6, 16, 61, 64, 71, 78–9, 86, 94, 126, 150, 152, 161, 186; WBC and 135

Hoffman, Trevor 51, 95
Horn, Brad 5, 89, 92, 95–112, 188
Houston Astros 74–5, 110, 172, 180
human rights 181
Hunter, Torii 20

IBAF *see* International Baseball Federation
Ichiro *see* Suzuki, Ichiro
identity 3–6, 10, 16, 20, 21, 36, 41, 53–4, 57, 59, 62–3, 65–70, 76, 94, 115, 118, 154, 186
injury 142, 145, 146
International Baseball Federation 132, 135–7, 140, 142, 144, 147–8
International Olympic Committee 132–3, 143–9
internet 5, 39, 78, 87, 93, 125, 173; *see also* online
Irabu, Hideki 119, 123
Italy 137, 142, 175, 177
Iwakuma, Hisashi 156

Japan 1, 6, 114–6, 117–31, 134, 149, 151–65, 170–86, 188; WBC and 134–42
Japan Professional Baseball Players Association 184–5
Japanese culture 118, 129, 131
Japanese fans 114–6, 117–31, 172–3, 178, 181–6
Japanese league 97, 100, 104, 114–6, 117–31, 150, 151–65, 179–86
Japanese players 1, 6, 97, 100, 111, 114–6, 117–31, 134, 151–65, 166, 168, 172–3, 178–86
Jeter, Derek 44, 51, 52, 91, 139
JPBPA *see* Japan Professional Baseball Players Association

Kansas City Royals 40, 66, 101, 180, 182
KBO *see* Korean Baseball Organization
Klinger, Patrick 31
Korean Baseball Organization 135–7, 164
Kukichi, Yusei 123, 183–5

LaFeber, Walter 1, 116, 117–8, 121, 128, 130–1, 150, 187
Lasorda, Tommy 127–8, 144
Latin America 7, 100, 120, 126, 134, 151–4, 158–60, 168, 170, 172, 174, 179–81, 185–6
LB-03 128
licensing 7, 12, 22–3, 47, 19, 59, 61, 64, 66, 73, 75, 85, 99, 120, 151, 154, 155, 168, 172–5, 178, 185
Little League 5, 96, 103–4, 112, 134, 177

logos 4, 59–76, 90, 154–5, 173, 174, 186
London 133, 144, 146, 158, 173, 177
Los Angeles Angels of Anaheim 12–3, 18, 32, 37, 65–6, 121, 122, 169
Los Angeles Dodgers 60, 63, 81, 130, 137, 144, 161, 169, 172, 182–3
Lowell, Mike 177

Majestic Athletic 173–4
Mantle, Mickey 54, 111
marketing 2, 4–7, 19, 21–39, 49, 43, 47, 60–3, 68, 72–3, 86, 98, 116–7, 120–8, 144, 155, 160–8, 171–7
Martinez, Buck 137
Matsuzaka, Daisuke 6, 97, 114–5, 117–22, 124, 127–8, 139, 153, 156, 166, 182–6, 188
McGuire, Bruce 12
McGwire, Mark 45–6
McPherson, Dallas 12
media 2, 5, 7, 10–2, 16, 19, 21, 36–8, 44, 49, 63, 67–8, 71, 77–93, 98, 101, 114–5, 117–9, 121–4, 127–30, 141, 148, 153–5, 168, 170, 172, 182, 185, 187
memorabilia 4, 38, 42–58, 89–90, 94, 108, 152, 173, 175, 186, 188
Mercer, Aleta 11, 17, 21, 22
merchandising 7, 30, 59, 66–8, 72–3, 115–6, 151, 153
Meridiano Television 126, 170
Mexico 137–8, 158–9, 166, 170, 172, 174–7, 181
Miami Marlins 38, 41, 65
Miller Park 11, 17, 21, 50
Milwaukee Brewers 12, 16–7, 21, 24, 38, 40, 51, 65, 68, 73–4, 145, 155, 157, 188
Minnesota Twins 31, 39, 65, 180
Minor League Baseball 3, 29, 91, 105, 112, 130, 137, 152, 159, 166, 169, 179, 184
"Mitchell Report" 88
MLB Advanced Media 78, 86–93,
MLB Café 173
MLB.com 31, 35, 48, 71, 80, 8–91, 124
"MLB.com at Bat" 87, 89
MLB Festival 177
MLB International 164, 170–1, 175–7
MLB Player Alumni 91
MLB: The Show 27
movie *see* film

National Baseball Hall of Fame and Museum 5, 50–1, 67–8, 89, 91–2, 94–113, 124, 152–3, 161, 187, 188
National League 85, 174
National Public Radio 11, 19
nationalism 6, 64, 67, 71, 124, 168

Native Americans 69–70
NBA 26, 86, 117, 144, 155, 156
NBC 62, 81–2, 122
Negro League 96, 100
NESN 85–6, 115
New Era 173–4
New York Mets 65, 172, 174
New York Yankees 37, 43, 49, 51, 61, 63–6, 69, 79, 84, 89, 94, 102, 120–2, 126–7, 130, 138, 153, 159, 161, 169, 172, 175
NFL 26, 80, 86, 155
NHK 125, 170
Nippon Ham Fighters 125, 162
Nippon Professional Baseball 128–9, 135–7, 140, 153–164, 182–5
Nomo, Hideo 114, 119, 123, 130, 182
Nomura, Don 182
Nomura, Katsuya 182
nostalgia 4, 25, 32–3, 54, 59, 62, 67–8, 70–1, 75–6
NPB *see* Nippon Professional Baseball

Oakland Athletics 33, 184
Obama, Barack 148
Okajima, Hideki 117, 127
Olympics 6, 132–5, 137–9, 143–50, 164
online 4, 18, 28, 41, 46, 56, 82–92, 110–2, 126, 128, 170, 185, 187
Opening Day 36, 155, 162, 168–9, 179
Operation Bullpen 46–8, 51
Operation Foul Ball 46
ownership 59, 70, 74, 76, 101, 133, 154

pastime 5–7, 14, 17, 24–5, 28, 30, 54, 64, 77–8, 80, 93, 96, 99–100, 103, 109, 111–2, 119, 134, 150, 186
patriotism 64, 72
Philadelphia Phillies 40, 49, 79, 147
Pitch, Hit, & Run Program 175
Pittsburgh Pirates 79, 130, 152
Play Ball! Program 175–6
Plesac, Dan 21
politics 6, 11, 96, 189
popular culture 3, 6, 9, 12–3, 19–20, 24–5, 28, 30, 41–60, 66–7, 94, 97, 133, 152, 154, 185
Posner, Mike 51
posting system 158, 184
post-season 171
promotion 9–10, 22, 28–31, 34–7, 4-, 68, 82, 102, 117, 120–1, 126, 138, 141, 153–4, 171, 174–6
Puerto Rico 83, 99–100, 158, 166, 168, 175–7, 181

radio 5, 11, 19–20, 22, 37, 77–81, 86, 93, 143

recruitment 7, 168, 177–81
replica 11, 39, 75, 116, 126, 128
Robinson, Jackie 99–100, 105, 161
Rodriguez, Alex 51–2, 91, 144
Rogers SportsNet 126
Rogge, Jacques 144, 147
Ruth, babe 44, 104, 129, 152, 161

Safe Neighborhood Act 169
St. Louis Cardinals 61, 65, 75, 79, 101, 174
San Diego Padres 4, 65, 172, 180
San Francisco Giants 31, 65, 79, 101, 107, 183
Schlesinger, Rick 16–18
Seattle Mariners 36, 65, 129, 157, 175, 183
Selig, Bud 6, 86, 95, 133, 150, 170
SESAC 22
Siemer, Jason 11
Simon, Dan 65
Small, Jim 151, 154–65, 167, 174–5, 178, 181, 185
Smith, Ozzie 161
soccer 2, 15, 91, 135, 149, 156, 162, 178
Son, Masayoshi 125
South Africa 92, 138, 164, 175–7
South Korea 128, 142, 146, 170, 173, 175–6
sponsorship 30, 33–5, 71, 82, 83, 155, 174–5, 178, 185
sporting culture 24
spring training 20, 32, 122, 130, 137, 142, 172
Steiner Sports Memorabilia 46, 49, 54–6
Suzuki, Ichiro 6, 46, 108, 111, 114, 117–24, 129–30, 152–3, 155–7, 175, 182, 184, 186
"Sweet Caroline" 14
sweet spot 43, 45

Taiwan 155, 168, 173
"Take me out to the ball game" 13, 14, 24
Tampa Bay Rays 34, 39, 89, 172
television 1, 3, 5, 9, 11, 22, 77–8, 80–6, 93, 104, 116–7, 124–7, 155–6

Texas Rangers 65, 72, 75, 84, 180
throw-back jersey 5
tickets 3, 21, 30–3, 35, 40, 70, 80, 87–9, 91–2, 110, 120–1, 130, 136, 140, 163, 169, 171, 175
Toronto Blue Jays 21, 65, 101, 176, 180
trading card *see* baseball card
translators 1, 97, 159

Uehara, Koji 127, 183
umpires 49, 58, 137
United States 2–3, 15, 47, 97, 99, 108–9, 114, 117–8, 123–4, 148, 153, 156–60, 163
use values 2, 10, 12, 17, 19–24, 28, 34, 41, 52, 154

Valentine, Bobby 162
Veeck, Bill 29, 41
Venezuela 134, 158, 168, 170, 172, 177, 180

Wagner, Honus 44–5
walk-on music 2–4, 9–25, 26, 30, 33, 42, 93, 186
Washington Nationals 51, 60, 72, 119, 183
"West Side Story" 126
Whiting, Robert 119–21, 239, 153–4, 165
Williams, Ted 54, 94
Winterball 176
women 35, 96, 100, 112, 128, 173
Women's Professional League 96
World Baseball Classic 6, 91, 132, 133, 136, 140, 141, 146, 148, 154, 163, 164, 172, 177
World Cup 38, 92, 135, 137, 162
World Series 5, 39, 69, 74, 79, 81, 85, 89, 95, 101, 104, 106–7, 117, 130, 134, 138, 145, 174, 187
Wrigley Field 14, 15, 24, 31, 55

Yankee Stadium 94, 122
Yomiuri Giants 125–6, 136, 153
Yomiuri Shimbun 126, 136
youth 4, 14, 33, 124, 173, 175, 181

www.ingramcontent.com/pod-product-compliance
Lightning Source LLC
Chambersburg PA
CBHW032056300426
44116CB00007B/768